Worked to the Bone
Race, Class, Power, and Privilege
in Kentucky

Worked to the Bone
Race, Class, Power, and Privilege
in Kentucky

PEM DAVIDSON BUCK

Monthly Review Press
New York

Library of Congress Cataloging-in-Publication Data
Buck, Pem Davidson,
     Worked to the bone : race, class, power, and priviledge in Kentucky /
Pem Davidson Buck.
          p. cm
     Includes bibliographical references and index.
     ISBN 1-58367-047-5 (pkb.) – 1-58367-045-7 (cloth)
     1. Kentucky–Social conditions. 2. Kentucky–Economic conditions.
3. Kentucky–Race relations. 4. Social classes–Kentucky. I. Title.

     HN79.K4 B83 2001
     306'.09769–DC21

                                                      2001045244
                                                      CIP

Designed and typeset by Terry J. Allen, Richmond, VT

Printed in Canada

10 9 8 7 6 5 4 3

CONTENTS

ACKNOWLEDGMENTS

The seed that eventually became this book was sown when, years ago, Faye V. Harrison told me it should be my task to "deconstruct whiteness"; as mentor, colleague, and friend she has nurtured both me and the seed she sowed. The Association of Black Anthropologists has been critical to my development as an anthropologist, both as an intellectual forum and as a support network for me as a white person examining racialized discourse. Anne Okongwu twisted my arm into submitting a book proposal and provided insight into social welfare policy as well as support and fellowship while I negotiated the slippery slopes of writing and publication. Late-night discussions with Yvonne Jones at American Anthropological Association meetings exposed me to a wide-ranging critique of books and issues and kept me in touch with her work on Louisville, Kentucky. Ann Kingsolver, with her knowledge of rural central Kentucky, reassured me for years that my views weren't crazy, and more recently did a deeply appreciated critique of this book. Discussions with Arthur Spears helped develop my understanding of fascism, and his support of the book itself has been invaluable. Helán Enoch Page's cutting-edge work on whiteness consistently pushed me to question my own assumptions. The intense discussion during the New York Academy of Sciences conference on Blackness and Whiteness organized by Page and Nina Glick-Schiller was a turning point in the evolution of the book. Other turning points resulted from my daughters' insights. Rachel Buck convinced me to go back to Bacon's Rebellion, rather than beginning the book with Reconstruction as I had intended. Naomi Buck convinced me to abandon my original focus on distinguishing various categories of the Far Right, a view reinforced by Loretta Ross's reaction to my work during a panel discussion sponsored by Project South. David Buck, my husband, helped with rewrites and made sure I didn't ignore the Wobblies and other labor challengers of capital. Dave, Rachel, and Naomi have all lived this book with me-and have done an enormous amount of work on it.

My parents, Hugh R. Davidson and Nancy Smith Davidson, sometimes in diametrically opposed ways, let me know it is all right to think outside the mainstream—a precious, if often painful, gift. Thanks to my brother, Jonathan Davidson, for unconditional support and for a memorable trip up a creek. My parents-in-law, Harry and Esther Buck, kept me well supplied with newspaper clippings and with their loving support over many years.

Many, many students have, consciously or unconsciously, caused me to rethink my assumptions about race and about life in Kentucky and on the edge of poverty. In particular there was a group of women who prodded me into learning about domestic violence and ultimately into beginning to learn about gender.

René Guarneros-Mata and Andrew "Chip" Maxwell both read incomplete versions of the book and gave me the reassurance I badly needed to be able to keep writing. Debbie Salsman and Angela Jenkins both read the manuscript, made helpful suggestions, and gave it their stamp of approval as people who have lived much that the book describes. Thanks also to the librarians who dealt with my innumerable inter-library loans, to the University of Kentucky for a sabbatical leave, and to the university and the Kentucky Humanities Council for several small grants for research and writing projects concerning local culture, and to Donna Lee Hill who worked with me on those projects. Doris Braendel's advice and support during the writing of the book was invaluable. Other people whose help or support I have appreciated are Diane Owsley, Joella Spataro, Terri Stewart, Mike Robinson, Richard Williams, Rose Garvey, Mary Bricker-Jenkins, Pam Sisler, Laurel Sisler, Allen Ashman, Debbie Narboni, Sandra Queen, Alexis Buss, Joan Haq, and the people at Monthly Review Press, especially Danielle McClellan, who took my book under her wing.

INTRODUCTION

THE VIEW FROM UNDER THE SINK

> Work your fingers to the bone,
> What do you get?
> Boney fingers!
>
> *—Hoyt Axton and Renee Armand*

The radio in our battered old pickup truck blared these words, set to one of those tunes that sticks in your head, over and over again during our first year or two in the rolling farmland of central Kentucky. You heard it in grocery stores, in hardware stores, even at the feed mill. It wasn't to be ignored. That was back in the early 1970s, and even now when I tell people my book is called *Worked to the Bone*, they often come back with, "Hunh! Well, I've sure got bony fingers!"

My first gut reaction to this song came early in our first spring after our move here from Pennsylvania. I was inexpertly wielding a pickax as a young mother, trying, with little visible success, to break through unbelievably intertwined sapling roots and rock-hard clay to make a garden. I remember hacking away with the tears rolling down my face, thinking about my husband's less-than-minimum wage, three-day-a-week farm labor job, and about my blistering hands, and the garden food we needed. I thought I was desperate, and as the words of that song kept cycling through my mind, I thought I understood about bony fingers. I have since discovered that the understanding I had gained was the merest glimmer. My desperation grew out of choices we had made when we decided not to pursue careers, but to buy land and try to live off of it instead, yet we still carried with us our background of white middle-class privilege. Years later we did take up that birthright when I returned to graduate school.

But in the meantime, I tried to get enough food grown, canned, and frozen to take us through each winter, raised pedigreed dairy goats and

dairy calves, and occasionally worked in tobacco, mostly cutting and housing it. My husband took various jobs, as a hod-carrier for a bricklayer and
then shoveling corn from one bin to another and stripping tobacco on the
large farm of a seed-corn producer. He eventually got a job working for a
plumbing and heating supply house. Five years later we started our own
small plumbing and heating business in which I worked as plumber's
helper. Like the women in many other local families running small con-
tracting businesses, I kept the books, but I also crawled around under people's houses, soldering, installing pipe, hanging heating ducts, wrapping
insulation, and holding the other ends of things for Dave.

Because deep down I had known I still had options when I was swing-
ing that pickax, my understanding of bony fingers had been incomplete.
But as we spent more and more years on the periphery of local working
class and small farm culture, I began to develop a form of double vision.
Part of me continued seeing things through the liberal middle-class eyes I
had inherited from my own family background. But, particularly after I
became a plumber's helper, I also began to develop what I now call the
"view from under the sink," another way of seeing the consequences of
continuous poverty and near-poverty—the if-it-ain't-one-thing-it's-another
low-intensity desperation expressed by "What do you get? Boney fingers."

It was while fixing plumbing leaks, lying on my back under kitchen
counters, soldering pipes while wedged between bottles of cleaning flu-
ids, that I learned about the view from under the sink. I often found
myself in fairly wealthy homes, looking up from under the sink at the
lady of the house and thinking about her life. She had furniture I could
not afford, dressed her children from stores I never entered, and complained about leaking plumbing at a time when what few pipes we had
in our own house froze and burst with remarkable regularity. I listened
to other contractors' interpretations of the world around them, a world I
was seeing for the first time, a world which I, like them, began to interpret as oppressive.

As I spent more and more time considering the view from under the
sink, I gradually saw stretching before me a life of involuntary poverty, no
longer the voluntary poverty of our earlier years. I began to be aware of
the underlying bitterness of dependency and forced gratitude I had felt
when the owner of that corn operation had butchered and given the
remains of last year's meat to the help, clearing his freezer for the new supply. Dave had come home with an enormous chunk of pork, the like of
which I had never seen. But my enthusiasm was dampened later when I
realized this meat was meant to help keep us grateful for a part-time, less-

than-minimum-wage job. I felt the same ambivalence when one of our daughters was given cast-off toys by a "lady of the house."

For ten or twelve years I lived under the poverty line and produced most of our own food. Toward the end of that time I quit plumbing and entered graduate school. There, I found my own experiences intersecting with anthropological and sociological theories about inequality. I began again to see things through new eyes, as I studied the creation of poverty for individuals and regions. My focus became the role of the elite and the policies they pursue in organizing a cheap labor force—producing bony-fingered people. As I began to understand this, my inherited middle-class liberal eyes underwent yet another upheaval, particularly when I began teaching and started applying these theories to the people I saw around me everyday, rather than to "other" people in Third World countries. I listened to student after student telling of their own or their family's struggles to survive on inadequate wages or inadequate income generated by low prices for farm products and high prices for farm inputs. I found myself going back to the "view from under the sink," the oppositional "big guys versus little guys" perspective I had heard from other contractors and the "boys" who worked for them. Since I am living in an area where nearly everyone except the local elites and those who identify with them buys some version of the oppositional "big guys versus little guys" view, my farming neighbors and many working class students in my classes had similar sentiments. "*They*—the big guys—are out to get us, and that is why we are having it so rough."

The liberal tradition I had inherited simply said owners of corporations *should* be nice, but did not question their *right* to be otherwise; after all, so people said, it is *natural* to want large profits, and poverty itself is a natural and inevitable result of lack of education or of economic change. But by now I no longer believed the liberal explanation of poverty. Nor could I continue to buy the liberal assumption that corporate capitalism is basically benevolent despite the problems that follow in its wake. How could I when I began formally researching issues in Kentucky and found that the tales I had heard informally were not isolated incidents?[1] In interviews and in informal discussions I heard story after story about injuries in the workplace, from dismembered limbs to ruined backs, from miscarriages to workplace deaths. I was told of illegally locked fire exits, exposure to chemicals without adequate protection, and safety mechanisms deliberately disabled. There were stories of friends and relatives required to work eighty or more hours a week, sometimes for months on end. There were students working "part-time" who hadn't had a day off in weeks. And others who worked two or three part-time jobs, unable to find full-time work. Others worked full-time and still couldn't support a family, while executives received raises. "*They* are out to get us" certainly seemed to be a reasonable explanation of the facts. Although I knew that conspiracy theories are definitely frowned upon in mainstream understandings of the world, as well as in mainstream social sciences, I nevertheless found myself concluding that the conspiratorial explanation from under the sink made at least as much sense of particular events as did mainstream explanations.

Social scientists can dispute the extent to which corporate owners have been conscious, now or in the past, of the consequences of their actions. And social scientists can argue about whether their policies have been coordinated. From the "view from under the sink," however, that argument is irrelevant and academic. I began to feel that the view from under the sink was justifiably different from that of the sink owners.

HISTORY, ANTHROPOLOGY, AND THE VIEW FROM UNDER THE SINK

It is only fair that I say up front that I have grown angry as I have learned more. I am angry at what I think the exercise of power has done to most people in the United States: angry at the way race, gender, and ethnicity have been used to divide and rule us, angry at the horrors that groups of people with slightly more power have inflicted on those with less power, and doubly angry at the horrors groups of elites have inflicted on us. Not only am I angry, I am often frightened as I contemplate our future, which, unless we do something, may hold even bonier fingers and greater horrors. This is a book with an agenda, an overt agenda rather than the sometimes unconscious, but in any case hidden, agenda of most "objective" social science. Quite simply, I don't like the future that may be coming, and I hope this book will help to circumvent it.

It is true that the future is shaped by the past. But it is equally true that the future is shaped by our *view* of the past. Our ideas of what happened in the past influence our ideas about what is possible in the future. *History* is a story constructed to explain the present. The dominant understanding of the past—an understanding shared by many Americans, the history taught first in grade school, and then in gradually more complex versions through high school and often early college—is one that justifies the distribution of power in the present. However, there are alternative histories, told from different viewpoints. Some, like the one I now espouse, take account of the view from under the sink. Such histories do not justify the unequal distribution of power by assuming that more powerful groups naturally deserve their position because of the value of their contributions to the general welfare and progress of a community. They look at what elite actions have meant for the lives of people under their various "sinks"— how ordinary people have constructed their lives to deal with or resist demands for their labor and their allegiance. And they talk about how ordinary people have dealt with elite strategies to pit them against each other in competition for nicer sinks to crawl under. Likewise, there are dominant and alternative versions of anthropology. In both history and anthropology, the dominant and the alternative versions are meant to empower different sets of people.

The dominant history of "South County," where I live, of "North County," where I teach, and of Kentucky generally, indeed of most of the United States, tells a story comforting to people of European descent.[2] It is a form of myth, but that doesn't make it meaningless. Histories of antebellum Kentucky downplay Native Americans, except as dangerous foes. The voices of slaves go unheard; their role as the foundation of Kentucky's wealth is not acknowledged. Little space is given to women and their roles. Poorer white families receive little attention. Such histories, along with countless other stories of the European takeover of this continent, help it seem natural that native Americans lost control of their land— after all, they were "savage" and "primitive," no match for the well-organized, advanced culture of Europeans who "developed" the country. By focusing on the activities of men who were European-American, these histories help people accept it as natural that European-American men now have higher wages and generally more power than anyone else in the country. The critical role played by women, be they Native American, European-American, or enslaved Africans, disappears from the record. In addition, these stories emphasize the role of a particular subset of those Europeans: those who initially "opened up" the country, and those who became powerful. Their power appears justified by the emphasis on the importance of their activities in leading the way toward "progress." That their wealth and power was built on the labor of their slaves and on the exploitation of poorer Whites, and even their own wives, is simply ignored. That many fingers, white, black, and Native American, became bonier under their leadership disappears from sight if the spotlight is focused on "progress."

This history has become the dominant version for a good reason: history acts as a lens, partially defining what is thinkable and unthinkable by limiting what we know and don't know. We can't act on an idea we haven't thought, so the control of history, of what we are likely to think and know, is a source of immense power. The dominant history—the generally accepted understanding of the past—in any society is the version that provides support, or at least damage control, for powerful people. The dominant history, in other words, is part of that propaganda that gains people's consent to the power gap between the elite and the rest of us. And when the elite are promoting policies that make for bonier fingers, the dominant history is crucial in our thoughts about resisting those policies. It encourages us to believe resistance has rarely worked in the past, except in our revolt against England, and that on balance corporate capitalism will eventually correct its temporary inequities, especially if people work with "the system" rather than trying to change it. But in fact, people in the past *have* come together across lines of race, gender, ethnicity, and class to resist, sometimes successfully, policies of the elite that were literally killing people. If we don't know this, we are much less likely to try it again, especially not in large enough numbers to be successful.

So, if my agenda is circumventing the future I am afraid may be coming, I need to provide an alternative history, one which emphasizes what I believe to be the *real* history of bony fingers, the policies that have created them, and resistance to them. It will be a history emphasizing the strategies used by the elite to fool people into agreeing to policies that hurt themselves and many other people. But my real interest is the present, not the past, so I will focus on those moments in the past that were critical in shaping lives in the present. This is where the anthropology comes in.

Anthropology provides ways to explain how the social structure people live in affects the way they see the world. And it provides ways of explaining why a social structure is organized as it is, relating one aspect of a society to another. Like the dominant version of history, however, the dominant version of anthropology has often been used to justify the unequal distribution of power. Tales of "strange customs" that the more powerful group describes as immoral, for instance, encourage the belief that weird or "primitive" people need to be brought under control. Forcing them to change appears to be the moral thing to do.

At the same time, anthropology has been a method for gaining useful knowledge for the control of conquered and colonized people. Knowledge of people's religion, family organization, inheritance patterns, economic and political systems, for instance, can allow administrators to devise more efficient methods for removing people's land rights without provoking a revolt. While many anthropologists have been deeply concerned about the welfare of the people they study, and in fact have at times fought damaging administrative policies, they cannot control how the knowledge they produce is used.

The dominant history and anthropology of Kentucky have played a similarly important part in justifying the loss of land rights and the creation of a cheap and exploited labor force, and continue to play an important role in "explaining" Kentucky to the rest of the nation. Accounts in novels, newspapers, television programs, and internet joke lists, in history, sociology, and anthropology books, and in missionary reports all have played critical roles at various points in Kentucky's history. These accounts have emphasized, in varying combinations, Kentucky feuds, drinking, incest, family violence, and general backwardness, barefootedness, improvidence, and rednecked cussedness.[3] Even now, my daughters and students talk of being teased when they leave Kentucky, with comments about outhouses, bare feet, early pregnancy, and incest.

These stereotypes, partially produced by the dominant history and anthropology, relieve consciences and explain to the rest of the nation that they need not question the role of the elite and corporate capital in creating Kentucky poverty, or their role in stimulating the attitudes described as "redneck." The actions of coal mine owners, of corporate tobacco buyers, or of manufacturing executives are irrelevant in explaining Kentucky's bony fingers if they can be explained by the problems in Kentucky's culture instead. These stereotypes have made it relatively easy for many people to dismiss the actions of tobacco farmers or coal miners when they have fought the corporations that controlled their lives. And this was not simply a problem of the past; the conditions that damage people and the dismissal of less powerful voices are ongoing. Miners' voices documenting the continued and disabling presence of black lung, for instance, went unheeded in the 1990s as the Kentucky legislature voted to dismantle workers' compensation benefits for that disease.[4]

ALTERNATIVE KNOWLEDGE

While anthropological knowledge has frequently been helpful to those who are organizing a cheap labor force, its ability to explain why people act as they do can be used in the opposite direction. An alternative anthropology, like an alternative history, takes account of the view from under the sink. First, the skills anthropologists developed for studying conquered, colonized, or exploited people can be used instead to study those who are doing the conquering, colonizing, or exploiting. Second, those skills can be used to help ordinary people understand their relationships to each other, and the attitudes they have about each other. It can show how some of these attitudes can make it easier to exploit us; if we are busy hating or blaming each other we aren't likely to band together to resist elite demands. This alternative anthropology, like the alternative version of history, does not justify the power gap between the elite and the rest of us. It does not assume bony fingers are natural; it does not assume racist or sexist or classist or homophobic attitudes are natural or innate; it does not assume elite leadership naturally leads in the general direction of a "progress" that benefits most of us. Instead, it attempts to show how these attitudes and the power relationships they justify have been constructed, and for whose benefit.

Alternative versions of history and anthropology, like the dominant versions, provide a lens through which to look at the world, one that is different from, but takes seriously, the voices from under the sink—or from behind the cash register, at sewing factory machines, in the tops of tobacco barns, bent under dairy cows, flipping hamburgers, canning tomatoes, hunting for work, stretching food stamps, serving time, filing workers' compensation claims, processing those claims, nursing in understaffed hospitals, or all the other things we do to keep body and soul together. The lens of an alternative anthropology and history is meant to empower a different set of people from the set empowered by the dominant lens. In other words, this alternative version will often contradict the dominant version. It is the purpose of this book to do just that.[5]

SETTING THE STAGE

South County, where I live in central Kentucky, is west of both the Appalachian Mountains and the fertile bluegrass. It is 92 percent white, according to census classifications; my local area in the northern end of the county is entirely white. The county's population of about fifteen thousand is classed entirely as rural, although there are several tiny towns. Most of the families identified as black are clustered on the outskirts of the towns, particularly in the southern part of the county. Many people don't farm, but depend for income on jobs fifteen to fifty minutes away. Some members of farming families make similar treks to supplement farm income. This pattern is common throughout South County, in West County, where my husband worked for several years at the local newspaper, and in large parts of North County, where I teach. There are a very few black farming families; during the summer and fall there are a small number of Latino migrant tobacco workers; and during the last fifteen years several Amish communities have been growing rapidly. The South County economy rests heavily on tobacco farming, on welfare and social security payments, and on income from jobs outside the county. North County is much larger and far more industrialized, particularly around the county seat. It has a total county population of about ninety thousand, approximately 10 percent black, 85 percent white, and a smattering of others, including well over two hundred people from Japan.[6]

In my county 27 percent of people live below the poverty line. Annual per capita income is a bit over $8,000; in North County it is approximately $2,500 higher. In the North County seat itself, per capita income is far higher, around $13,000. Most jobs in South County are in the service sector or in low-wage industry such as sewing factories. For some women this means a triple shift: the job, the farm, and the house. Likewise some men have a triple shift, with a job, farming, and either enormous amounts of involuntary overtime or a second job. Contrary to the stereotypes, workaholics are common in Kentucky. Many people rarely get enough sleep. Some rarely see their children awake. As one young mother put it, she and her husband don't even see each other long enough to fight.

My Agenda: Kentucky as a Piece of the Whole

Some of the readers of this book, I hope, either are themselves or know well bony-fingered people who engage in the oppositional "big guy versus little guy" analysis. But because the view from under the sink has been so suppressed many other readers will be unaware of its existence, as I was before I began crawling around under sinks as a plumber's helper. My research has focused on bony-fingered white people, many of whom use "big guy versus little guy" analysis; their voices from Kentucky will show up in the pages of this book.

This book focuses on Kentucky. However, I want to make it very clear that what I am describing is not limited to Kentucky. Kentuckians are not the only people in the United States burdened by a damaging history and anthropology. Nor are Kentuckians the only people in the United States with bony fingers. Kentucky is not separate from the rest of the United States. If I can explain why so many people in the counties where I live and teach are experiencing the desperation and frustration of working their fingers to the bone and getting nothing but bony fingers, if I can show how people's attitudes about race, class, gender, ethnicity, and sexuality may contribute to efforts to divide and rule us, getting us to fight each other in order to raise profits, then I will have fulfilled my agenda. This alternative to the dominant version of history and anthropology can be applied by people in other places to their own situations. And perhaps together we can circumvent a future of even bonier fingers in which we desperately fight each other for the right to basic human necessities while corporate profits soar.

1

MAKING SWEAT TRICKLE UP:
ORGANIZING THE FIRST STEPS TOWARD
UNDERDEVELOPMENT IN THE U.S. SOUTH

The sun shines bright on the old Kentucky home,
Tis summer, the darkies ["people," in recent versions] are gay,
The corn top's ripe and the meadow's in the bloom
While the birds make music all the day.
The young folks roll on the little cabin floor,
All merry, all happy and bright:
By 'n' by Hard Times comes a knocking at the door,
Then my old Kentucky Home, good night!
[Chorus:]
Weep no more, my lady,
Oh! weep no more today!
We will sing one song
For the old Kentucky Home,
For the old Kentucky Home, far away.

—Stephen Foster

Т he power of dominant understandings of the past and of the dominant stereotypes of Kentucky–including the state song's description of slavery–lies in their inaccuracy. What is it that this remarkably unified dominant understanding of Kentucky is covering up in order to perform the usual function of such dominant views of the past–supporting the authority of those who hold power in the present? To answer this question, we first have to look at the meaning of *development*, the process that has brought Kentucky to its present position at the bottom of the barrel on most socioeconomic indicators while at the same time concentrating wealth in the hands of a small number of people.

THE TRICKLE-UP THEORY OF DEVELOPMENT

Former President Reagan was known for his support of the trickle-down theory of economics—which George Bush Sr., running against Ronald Reagan in the primaries, referred to as "voodoo economics." But this wasn't voodoo: Reagan had just gotten things a little mixed up. What he should have said was the trickle-up theory, which is what development is all about.[1] To explain what I mean, let me go back to the plumbing business.

Plumbing deals with drainage systems, and organizes the flow of water in and out of a house. Development likewise deals with drainage, organizing the flow of value produced by work—the flow of sweat—out of the hands of workers and through the hands of successive layers of elites. In a plumbing system, pipes get bigger and bigger toward the bottom of a house as they carry more and more water, and continue getting bigger as larger pipes under the street collect water from more and more houses. Plumbing systems get reorganized from time to time as new technologies are developed. When the outhouse is replaced by a flush toilet and septic tank, the house develops a drainage system connecting it with a spot a short distance away, and much more liquid is handled than in the old system. As additional bathrooms are installed, new plumbing is needed and the amount of liquid increases. When the septic tank is replaced by a sewer system, drainage again has to be reorganized. The house is now connected to a much larger system that includes all the other houses in the neighborhood. Each house now contributes to a huge flow of sewage going toward a central point at a considerable distance. Likewise development involves reorganization of the flow of sweat, of the flow of value produced by work. Like the progressive changes in plumbing systems, historically development has meant a bigger and bigger flow out of the household and an increased concentration of that flow into fewer and fewer, but bigger, pipes. And development, like the reorganization of plumbing systems (as I can personally testify!), involves a lot of dirty work.

We ordinarily visualize social structure as a pyramid, however, with lots of ordinary people at the bottom, and fewer and fewer people higher on the pyramid, with a few extraordinarily wealthy and powerful people at the very top. So since we think of powerful people as being "up," to make my plumbing analogy work, think of that flow of value as an uphill flow, going up in bigger and bigger concentrations into the hands of level after level of fewer and fewer but increasingly wealthy people. Sweat, in other words, is made to trickle up.

Development is a process by which sweat is made to trickle up. Each stage of development is a reorganization to produce a larger flow of sweat into the hands of an elite. This is not voodoo, and Reagan's "trickle-down" economics did increase the flow of value up the socioeconomic scale into the hands of the already wealthy. During his administration the rich got significantly wealthier, the poor got significantly poorer, while those in the middle saw drops in their standard of living.[2] But Reagan didn't invent this system, nor did it stop under a Democratic administration. The plantation of "My Old Kentucky Home" in reality merely represented a different organization of the drainage system. It was one of the stops along the pipe that eventually drained small white farming households as well as slave households. But before any of this could happen in Kentucky the Native American culture already there had to be dismantled, because it was not organized to provide drainage.

THE NATIVE AMERICAN EGALITARIAN SYSTEM

The dominant history says Native Americans described Kentucky as a "dark and bloody ground," used merely for fighting and occasional hunting forays. This is a variant of the common colonial claim that an area was unused, misused, or under used by its indigenous inhabitants. This claim makes colonization appear to be a more "efficient," and therefore a "better," use of the land, and taking it away would have little consequence for indigenous survival.[3] In fact, the Cherokee and Shawnee used Kentucky extensively. The Cherokee hunted here and had a few permanent settlements. For the Shawnee it was an integral part of the annual subsistence strategy; they left their permanent settlements and migrated into Kentucky during the winter in small family encampments.[4]

The Cherokee and Shawnee were not organized before colonization to produce a surplus that an elite could take away from the households that did the work. Neither Cherokee nor Shawnee had a real elite or ruling class. Cherokee households consisted of kin all related to each other through their mother's side of the family; at marriage, men moved in with their wives' families.[5] The older women in the household directed the work of the younger women, their daughters and granddaughters, nieces and younger cousins. The crops they grew together belonged to the entire household. The clan to which each household automatically belonged distributed land to its members. All women had the right to farm on the land used by their household. And since all women were automatically born as part of a household, this meant they all had the right to farm somewhere. The men who lived with them, husbands and unmarried sons, brothers, and nephews, had a right to food from the crops because they were married to or related to the women who had direct use rights to clan land. This meant that all men had the right to eat somewhere, either in the household where they were born or in the household of their wives. Men cleared land for farming, helped with planting and harvesting, did a lot of hunting, providing meat for the household in which they lived, and conducted warfare. The senior men and women of each clan had positions of considerable authority in guiding decisions for the conduct of internal and external affairs of each village, including decisions relating to war.

The Shawnee system was similar, although there is far less anthropological and historical information about them than about the Cherokee. Shawnee households were nuclear rather than extended like those of the Cherokee, and apparently village rather than clan organization determined land use. But like the Cherokee, women controlled the crops they grew and held positions of political power in a system of chiefs that paralleled that of the men. These chiefs participated with male chiefs in policy decisions relating to both war and peace, and directed the conduct of those affairs, such as farming, that were exclusively female.

Neither chiefs nor anyone else among the Cherokee or Shawnee had the right to demand tribute or tax from other households. Chiefs did the same work and lived in the same way as everyone else. Nor was there any method for hiring someone to work to produce wealth for you. Households that didn't have enough male or female labor to support all their dependents—the very elderly and the young or incapacitated—could adopt or enslave war captives. Some of the chiefs—like monarchs in Europe—had to come from the right lineage, but were chosen from the available men or women of that lineage according to ability, not by being firstborn. Other chiefly positions, such as war chief, were awarded according to ability, not by lineage. Chiefly households were not materially better off than other households. Chiefs themselves received prestige and had some power, but could not act without the agreement of a council composed of clan elders.

Kentucky had not always been free of a drainage system or of an elite. Earlier in Native American history, things may have been somewhat different. Archaeological evidence indicates that people here—who preceded the Cherokee and Shawnee—were involved in chiefdoms that are now called Hopewell and Mississippian.[6] Hopewell chiefs may have received gifts and later Mississippian chiefdoms may have demanded a small amount of tribute. The most powerful Mississippian paramount chiefs at Cahokia (near present-day St. Louis) may have stored tribute and weapons in warehouses on the huge central temple mound. Similar, but smaller, mounds are found throughout Kentucky. These were much more complex and less egalitarian chiefdoms than those of the Cherokee and Shawnee, and did involve some drainage. It was the work of the household that produced those gifts and tribute, and that work went to increase the prestige and power of the chief. Nevertheless, the drainage was slight, since only a very small proportion of the household's work went toward producing or procuring the gift or tribute. Everyone in Mississippian societies had direct access to land. However, this was not true of Native American states such as the Aztec or Inca where, as in the European kingdoms from which the early colonizers came, an aristocracy controlled the land and took much of the produce grown by people living on it. However, by the time the first Europeans and Africans arrived in Kentucky in the mid-1700s, Native Americans–like the Cherokee and Shawnee–had established a more egalitarian society in much of the former Mississippian area.

Most of what is now the United States was organized in ways comparable to those of the Cherokee and Shawnee, without a major drainage system like that of the Inca and Aztec empires. The Europeans here could not simply conquer a king or paramount chief, substitute themselves at the top of an already-established drainage system, and receive the tribute that was already organized to flow to the top, as they did when they conquered the Incas and Aztecs.[7] Nor could they control the labor of these Native Americans who–unlike those in the empires–had clear and direct rights to land, and were not organized to give labor or wealth to nobles. So in Kentucky, as in much of the rest of what is now the United States, a drainage system had to be established before anyone was going to get wealthy. And wealth was, indeed, the intention of the first European landowners in Kentucky, the speculators who took up vast tracts of the best land.

ORGANIZING THE INITIAL DRAINAGE SYSTEMS IN VIRGINIA

To make sense of what happened in Kentucky it is necessary first to take a good hard look at Virginia. What is now Kentucky was part of Virginia during the colonial period, and events in colonial Virginia shaped the future of drainage in the South. Drainage requires access to resources and to a controlled labor supply, to people who will, voluntarily or involuntarily, allow their sweat to flow up to enrich others. With the invasion of what is now Virginia, Europeans simultaneously organized two methods of drainage. They tapped the coastal plains by growing tobacco using the forced labor of Europeans, Native Americans, and Africans on confiscated or ceded Powhatan land. They tapped the more distant hills and mountains through trade for deer and other skins with indebted Native Americans, particularly the Cherokee.

Deerskin, debt, and indirect control of Native American labor

Europeans on the coast, bent on raising tobacco rather than food, were not at all reluctant to back up their negotiations for land and for food with force.[8] Tobacco was a medium of exchange within the colony, used regularly for purchases; growing tobacco was almost like growing dollar bills. And it was the source of profits for investors in the Virginia Company and later for independent planters. Devoting land and labor to tobacco, rather than to growing food, was a policy that forced European dependence on Native American cornfields and women's labor, and on Native American meat hunting and men's labor. Since tobacco depleted the soil rapidly, it also forced dependence on continuous new supplies of Native American land. Massacres of reluctant villages were not uncommon; neither was Native American retaliation and resistance.

Trading was often forced by violence, but Native Americans soon had their own reasons to trade. Not least among these reasons for people living back from the coast was the need for rifles to hold back the rising tide of Europeans. Furthermore, Europeans purposefully gave alcohol in trade in order to addict Native Americans; once addicted they became willing traders. Again purposely, European traders gave goods on credit in order to create debt. As trade increased, so did the need for European goods, particularly the metal axes and hoes needed to increase the production of corn and the rifles and knives that helped produce meat and skins. Deerskins for Europe's leather industry followed tobacco as the second most lucrative colonial product. In a series of vicious circles, as deer became scarcer, men devoted more time to hunting and less to clearing farmland. As women devoted more time to tanning hides, they became more dependent on manufactured goods and tools. At the same time, an enormous death rate contributed to the destruction of the former Native American social structure. Deaths skyrocketed as a result of exposure to European diseases, from wars with the Europeans, and from wars with other Native Americans over the land that was left. Gradually Appalachian Native

American communities, pushed by debt and growing dependence on European goods, became part of an export economy. Many people, however, continued to argue that they should push the Europeans back into the sea or cut off all contact with them.

Tobacco and direct control of forced labor

Tobacco was the greatest source of wealth for the owners of the Virginia Company and later for independent European planters. In addition it was often the more powerful planters who monopolized the deerskin trade, concentrating the two greatest sources of wealth in the hands of a fairly small number of Europeans. However, tobacco was then, as it is now, an extraordinarily labor-intensive crop. For large tobacco planters to maximize their profits, they needed a huge labor supply. Their system, like the drainage system in England, was based on the denial of land rights.[9] Any system similar to the Native American egalitarian system in which land rights were treated as human rights would not produce drainable people. The planter elite met their labor and profit requirements with a flexible and constantly evolving system of unfree labor. While this system itself was never static, its fundamental principle was always "the assumption of the God-given right to mistreat others" in the name of profits.[10]

Initially unfree labor was organized for a vast array of people from three different continents in an equally vast array of unfree arrangements. Europeans defined unfree labor for people captured in a "just war" as legitimate. This definition was common around the world, permitting the buying and selling of captives under sentence of lifelong, but not hereditary, servitude. The result was a flow of exported captives around the world as neighboring enemies sold each other on the centuries-old international market. England had sold Irish captives to the Spanish army; Germans had sold Slavs; African kingdoms sold captives from other kingdoms and tribes . . . the list includes slaves and slave-traders from every continent.[11] In the North American colonies thousands of captive Native Americans were forced into lifelong unpaid servitude in a system close to slavery; others were forced into shorter unpaid contracts, closer to indenture. Some were captured by Europeans. Others were captured in inter-tribal wars and sold by the winners to Europeans. The Europeans quickly established a policy of fomenting inter-tribal war and of supplying arms to both sides. This policy provided an increased number of captives, depleted Native American fighting strength, and focused their anger on each other instead of on European invaders.[12]

However, Native Americans were not an ideal labor source from the planters' point of view.[13] Since many Native Americans still had access to land themselves, they had no need to work for others. Captured Native Americans could disappear, joining other Native Americans further from white settlement. Perhaps even more importantly, Native Americans had friends and family with some power nearby; Europeans frequently had cause to regret enslaving Native Americans when a captive's relatives staged retaliatory raids.

Since the attempt to directly control Native American labor on the continent was relatively unsuccessful, other sources of labor were needed if tobacco was to be lucrative.[14] Tenants, both African and European, were part of the answer. But tenants demanded a portion of the crop they raised or helped to raise, a big labor cost to landowners. As the elite consolidated more and more land in their own hands, they began to force tenants into accepting contracts that turned them into nearly unpaid laborers.[15] With this adjustment, landowners considered tenancy a practical arrangement for land they couldn't oversee themselves, particularly in areas vulnerable to Native American attack, or where land had to be cleared and the crop would be small. But in prime tobacco-producing areas, landowners wanted even cheaper and more abundant gang laborers. However, hiring gang labor was difficult since European workers tended to leave these jobs so long as land, and therefore a degree of independence, was still somewhat available to them.[16]

Forced and unpaid labor was the planters' preferred choice, and those most easily available for forcing came from Europe. The poor of England and the youth of rebellious Ireland were rounded up, frequently by force, and shipped to the colonies under conditions so awful that Bennett describes them as "the White Middle Passage."[17] They, as well as desperately poor people from other parts of Europe and some captives from Africa, became indentured servants. Laws were written or revised to increase the supply of people who could be shipped involuntarily. Vagrancy laws now could be applied to anyone who couldn't find a job, and people could be convicted and shipped for sale for seven years if they stole a loaf of bread.[18] For the first seventy years of colonization unfree Europeans performed most of the work of the colonies. Indeed, until 1660, Africans were probably not more than 5 percent of the population of Virginia.[19] And during those early years, neither slavery, indenture, nor race were clearly established; all three evolved together to meet changing elite needs for forced unpaid labor.

EARLY EVOLUTION OF UNFREE LABOR

Initially the Virginia Company paid workers' passage and supplied them with food for a year.[20] After that year they were freed, given land, and could get more land by importing other workers under the headright system. However, contracts soon shifted the cost of the passage and supplies to the servant, creating debt and debt peonage. Indentures were rapidly lengthened far beyond covering the cost of the passage and food. Laws governing the relationship between owner and servant gave the owner more and more control over the life of the servant. During their indenture, servants could be sold to other masters; they could be whipped for disobedience; they had to have their masters' permission to marry. Women who bore children while indentured were forced into two and a half additional years of service to pay their masters back for the time they "lost" due to pregnancy and child care. Eventually children whose indentured mothers were unmarried were themselves indentured until they were in their twenties, so that to some extent indentured servitude took on the hereditary aspects of true slavery. As indenture laws became harsher, owners of women found it advantageous to permit or to make sure they became pregnant. Raping, coercing, or seducing their servants gave owners the labor of their own illegitimate children, to use themselves or to sell, until the children were adults.

Indenture during the 1600s thus gradually became a closer relative of slavery; indentured servants were often sold on the same auction block as slaves. During the early years, most indentured people were European. However, Africans were also sometimes indentured, and slavery for those Africans who arrived already enslaved from the West Indies was not as different from indenture as it later became. Children of slaves were often free, or became free at adulthood, as did the children of indentured servants. Slavery wasn't even necessarily lifelong, but was instead an indenture that was a lot longer than the usual version. Free Africans and Europeans frequently married; some free Africans owned land and indentured servants. The two groups were not clearly demarcated, either in terms of ancestry or in terms of their position in early colonial social structure. Oppression at this point wasn't racial.[21]

It is difficult to know how many were unfree at any one time, but it was certainly a large number. In 1627, for example, fifteen hundred captured children were shipped to Virginia and in 1636, of the five thousand non-Native inhabitants of Virginia, approximately three thousand had come as indentured servants. The legality of all this was established at the very first session of the Virginia House of Burgesses, with democracy for a few and unfree labor for nearly everyone else.[22]

REVISING THE SYSTEM: CONSTRUCTING SLAVERY

In shifting away from dependence on tenants to dependence on indenture, big landowners destroyed the middle class, those people with a stake in the system who would act as a buffer between the landowners, their forced laborers, and the free but desperately poor.[23] As the European population of the colonies increased, this became a more pressing problem. It became harder and harder to isolate European indentured servants from the free European population, so that even temporary enslavement became harder to enforce. European indentured servants could and did run away, blending in with the rest of the Europeans.[24]

From the masters' point of view, another problem with indentured servitude was of even greater concern. European and African indentured servants frequently identified with each other and exhibited what was to their masters an alarming tendency to join together in rebellion and resistance. The tendency of African and European indentured servants to join poor and disgruntled, but free, Europeans and Africans to make common cause against the elite was an even greater cause for alarm.[25] And the ranks of the poor and disgruntled were growing as more people finished their indentures. Since the financially advantaged got most of the remaining land, little remained for newly free people. Earlier, perhaps one-half of those gaining their freedom had been able to get land. By the 1670s, it was closer to one in twenty, and many small landowners were in debt to the larger ones.

Before 1670 all free men, African and European, had the vote. But the elite worried about the potential for rebellion among those Governor William Berkeley described as the six out of seven "people [who] were 'Poor Indebted Discontented and Armed,' " and in 1670 the legislature took away the voting rights of landless men.[26] Bacon's Rebellion followed in 1676 on the heels of this withdrawal of privilege and was the culmination of years of increasing discontent.[27] Nathaniel Bacon, a frontier landholder, organized a militia for an attack against Native Americans. Organizing armed and desperately poor freemen was counter to Governor Berkeley's policy, given elite worries about revolt. Bacon was charged with treason, and he retaliated by marching against Jamestown, joined by a multitude of African and European indentured servants. It was a dramatic exhibition of the tendency of poor free people and indentured servants, all angry, to make common cause regardless of ancestry. While Bacon apparently intended to use this anger to propel himself from local elite status into the ruling core, his followers were intent on using the rebellion to force land redistribution and to regain the vote. Nearly the entire Virginia population was at least peripherally involved. Jamestown literally went up in smoke. On top of all this, tension between larger and smaller landowners was increasing, although that didn't develop into outright conflict until the early 1700s when elite and small farmers fought over tobacco sale regulation.[28]

People with power, in other words, were having trouble getting everyone else to believe their power was legitimate and natural. Poorer people of similar class position joined together, understanding that they had a common oppressor in the elite. A royal commission after the rebellion concluded that controlling the unrest, forcing local elites and the rebellious poor to accept the legitimacy of the governing elites, would require the permanent presence of an army.[29] From the point of view of the elite, a new system was needed.

Let us be clear here: the course the elite chose was not their only option.[30] They could have abandoned forced labor. They could have redistributed land and power so that all would have enough, in a system more like the Native American one they had destroyed. They could have stopped importing European and African labor so that the population would not grow so dramatically. Then it might have been possible to provide land for all without threatening Native American survival, thereby avoiding Native American reprisals. The elite chose not to go this way. To do so would have meant renouncing the drainage system that made them wealthy and powerful; they would no longer be an elite. This they were not willing to do. Instead, they chose to reorganize the drainage system and to create the racial divide from which nearly all Americans have suffered, to varying degrees and in varying ways, ever since. They created this divide in order to manufacture consent to poverty or powerlessness, or both, for most Europeans, and absolute powerlessness for most Africans. They created a drainage hierarchy to benefit themselves, to provide maximum profits with minimum rebellion. This hierarchy ranged from smaller landowners to tenant farmers, laborers, apprentices, servants, convict laborers, and slaves.

One strategy was simply to lengthen the term of indenture and tighten the laws surrounding it. This progressive removal of English rights for servants had begun before Bacon's Rebellion, as had the first steps toward slavery.[31] It accelerated after the rebellion, and, as a stopgap measure, it was helpful. However, it produced even angrier servants and angrier freed men and women at the end of their indenture. But its biggest flaw was a demographic one. As more indentured servants began surviving long enough to become free, even with the extended indenture period, the free population wanting land was increasing rapidly.

Earlier, when half the new arrivals to the colonies survived for less than five years, masters had preferred the cheaper, short-term purchase of indentured servants, rather than spending more for a lifetime servant who might die within a few years. Later, however, turning to lifetime purchase made economic sense for landowners since new arrivals were likely to live longer.[32] But constructing permanent slavery for Europeans in the colonies would have been difficult. Like Native Americans, unfree Europeans had free friends and relatives with some degree of power; some of them wrote home to England. If Europeans became slaves, ferment in England might lead to laws cutting off the flow of laborers to the colonies. To some extent this problem was avoided by describing the assignment of unfree laborers as marriage. In the earliest colonial years, the Virginia Company simply imported women and sold them, at a profit, for marriage to men who could afford the very high price.[33]

As the next chapter will describe, the solution the planters eventually chose was two-pronged: permanent, inherited slavery for those identified by African descent, and varying forms of temporary unfree and semi-free labor for many of those identified by European descent. Altogether this system had disastrous consequences for both Europeans and Africans. [34]

2

DERAILING REBELLION: INVENTING WHITE PRIVILEGE

Anger increased among landless Europeans as their numbers contin-ued to increase after Bacon's Rebellion. By 1720 in Christ Church, Virginia, for instance, over 40 percent of households were landless.[1] Jobs other than low-paid labor or farm tenancy were scarce, and a new series of laws crim-inalized joblessness: "vagrants" were sold as unfree servants. In fact, many European tenants, day laborers, indentured servants, and apprentices were only partially free. Smedley points out that "convicts, vagabonds, orphans, illegitimate children of all 'races,' and debtors were frequently bought and sold and even referred to occasionally as 'slaves.'"[2] The misery resulting from landlessness was very real, and therefore so was the danger of rebel-lion, but using direct force struck the Virginia elites as problematic for con-trolling Europeans. Instead, they defused the danger of European rebellion in the century following Bacon's Rebellion through strategies focused on getting Europeans, regardless of their class position, to identify with the elite—to believe that what was good for the elite was good for them.

While there was still some fertile, if expensive, land left, this operation was relatively straightforward. The elite, through their own credit in England and Scotland, provided loans to small farmers. In return for cred-it, these farmers provided deference and political support to the elite. But the landless were not tied into this system, and by the 1760s even smaller landowners were becoming less submissive.[3] An alternative mechanism was needed to get the poor to accept elite leadership; the solution lay in creating the first of what would be many versions of an evolving white privilege. The drainage system after Bacon's Rebellion was gradually revised into a two-pronged system of slavery for those of African descent and "freedom" for those of European descent. In reality, however, the least powerful among those of European descent were bound into varying degrees of unfree labor, and even those with somewhat more power continued to be drained by those above them.

Because of the rather mythical quality of their freedom, and because of a several generation history of cooperation between African and European laborers, it wasn't immediately obvious to many poorer Europeans that *whiteness* was their defining characteristic. They had to be persuaded to buy into the new dual system, persuaded that whiteness made them like the elite. If oppressed European and African laborers could be divided this way—if their solidarity could be broken—the elite would have an adequate, controllable, and cheap African labor supply and drainable class categories of Europeans.

Constructing Race

Improbable as it now seems, since Americans live in a society where racial characterization and self-definition appear to be parts of nature, in the early days of colonization before slavery was solidified and clearly distinguished from other forms of forced labor, Europeans and Africans seem not to have seen their physical differences in that way.[4] It took until the end of the 1700s for ideas about race to develop until they resembled those we live with today. Before Bacon's Rebellion, African and European indentured servants made love with each other, married each other, ran away with each other, lived as neighbors, liked or disliked each other according to individual personality. Sometimes they died or were punished together for resisting or revolting. And masters had to free both Europeans and Africans if they survived to the end of their indentures. Likewise, Europeans initially did not place all Native Americans in a single racial category. They saw cultural, not biological, differences among Native Americans as distinguishing one tribe from another and from themselves.

Given the tendency of slaves, servants, and landless free Europeans and Africans to cooperate in rebellion, the elite had to "teach Whites the value of whiteness" in order to divide and rule their labor force.[5] After Bacon's Rebellion they utilized their domination of colonial legislatures that made laws and of courts that administered them, gradually building a racial strategy based on the earlier tightening and lengthening of African indenture. Part of this process was tighter control of voting. Free property-owning blacks, mulattos, and Native Americans, all identified as *not* of European ancestry, were denied the vote in 1723.[6]

To keep the racial categories separate, a 1691 law increased the punishment of European women who married African or Indian men; toward the end of the 1600s a white woman could be whipped or enslaved for marrying a Black. Eventually enslavement for white women was abolished because it transgressed the definition of slavery as black. The problem of what to do with white women's "black" children was eventually partially solved by the control of white women's reproduction to prevent the existence of such children. The potentially "white" children of black women were defined out of existence; they were "black" and shifted from serving a thirty-year indenture to being slaves. To facilitate these reproductive distinctions and to discourage the intimacy that can lead to solidarity and revolts, laws were passed requiring separate quarters for black and white laborers. Kathleen Brown points out that the control of women's bodies thus became critical to the maintenance of whiteness and to the production of slaves.[7] At the same time black men were denied the rights of colonial masculinity as property ownership, guns, and access to white women were forbidden. Children were made to inherit their mother's status, freeing European fathers from any vestiges of responsibility for their offspring born to indentured or enslaved African mothers. This legal shift has had a profound effect on the distribution of wealth in the United States ever since; slaveholding fathers were some of the richest men in the country, and their wealth, distributed among *all* their children, would have created a significant wealthy black segment of the population.

At the same time a changing panoply of specific laws molded European behavior into patterns that made slave revolt and cross-race unity more and more difficult.[8] These laws limited, for instance, the European right to teach slaves to read. Europeans couldn't use slaves in skilled jobs, which were reserved for Europeans. Europeans had to administer prescribed punishment for slave "misbehavior" and were expected to participate in patrolling at night. They did not have the legal right to befriend Blacks. A white servant who ran away with a Black was subject to additional punishment beyond that for simply running away. European rights to free their slaves were also curtailed.

Built into all this, rarely mentioned but nevertheless basic to the elite's ability to create and maintain whiteness, slavery, and exploitation, was the use of force against both Blacks and Whites. Fear kept many Whites from challenging, or even questioning, the system. It is worth quoting Lerone Bennett's analysis of how the differentiation between black and white was accomplished:

The whole system of separation and subordination rested on official state terror. The exigencies of the situation required men to kill some white people to keep them white and to kill many blacks to keep them black. In the North and South, men and women were maimed, tortured, and murdered in a comprehensive campaign of mass conditioning. The severed heads of black and white rebels were impaled on poles along the road as warnings to black people and white people, and opponents of the status quo were starved to death in chains and roasted slowly over open fires. Some rebels were branded; others were castrated. This exemplary cruelty, which was carried out as a deliberate process of mass education, was an inherent part of the new system.[9]

Creating white privilege

White privileges were established. The "daily exercise of white personal power over black individuals had become a cherished aspect of Southern culture," a critically important part of getting Whites to "settle for being white."[10] Privilege encouraged Whites to identify with the big slaveholding planters as members of the same "race." They were led to act on the belief that all Whites had an equal interest in the maintenance of whiteness and white privilege, and that it was the elite—those controlling the economic system, the political system, and the judicial system—who ultimately protected the benefits of being white.[11]

More pain could be inflicted on Blacks than on Whites.[12] Whites alone could bear arms; Whites alone had the right of self-defense. White servants could own livestock; Africans couldn't. It became illegal to whip naked Whites. Whites but not Africans had to be given their freedom dues at the end of their indenture. Whites were given the right to beat any Blacks, even those they didn't own, for failing to show proper respect. Only Whites could be hired to force black labor as overseers. White servants and laborers were given lighter tasks and a monopoly, for a time, on skilled jobs. White men were given the right to control "their" women without elite interference; Blacks as slaves were denied the right to family at all, since family would mean that slave husbands, not owners, controlled slave wives. In 1668, all free African women were defined as labor, for whom husbands or employers had to pay a tithe, while white women were defined as keepers of men's homes, not as labor; their husbands paid no tax on them. White women were indirectly given control of black slaves and the right to substitute slave labor for their own labor in the fields.

Despite these privileges, landless Whites, some of them living in "miserable huts," might have rejected white privilege if they saw that in fact it made little *positive* difference in their lives, and instead merely protected them from the worst *negative* effects of elite punishment and interference, such as were inflicted on those of African descent.[13] After all, the right to whip someone doesn't cure your own hunger or landlessness. By the end of the Revolutionary War unrest was in the air. Direct control by the elite was no longer politically or militarily feasible. Rebellions and attempted rebellions had been fairly frequent in the hundred years following Bacon's Rebellion.[14] They indicated the continuing depth of landless European discontent. Baptist ferment against the belief in the inherent superiority of the upper classes simply underscored the danger.[15]

So landless Europeans had to be given some *material* reason to reject those aspects of their lives that made them similar to landless Africans and Native Americans, and to focus instead on their similarity to the landed Europeans—to accept whiteness as their defining characteristic. Landless Europeans' only real similarity to the elite was their European ancestry itself, so that ancestry had to be given real significance: European ancestry was identified with upward mobility and the right to use the labor of the non-eligible in their upward climb. So, since land at that time was the source of upward mobility, land had to be made available, if only to a few.

Meanwhile, Thomas Jefferson advocated the establishment of a solid white Anglo-Saxon yeoman class of small farmers, who, as property owners, would acquire a vested interest in law and order and reject class conflict with the elite. These small farmers would, by upholding "law and order," support and sometimes administer the legal mechanisms—jails, workhouses and poorhouses, and vagrancy laws—that would control other Whites who would remain a landless labor force. They would support the legal and illegal mechanisms controlling Native Americans, Africans, and poor Whites, becoming a buffer class between the elite and those they most exploited, disguising the elite's continuing grip on power and wealth. This strategy—co-opting a few, giving them privileges and advancement in return for controlling the rest of an exploited group—has been used in many parts of the world when an elite wishes to avoid the use of military might to put down the rebellions their exploitation arouses.[16]

With land or the hope of land of their own, these white people would become a buffer between the elite and those they most severely exploited. And some, at least, would see white anger from those at the bottom as unjustified. Elite legitimacy would be reestablished. But providing the land to create this white buffer class remained difficult until after the Revolutionary War.

KENTUCKY, LAND, AND A MATERIAL BASIS FOR HOPE

Kentucky, with its first permanent European settlement in 1774, became a relief valve for the East Coast European landless. It provided that missing material basis—land—for an apparently realistic hope of upward mobility and a corresponding identification with elites. The potency of that hope, and the desperation that prompted it, is hinted at in contemporary horrified descriptions of poor Whites flooding over the mountains.[17] These descriptions bring to mind stories of Okies heading to California, or television images of refugees fleeing starvation, carrying children and possessions, without money for land or food, enduring the trek in the hopes that conditions elsewhere will be better.

The first white explorers had crossed the mountains around 1750, when the lack of land east of the Appalachians was reaching crisis proportions. They returned with tales of incredible land in Kentucky. John Filson described Kentucky as an earthly paradise "where afflicted humanity raises her drooping head; where springs a harvest for the poor; where conscience ceases to be a slave, and laws are no more than the security of happiness."[18] This was a land where poor but intrepid white men like Daniel Boone could become heroes, according to Filson, a land speculator, who published this widely distributed description in 1784 to attract buyers.[19] The myth of Kentucky as a wondrous Garden of Eden gripped public imagination, and the rumor circulated that land would be available to all Whites. Instead there were land grants to veterans, but only to those nonveterans who arrived before 1778. For a brief time, laws made land relatively easy to purchase south of the Green River. The rumor and the occasional reality of free or cheap land combined with the widely circulated descriptions of paradise to become the basis for the hope that led tens of thousands to Kentucky. What most poor Whites actually found upon arrival in Kentucky bore little resemblance either to the myths or to the bonanza that the wealthy had already claimed.[20] Nevertheless, by providing a material basis for hope the Kentucky myth helped consolidate whiteness and played a critical role in creating a buffer class.

DISPOSSESSING NATIVE AMERICANS IN KENTUCKY

The deerskin drainage system had by this time reached across the mountains into what is now Kentucky. That system had depended on Cherokee and Shawnee control of hunting and farming grounds, and was protected for a time by the British Proclamation Line that forbade white settlement across the Appalachians. When it became necessary to allow European access to land in Kentucky, this older drainage system, as well as the remains of the indigenous egalitarian system, had to be dismantled. First, Shawnee and Cherokee land rights had to be denied. Military force was critical in this process, since Native Americans mounted a fifty-year armed resistance.[21] Also critical was the onslaught of European disease, and the signing and abrogating of treaties. Dragging Canoe was right when he said the European invasion would *make* Kentucky "dark and bloody."[22]

Second, despite military and biological assault there were still Native Americans left in Kentucky. And as long as they held land in common, no individual could sell it to white settlers, because no one actually owned it. To deal with this, Congress and Thomas Jefferson, both as president and as governor of Virginia, organized individual private property *ownership* to replace the land *use* rights vested in clan, village, and household. Men (not women) had to farm their own farms and become patriarchal heads of households. Women lost control of land, crops, and their official positions of authority, becoming dependent on men for their right to sustenance. Men would not be subject to what some Europeans, in disgust, called "petticoat government," and would control decisions about their land.[23] And, as Jefferson explained to Congress, once individual Native Americans privately owned land, the sale of manufactured goods could be used to tempt or fool them into debt. Once indebted, Jefferson pointed out, they could be forced to sell those privately owned farms to Whites. Jefferson advocated the use of federally owned trading houses to accomplish this goal, since they would not need to make a profit, as would private businesses.[24]

Some Cherokee bought into this system. They accommodated themselves to private property ownership and white ideas about farming and established farms on land Whites didn't want at that time. Owners of large tracts needed more laborers than a family could provide in order to accumulate the wealth that their private ownership theoretically made possible. Since Cherokee culture didn't provide people "willing" to allow the owner to use their labor to become wealthy while the person doing the work did not, some large Cherokee landholders bought African slaves.[25] These Cherokee landowners now played a part similar to that of many Whites in the new drainage system. Once Whites wanted their land, however, U.S. troops forcibly removed them and sent them on "The Trail of Tears" to land Whites did not want in Oklahoma.

REPOSSESSION BY WHITES

During the 1750s, wealthy land speculators began breaking treaty agreements with Native Americans and with the French. They obtained vast land holdings for future sale and as a resource to be used in the production of goods for sale. Much of what remained later went to veterans in lieu of wages. Officers' grants were often many thousands of acres, far more than the 100 to 300 acres enlisted men generally received.[26] Since higher rank in the military tended to go to the already better-off, this policy maintained the class structure of the East while at the same time providing hope of upward mobility for those at the bottom of the white hierarchy.[27]

The legal system provided further protection for the class structure. Since grants were initially made without surveying, Kentucky became a crazy patchwork of overlapping claims. While any grant gave the grantee the right to defend his claim against other claimants, then, as now, litigation was expensive and the already better-off stood a greater chance of establishing ownership. Poorer people often lost their title or were relegated to more marginal land, unsuited for plantation agriculture.[28] And Jefferson's system for dispossessing Native Americans through debt worked equally well for dispossessing poorer Whites.

Not only was class differentiation solidified through the land grant system; so was white privilege. Large grants went only to people of British or Irish ancestry; presumably the 5,000 Africans who had fought in the Revolution received none.[29] To make land more available to themselves, many Whites supported the continued elimination of African competition for land, and even non-slaveholders supported slavery in hopes of joining the slaveholding class themselves. And if Whites were to utilize their grants they had to define their interests as contrary to those of Native Americans. Further, treaty requirements and payments to Native Americans for the capture and return of African slaves undoubtedly encouraged Africans and Native Americans to define their own interests as conflicting, helping in the process of divide and rule.[30]

And finally, the land grant system contributed to male supremacy, since land was generally granted to men, leaving women dependent on men for the right to use land, unlike the female independence built into the Cherokee and Shawnee systems. Whites hid this difference with their portrayal of Native American women as "squaws" whose independent farming for female-organized households was described as drudgery inflicted by brutal savages upon "their women," whom they treated like slaves.[31]

This was quite a construction, considering that it was Whites who enslaved African women, and that European-American women in small farm families on the frontier probably worked longer hours than did Native American women. Even elite white women had less control over the affairs of their government than did Native American women!

Much of the best land in Kentucky was already taken up by wealthy speculators before 1795, when ordinary people began flooding into Kentucky. One of these speculators owned over 830,000 acres.[32] Family ties connected the owners of these huge estates and family networks enhanced their ability to act in a fairly cohesive manner, giving an extremely small number of people immense power. Their names are familiar ones in Kentucky history: Breckinridge, Shelby, Trigg, Brown, Preston . . . [33]

Land grants to veterans helped defuse discontent back east, permitting elites to maintain control.[34] Equally important, they attracted men and women who were desperate enough to act willingly as shock troops, making Kentucky safe for the westward expansion of plantation production. Veterans, especially officers, were given far more land than a family could farm because they had something the elites wanted more than money: military experience and the willingness to use it against Native Americans. In return for donating their experience, and often their lives or the lives of their wives and children, they received the right to build a fort, settle a group of tenants on their grant, and try to wrest it from Native Americans. In essence they became a military buffer between Native Americans and advancing white settlement. For people without access to capital or land in the heavily settled East, the chance for upward mobility –if they survived–made the risk worthwhile. They now had reason to treasure white privilege.

Early white and black settlement in North and South County

The general outline of settlement policies is visible in the early history of North County.[35] North County originally included part of what is now South County and parts of several other counties–an area about the size of Connecticut. There were some extremely large grants in this area; one was about 150 square miles. Most, however, were much smaller. By 1780 three forts were established around what is now the county seat. Revolutionary War officers held these forts and organized the "defense" of the area, resisting Native American raids and implementing their own. Within twenty years the non-native population of North County had exploded to about 3,500; nearly 10 percent were of recognized African ancestry. The fort system was clearly accomplishing its purpose of Native American destruction, removal, and control, making North County safe for white invaders and their slaves.

North County was organized in 1792, and one of its first official acts was to get a jail built, which became the county's first public building. Overseers of the poor were appointed almost immediately, and "vagrancy" was a de facto racially defined white crime. Only free people could be vagrant, since wandering slaves and bond-laborers were simply returned to their masters. Thus the only non-Whites who could possibly have been declared vagrant were North County's eleven free people of color. The presence of overseers of the poor and of vagrancy indicates that poverty became an issue for Whites almost immediately, reflecting the class structure built into the land grant system. Whites convicted of "vagrancy" were sold for a year to the highest bidder at the courthouse door. Orphans and illegitimate children were bound-out as "apprentices" in a system very close to slavery, so that there was a continuum of unfree, semi-free, and free people in North County.

By 1820, after North County and South County separated, slightly over a quarter of the Whites in North County owned slaves, and almost 14 percent of the population was enslaved. Slave ownership in South County was slightly more concentrated. There a slightly smaller percentage of white families owned slaves, and a slightly bigger proportion of the population was enslaved. The census doesn't clearly specify unfree white labor, those who had been sold for vagrancy or bound-out, but it is clear that during the early years of white settlement lack of freedom was a fairly common condition, including both enslaved Africans and some Whites. Unfree labor, whether of the temporary white variety or the lifelong inherited African variety, provided a significant proportion of each county's labor, part of the system of making sweat trickle up.

QUELLING REBELLION BY REINFORCING WHITE PRIVILEGE: VOTING RIGHTS

So the provision of land as the material basis for white privilege turned out to be a partial mirage. Consequently class divisions and protest appeared almost immediately. By the 1780s, perhaps 75 percent of Kentucky residents were poor and landless, more in the Bluegrass than elsewhere, often working as tenants for the huge landowners.[36] Henderson's Transylvania Company attempted to reestablish a form of feudalism, with perpetual rents for those who worked the land.[37] In Harrodsburg one group of protesters assembled to set aside Virginia law in order to divide land among themselves equally rather than according to their wealth and ability to buy land. They were dispersed by a militia officer aided by people opposing the protesters.[38] Resistance to service in militia units was intense; most men wanted to guard their own families, and raise their crops, rather than spend the summer risking their lives following elite orders to defend elite property.

Since most people had little access to cash without wage labor, and land prices rose as the frontier became safer, buying land became doubly difficult. Many landless Whites saw themselves in competition with slave labor, both in agriculture and in manufacturing, as well as in their frustrated ambitions of land ownership. They resented both the slaves and the elite who used those slaves to enrich themselves at the expense of poorer Whites. Not all poor Whites bought into this system, however; landless Whites who worked with Blacks and lived similarly to them occasionally crossed racial lines to defy the right of those higher on the drainage system to order white people lower on the drainage system around.[39]

In general, although whiteness ultimately helped maintain elite power, many Whites objected loudly to the "aristocrats" who had grabbed so much land and power. So the elites writing Kentucky's state constitution undid the property qualification that had helped spark Bacon's Rebellion and gave all white men the vote instead of accepting Jefferson's solution—giving them land.[40] The right to vote, to participate in deciding which of contending elites would represent them, became a critical piece of white privilege. Voting defused rebellion by giving angry people a stake in the government.[41] Equally important, it allowed white male tenants to define themselves as independent and free at a time when most white men of similar status on the East Coast still couldn't vote.

The whiteness that poorer people of European ancestry now accepted would continue to provide a smokescreen behind which the elite reorganized the drainage system as necessary to maintain their own control, to the detriment of black and most white households.

3

LIFE IN BLACK AND WHITE

It had been a long struggle in the century following Bacon's Rebellion, but by sometime after 1750 most people who were identified by their European descent had finally come to fully believe that their skin color was a basic aspect of their character and identity, as integral to who they were as their gender.[1] That belief was basic to the construction of the new system, clearly visible in Kentucky in the reality of plantation, slave cabin, and log cabin, of landlessness and landholding, of free, semi-free, and unfree white labor and of slavery for almost all Blacks. All lived lives that, perforce, accommodated differing positions in the drainage system through the organization of very different household structures and gender roles. And, as the next chapter will describe, neither Blacks nor poorer Whites submitted passively.

Before we can see how people in Kentucky and elsewhere in the South attempted to resist trickle-up, however, we need to see just how the drainage system they were fighting was organized. To do this I will use several now-mythologized sites to illustrate common central Kentucky patterns in the general area of North and South County. One is Federal Hill, the plantation owned by John Rowan and eulogized in the state song, "My Old Kentucky Home," built in the first years of white settlement. The Lincolns also arrived in the early years of white settlement. Sinking Spring was Abraham Lincoln's birthplace, Knob Creek Farm his boyhood home. Both of Lincoln's log cabins and Federal Hill are critical in state and national self-definition. They have been quite literally enshrined; Federal Hill by an act of the Kentucky legislature, and Lincoln's birthplace in a national park where the (presumed) cabin in which he was born rests inside a replica of the Lincoln Memorial in Washington. Both are figuratively enshrined in the mythology of plantation and log cabin.

FEDERAL HILL: THE PLANTATION REALITY

Federal Hill was built in 1795–1797, just as the area was becoming safe for Whites and their slaves.[2] It is an imposing brick structure built on a rise. The circular front drive leads to an enormous front door, a door without an outside doorknob, for those entering through that door never expected to open it for themselves. The slave quarters were originally behind the mansion. It was here that the people who did the work that maintained the household and produced the crops struggled to organize their own households and kinship groups. The six cabins that remained in the 1950s were torn down. Their preservation apparently was not judged to merit the expense and effort that has gone into enshrining the lives of the elite who owned the people living in them.

The land on which Federal Hill was built had belonged to Mrs. Rowan's father, a warrant and land grant speculator, and was probably passed through her to John Rowan as dowry in 1794. Rowan was a lawyer, a member of Kentucky's constitutional convention, Kentucky's secretary of state, a frequent member of the state legislature, a representative to Congress in 1806, and a U.S. senator in 1824. He had business interests and property in Louisville and Washington as well as his plantation—a bona fide member of Kentucky's ruling elite. Thirty to forty slaves worked his 1300 acres. Initially the enslaved Africans at Federal Hill grew corn, livestock, fruit and other crops, producing most of what was used on the plantation. Surpluses were sold; later cash crops like tobacco and hemp apparently played a larger role.

The diversified production at Federal Hill was typical of antebellum Kentucky. Tobacco came across the Appalachians with slavery, and by the early 1800s was an important Kentucky export. Until the Civil War, however, hemp for rope and for cotton-bale bagging took first place in Kentucky's manufacturing and agricultural production. Like tobacco, hemp was a labor-intensive crop, well adapted to plantations. But until the spread of the new white burley tobacco after the Civil War, Kentucky's agricultural production remained fairly diversified, even on plantations. It ranked first or second nationally in the production of hemp and high in production of tobacco, corn, wheat, horses, mules, swine, cattle, and sheep.[3]

The importance of fairly large-scale, labor-intensive, plantation-like monoculture appears to have been more developed in South County than in North County. However, it never gained the overwhelming predominance here that it gained in the Bluegrass, with its hemp production, or in western Kentucky, the heart of antebellum tobacco growing, or in the Deep South. As the Civil War approached, South County increasingly concentrated on plantation crops—tobacco and a little hemp. By 1860 it produced 5.5 times more tobacco per farm than North County and far less of the diversified subsistence crops such as grain, fruit, butter, cattle, and hogs. By 1860, 11 to 12 percent of slaveholders in both North and South Counties had over ten slaves. But except in the inner Bluegrass, few Kentucky owners had as many slaves as John Rowan.[4]

Large land-and-slaveholding, like that at Federal Hill, predominated on the land best suited to the labor-intensive row crops—hemp, tobacco, cotton, sugarcane—that made slavery profitable. Southern South County seems to have fit this pattern more closely than northern South County or than North County. Southern South County supported the Confederacy in opposition to the rest of the county, and according to a local historian, the area around the northern part of the county grew little tobacco until after World War I.[5] Yeoman families like Lincoln's, farming their own land using primarily their own labor, dominated areas where land was less suitable, like the narrow bottom land at Knob Creek, or that was far from rivers or roads and transportation to markets, like northern South County and much of North County.[6]

Plantation economy: the beginnings of underdevelopment

A split between large-scale export production and small-scale, more subsistence-oriented production is typical of regions with economies that have been developed for the benefit of outside elites. There are many names for such places: Third World, peripheral, underdeveloped, colonized. What characterizes these regions is their position in the national or international drainage system. Their economies and social structure have been reorganized to produce cheap labor, raw materials, and resources for more powerful external elites.

Kentucky and the U.S. South gradually became underdeveloped in response to the control exercised first by British and later by Northern investors in export crop production.[7] Since crop prices fluctuated wildly, planting was financially risky and growers were dependent on kinship and friendship connections, such as the Rowans had in Louisville and

Washington, for credit with Northern bankers. Plantations thus became part of Northern financial structures. This explains the extensive support for slavery among Northern business people as well as Southern planters' resentment of Northern domination. Planters often found themselves pushed into growing export crops even when they weren't particularly profitable, benefiting Northern manufacturers further up the drainage system who needed the South's cheap raw materials and slave labor.

Slave labor was critical to both the Northern and Southern economy and was the foundation, along with the earlier forms of unfree labor, on which the United States was built. Slaves produced 80 percent of the nation's overseas trade goods. Until the 1820s, some of those slaves lived in the North, and during the entire antebellum period even Northern manufactured exports depended on raw materials produced in the South.[8] As Mintz pointedly describes, two sets of workers, slaves and overworked and underpaid English wage laborers, produced the goods needed to keep the other set under control and producing: cotton, sugar, and addictive substances such as alcohol and tobacco on the one hand, and manacles and tools on the other.[9] British and U.S. elites profited on both ends of the trade: as users of labor they gained control of overworked wage laborers who used sugar for quick energy and consumed alcohol and tobacco products or of slaves threatened with manacles and whipping. As sellers of manufactured goods or raw materials they gained markets. Kentucky entered into this system at several points. It was, and still is, a major drug producer. Both tobacco and whiskey have been important exports since European settlement; marijuana was added later. Kentucky provided some of the hemp ropes for ships transporting goods to England and back. Its bagging wrapped the cotton that went to England, and later to mills within the United States. And Kentucky was a major supplier of the labor power for Deep South agriculture, exporting for profit both humans and mules.[10]

Federal Hill and welfare dependency

The Rowans, like other plantation owners, depended on a variety of forms of welfare. This welfare was given by the state, beginning with the initial land grant itself. The enslavement of Africans required legal structures defining humans as property and granting property rights to landowners of far more land than was needed to support a family. These same legal structures provided welfare by allowing owners to have valuable property—children—raised for free by enslaved families and communities behind the Big House. The state authorized the daily exercise of force that was needed to keep people in misery working without revolting. But should that force fail, there was government military assistance to prevent slave revolts and to prevent poor Whites as well as Blacks and Native Americans from claiming a share of the land. Plantation owners depended on their own control of local government, the courts, and the media for legitimation and authority. Newspapers of the time consistently presented slaveholders as a superior and paternalistic class, deserving of their position in relation to poor Whites.[11] Even with all this state provided welfare, the elite also depended upon the private welfare that came from access to financial backing and business connections that could be depended upon to help carry the plantation owner through years of financial loss.

Further, slaveholding depended on a gendered system of welfare enforced by the state, giving slaveholding men legal control over their own wives. Without such laws slaveholding would have been much more problematic: white women were far more likely than men to side with slaves against an owner's violence, and frequently objected to their husbands' adultery with slaves.[12] Since husbands could enforce wives' obedience with some of the same violence used against slaves, and since wives could only rarely leave their husbands, wives of slaveholders often expressed their anger and jealousy not at their husbands, but with violence against their husbands' victims. Regardless of their personal attitude toward slaves, whether or not they approved of slavery for their own racial and class interests, their complicity was legally enforced. Legally slaveholders' wives were obligated to play a significant role in controlling slaves, usually as directors of slave household labor. They participated in, or at least tolerated, the daily personal intimate violence on which slavery depended: the sexual abuse, child abuse, rape, and battering, the enforced neglect of children and spouses, and the destruction of families through sale that constituted a psychological as well as physical reign of terror. The preservation of slavery and the submission of white women to their husbands were explicitly intertwined in pro-slavery arguments. White women must not set slaves an example of resistance; patriarchal rights to obedience of both women and slaves were implied in the frequent statements by slaveholders about their slaves as "family."

The economy of slavery

When first settled by Whites, Kentucky had been a slave importing state. But around 1820 Kentucky became the first state west of the Appalachians to become an exporting region, sending slaves to the Deep South or to the rapidly expanding Southwest, the fate of the man supposedly comforting his mistress in Foster's "My Old Kentucky Home." Neither area "raised" enough slaves born locally to meet its landowners' insatiable appetites for more and more slaves. Both depended on the purchase of slaves from Kentucky, and elsewhere in the Upper South, where land and climate limited plantation production; Upper South slaveholders found it more profitable to sell "excess" production of their "breeding women," who were not overworked to the point of miscarriage as they often were in the Deep South.[13]

Slaves in the Upper South were in and of themselves important status markers for their owners, and a source of wealth and economic security whether or not plantation production made a profit. Despite their frequent protestations about the inefficiency of slave labor, and despite their objections to Northern domination, slaveholders included some of the richest and most powerful people in the United States. Their income was so high that white per capita income in the South averaged twice that of Whites in the Northeast despite poverty among landless southern Whites.[14] Because there was such an extensive market for slaves, slave labor in Kentucky didn't have to be cheaper than hired labor as long as it covered the costs involved in keeping them. To help cover these costs, plantations often provided slaves with small garden plots to work on their own time. Some coal mine owners followed the same strategy later when they provided severely underpaid miners garden plots for their wives to work.[15] In addition, slaves could be sold or used as collateral, and became more valuable when the legal importation of Africans ended in 1808. Slaves could be hired out to farmers and businesses; they could be set to running their own businesses on shares. And leasing slaves to industry, particularly in manufacturing iron and rope, was profitable and increasing during the decades before the Civil War.[16]

Local planter control

Huge landowners used the fortunes they built from their drainage of slaves and tenants to control both slaves and tenants. And they developed patron-client relationships in which they extended credit to small landowners in return for deference and votes. The result was a Southern oligarchy—7 percent of the population owned about three-quarters of all slaves, nearly as large a percentage of the best agricultural land, and controlled the local political system.[17] Big landowners in the Bluegrass, Kentucky's best farmland, surrounded themselves with "genteel" trappings as the plantation system and slaveholding moved across the Appalachians, forming a "cohesive agrarian landed aristocracy which retained political leadership and held itself aloof from other elements of the state's population."[18]

However, the patron-client relationship and the aristocratic nature of elite control were somewhat disguised in relations between white men across class lines.[19] The big landowner and his poor neighbor could meet on terms of apparent equality outside their homes. White men could all define themselves as equally free, as heads of households with non-citizen dependents, and as at least potential property owners, but to do so they needed to define a large portion of the population as ineligible for equality. They needed slaves and white women against whom to measure themselves. In addition, this fraternization across class lines was distinctly *fraternization*; women didn't participate in equivalent cross class socializing. They made certain that class markers were clear when men returned to their homes or socialized within their homes, and that children grew up with a clear sense of position. Inside their homes, the aristocrats and their wives and heirs were safe from the polluting influences of the working classes.

KNOB CREEK FARM: THE LOG CABIN REALITY

The Knob Creek Farm where Abraham Lincoln spent his early years nestles between high hills with a creek running through the hollow within sight of the cabin. The cabin probably had a single room with a fireplace at one end and a loft overhead. Undoubtedly there would have been outbuildings scattered around, and fields stretched back behind the cabin away from the road. Lincoln spoke of taking corn up the steep winding road to the nearest mill. Life here would have been very different from life at Federal Hill.

The roots of this difference were established at the beginning of white settlement. Twenty-one land barons claimed one-fourth of Kentucky by the end of the 1700s. Other settlers would have to buy from them, and prices were usually too high for small farmers. Speculators frequently refused to sell, waiting for prices to rise, so new settlers competed with each other to establish claims on the remaining land, and found that the best agricultural land was unavailable to them. Once elites consolidated this kind of power, they were able to pass their power and position on to their children, so that entrance into the upper class became difficult for people not born to it. Those who were left landless frequently became tenants, although landownership was far more common in outlying non-plantation areas like much of North and South County.[20]

Landless white farming

Landless families were welcome in the eyes of large landowners who wanted to open up new tracts of frontier land.[21] Given the danger posed in outlying areas until the mid-1790s by Cherokee or Shawnee defiance of land snatching, it made sense economically to keep expensive slaves in more protected areas. Tenants' deaths, however, would be of little economic consequence to landlords, and their presence in frontier militia units was essential in wresting the land from Native Americans.

Landless Whites and small landowners acted as the frontier buffer between Native Americans and the developing white slave-dependent society that gradually spread out from its center in the Bluegrass. Tenants produced some crops and enhanced the value of the landlords' holdings by clearing land, attracting additional population, and securing the land against other claimants and squatters. None of this was particularly lucrative. Five acres a year was about all a family could clear, but land produced little of commercial value until the process had been completed.[22] Once land began producing and tenants might begin making a profit, however, landowners often found it more lucrative to switch to sharecropping, depriving growers of much of their potential profit. Where there was no further danger of Native American attacks and farming had become productive, landowners generally replaced tenants with slaves.

So, in reality, many of those log cabins were not inhabited by equal and independent families on the road to wealth, unaffected by an elite or by the presence of slavery, as the romantic log cabin myth implies. Instead, many were home to dependent tenants or sharecroppers risking their lives and spending their sweat to enrich a landlord living miles away in luxury. Many of these families never would establish claims to land, and would soon leave Kentucky in a continued search for a promised land that kept its promises.[23]

Landowning: diversified subsistence farming

For others, landowning was a reality, although for some ownership was only temporary. Many of the earliest settlers had high hopes of quick riches through the large-scale production of commercial crops; such hopes apparently declined as farms were subdivided among heirs and as much of the good land became concentrated in the hands of local elites.[24] Many families, including the Lincolns, apparently saw diversified subsistence farming as a more reasonable strategy than either a thoroughly commercial family farming orientation or true subsistence farming. They focused on producing to supply their own needs *as well as* to sell on the market, rather than on commercial production for sale *at the expense of* production for home use.[25]

Diversified subsistence households grew enough of a wide variety of crops, including grains, vegetables, and fruits, to supply their own needs and to have enough to sell. In those early years "home manufactures" made by women—cloth, butter, cheese—were important sources of income. Stores accepted hogs, hides, tobacco, whiskey and other country produce in payment, and then exported these goods down river to New Orleans. Bartering and work trading, especially among kin, helped to make diversified subsistence farming practical. It was a common pattern in smallholder sections like the area around the Knob Creek farm, and dominated North and South County except where river transportation made the plantation production of tobacco feasible.[26]

Whiskey production appears to have begun with the first white settlers; it was produced commercially in the 1790s in North County. The first business in the county seat was probably a tavern, and the court established tavern prices for whiskey in 1793. Whiskey doubled as a medium of exchange in the early years when little currency was to be found in Kentucky. Abraham Lincoln's father, Thomas Lincoln, appears to have been paid in whiskey when he sold Knob Creek farm. Small-scale whiskey production combined well with diversified subsistence farming since it required relatively little labor compared to other saleable crops such as tobacco and was more practical to transport without rivers since it was far more valuable for its bulk than tobacco.[27] Another common source of income, also involving comparatively little labor, was the sale of livestock. Hogs, cattle, sheep, and chickens roamed the hills, fenced out of crops and gardens. Foraging for themselves for most of the year, they cost little to raise and could be driven to market on the hoof, so that lack of roads and railroads didn't prevent selling them.[28]

The entire household provided labor in diversified subsistence farming. While neither Lincoln nor his biographers say so, it is quite likely that the entire Lincoln family—Abraham's mother and sister along with the men—worked on cultivating the 14 acres of corn and pumpkins along the creek bottom.[29] More prosperous households might get additional labor by buying or renting a slave or by hiring sons or daughters from smaller farms.[30]

The varying constructions of gender

Families pursuing a diversified subsistence strategy probably had more egalitarian family structures than did plantation owners or commercial family farmers.[31] Although men had the right to appropriate the value produced by their wives and children by claiming the cash from sales, in reality there was little cash to appropriate. Family members benefited equally from the food they produced, from the roof over their heads, and from the clothes they made. Women probably worked somewhat harder than men, as they do in most stratified societies, but men also worked hard. Theoretically, diversified subsistence farming men did have more power than their wives because they actually owned the land on which women depended and the law constructed the husband as a citizen with rights and his wife as a dependent under his control. However, ownership of the land was to a significant extent offset by other aspects of the structure of diversified subsistence farming. The first of these was men's dependence on kinship networks in which women played major roles; the second was women's independent production and marketing.

Kinship networks provided economic security—help in time of trouble, as well as routine cooperation—and were a source of companionship and political organization. Women generally played important roles in these networks, giving weight to their opinions and actions. Moreover, women on diversified subsistence farms produced home manufactures on their own and sold these goods directly to consumers or bartered them at stores. One early North County historian writes of his future brother-in-law as a child accompanying a group of women in 1804 on one such independent expedition. They took a load of cloth on horseback to a merchant and selected the goods they wanted in return.[32] From this independent production, which in many ways paralleled that of the men in their families, they had a source of power that women growing tobacco on commercial family farms didn't have.

In both diversified subsistence farming and commercial family farming, women's labor was critical to success, but simply being necessary and productive doesn't in itself lead to power or equality—as slaves could certainly testify. Nor did elite women, who also performed critical labor in plantation management, gain power or equality with the men in their families. But in diversified subsistence farming, women themselves to some degree controlled what they produced. In societies around the world this type of control correlates with relative equality between the sexes.[33] This would have been far less true in landless farming families. In those families women and children were unpaid and involuntary labor for landowners. Contracts were made between men, and all payments were made to men. The contract included not just the tenant head of the household, but also his dependents.[34] The male head of household became the foreman, obligated and authorized by the contract itself to produce household labor; a household that failed to fulfill the contract could lose both housing and payment for work already done.

In diversified subsistence families, however, the role of "head of household" was not as thoroughly constructed. Men were not in a position to act as conduits feeding large amounts of household labor into the drainage system, as they were in tenant families. The combination of subsistence and cash cropping allowed families to avoid intense entanglement with the drainage system by staying out of debt and keeping for themselves a fairly large proportion of the value they produced. Indeed, it still performs the same function for a few of my small-scale tobacco-growing, beef-selling, gardening, meat-freezing, egg-producing neighbors.

Selling Yourself Piecemeal

Into this mix of landholders, renters, merchants, and enslaved workers, we need to introduce two other elements: the unfree and semi-free, mainly white, working class, and the "free" waged working class who sold themselves piecemeal rather than being sold whole.[35]

Unfree and semi-free labor

Before the Revolutionary War, relatively few people worked for hourly or daily wages. Hiring white labor for manufacturing or farming in Kentucky's early days was rare. There simply wasn't enough cash available to use for wages, and in dangerous or particularly onerous work, such as that in many frontier salt and iron works, skilled Whites demanded high wages. Owners avoided hiring them when possible, or combined white and black labor, as the owners of a South County iron furnace did.[36]

Involuntary indenture and apprenticeships provided a source of unfree labor in Kentucky and the rest of the South. Orphans and children removed from their families because of abuse were indentured or apprenticed by the court until they were eighteen or twenty-one years old, often as farm laborers or as unpaid craft or manufacturing workers, while others became household servants. Many of these "orphans" were the free black children of white women, or the children of people adjudged unable to support their children, or illegitimate. Adults who were defined as paupers or vagabonds could be indentured. This was not an insignificant source of labor. One North Carolina County, for instance, apprenticed about one hundred children a year.[37] Those Whites in the semi-free working status assumed that they would go on to become free, perhaps landowners. Apprentices and journeymen hoped to become free master artisans and mechanics.

The dilemma of wages/freedom/whiteness

After the Revolutionary War, however, the earlier wide continuum of free, semi-free, temporarily unfree, and permanently unfree statuses began to change. Indenture and apprenticeship were gradually replaced by various systems of hiring labor and eventually by slave labor in a number of industries. Artisans and mechanics turned to wage labor; workers were less likely to become independent craftspeople without the apprenticeship process.[38] The temporary lack of freedom in the middle of the old labor continuum was disappearing, making a greater gulf between black and white, free and slave.

As wage labor became a lifelong status after the 1820s, rather than a presumably temporary one for men on their way to independence, hired workers began to worry about being "wage slaves" or "white slaves."[39] Freedom was still associated with whiteness and self-sufficiency, while blackness was more clearly associated with permanent lack of freedom. Whites without property were left in a serious definitional bind. How could they be free if they weren't self-sufficient, supporting themselves on their own property, dependent instead on an employer? And if they were working under the control of someone else, how were they white, particularly if they were doing the same kind of work free or enslaved Blacks were doing? Whites despised wage labor for the conditions of work it entailed, for the poverty that followed in its wake, and for its threat to the status of free men.

The dilemma presented by permanent hired labor arrived in force with industrialization, striking the North earlier than the South. It was hidden at first, in North and South, by hiring primarily women and children from farming families in the early textile factories and cotton mills. So long as this was thought of as a temporary arrangement, particularly for women while awaiting marriage and a return to farming as a wife, it threatened neither patriarchy nor the association of whiteness with self-sufficiency and freedom.[40] But the dilemma continued to grow. In the North, a flood of immigrants—who shunned the South where slavery reduced the number of paying jobs—joined free Blacks and some of the "native" Whites to form a large, landless working class.[41] By the late 1830s many more native

Northern men were relying on wage labor, finding themselves in competition with native women and with immigrant men and women. Immigration had ended the labor shortage, and employers took advantage of the situation to allow working conditions for women and men to become even worse.[42]

The dilemma took shape somewhat differently in the South, corresponding to the difference in the labor system. In the North, a goodly percentage of hired labor was immigrant, unaccustomed to being white. About half the immigrants were Irish, fleeing first near-enslavement in Ireland and later the potato famine of the 1840s.[43] They were defined as a racial group, not quite white and inferior to "native" Whites. But in the South those drawn into wage labor were more frequently "native" and believed in their whiteness and in white privilege. Since industrialization came later to most of the South, they had had an extra generation or so beyond "native" Northerners to identify with their whiteness. In addition, many Southern laborers had been landowners themselves, came from landowning families, or owned farms that were too small to support them. Many believed they had lost their land or their ability to make a living off their land because of the machinations of the slaveholding elites who had placed them in direct competition with slave labor.

The Lincolns and wage labor

This progression can be seen in the history of the Lincoln family.[44] Both the Lincoln and the Hanks families arrived in Kentucky in the 1780s. Abraham Sr., the president's grandfather, came from a well-to-do Virginia family. He moved to Kentucky and ended up owning 5,544 acres of Kentucky's richest land. However, in 1786 he became one of the hundreds of Whites in Kentucky killed by Native Americans, and apparently his estate went to Thomas Lincoln's older brother, Mordecai, leaving Thomas landless.[45] Thomas became an artisan and laborer in North County in the early 1800s, working for low daily wages. As an artisan, he competed with slave labor, since slaves, unlike free Blacks, could now engage in skilled crafts.[46] Enslavement in North County was growing dramatically during this time, and there were few people paying wages. Between 1800 and 1810 a few new businesses did hire a few employees. There was a mill, a tavern, a tanner, a shoemaker, at least two dry-goods stores, and a brickyard. The War of 1812 provided business for iron furnaces, and by the 1830s Kentucky was one of the larger iron-producing states.[47] Several furnaces in rural South County employed and housed a number of white families;

slaves did much of the work, however. At about the same time there was an increase in textile manufacturing. There was a mill in what was then still a part of North County, employing forty to sixty Whites indoors while slaves did all the outdoor work.[48] Even at their peaks the mills and furnaces would have been but a limited source of employment.

While Thomas was working as an artisan, however, most of even this limited source of employment was still in the future. The North County seat remained very small during this period, with a total enslaved and free population of nearly 150 in 1800 and only slightly more in 1810. It is therefore unlikely that jobs for Whites in the county seat increased at anything like the county-wide increase in enslavement. White "vagrants"—men who were landless, jobless, poverty-stricken, and sometimes wandering—were becoming an issue in the county seat. Imprisonment for debt was also common.[49] However, the increase in enslavement did create additional jobs in one area: slave control. These jobs tended to go to landless or poor Whites, and, like the Federal Hill overseer, Thomas benefited. In 1805 he briefly became a paid slave patroller under the command of his future second father-in-law. However, the paid patrol was replaced within a year by a much larger but unpaid patrol; Thomas was not a member.[50]

At about this time Thomas married Nancy Hanks and bought a farm, perhaps using savings, perhaps with help from Mordecai. Abraham was born on their second farm, Sinking Spring, which they left because of its infertility, and moved to Knob Creek, in an almost entirely white area. However, at this point elite structuring of the economy again caught up with them. Despite the fact that by 1814 Thomas Lincoln was listed as fifteenth out of ninety-eight in wealth in his county, in 1816 he was unwilling or unable to pay to establish his ownership of Knob Creek farm. He had been issued a suit of ejection by a non-resident, and lawyers had raised their fees, taking advantage of the constant litigation that consolidated land in the hands of the wealthy. By 1821, one-third of Kentucky belonged to banks and non-residents, acquired through foreclosure and forced sales.[51] Thomas sold out and the Lincolns went to Indiana, to get away from slavery according to Abraham, but perhaps also to get away from the "despotic influence" wealthy slaveholders exercised over poorer Whites.[52]

In fact, the Lincolns were part of a flood of poorer Whites leaving slave states. W. E. B. Du Bois calls this exodus the "revolt against the dominion of the planters over the poor whites," expressed, "just as the revolt of the slaves, . . . through migration." Slaves exercised the "Safety Valve of Slavery" through running away, escaping north at the rate of about one thousand a year, three hundred of them from Kentucky, by the 1850s.[53]

Whites also "ran away." By the turn of the century more people were leaving Kentucky than moving in.[54] So long as land continued to be available, Whites who were landless or had lost their land could move on, and move on they did, in such large numbers that there was a constant labor shortage in Southern white smallholding areas. While the frontier was still fairly accessible to Whites, and the hope of landowning seemed to be fairly reasonable, Northerners as well as Southerners exercised the "safety valve" of running away from bad conditions. However, as poverty increased in both North and South, obtaining the money to buy land and start farming became increasingly difficult. By the 1860s between one-quarter and one-half of the population of the United States was too poor even to become tenants on an eighty-acre farm, much less to buy one.[55] More and more Whites in the North found themselves working for wages, more and more white Southerners found themselves renting farms, and Irish workers in the South were sometimes hired for situations so dangerous that slaveholders didn't want to risk losing their valuable slave investments.[56]

But during the first part of the 1800s the "safety valve" still functioned, helping to prevent the buildup of discontent among Whites. The ability to "run away" safely and legally was an important piece of white privilege. But it would not function forever.

4

RESISTING TRICKLE-UP
WHILE ACCOMMODATING WHITENESS

White resistance to trickle-up in the 1800s was shaped by racial politics. Before the consolidation of white privilege with the "opening up" of the Kentucky frontier, people whose sweat trickled up had frequently joined forces without regard to which continent their forebears had come from, or to the color of their skin. But now such alliances, with their enormous threat to elite control, attracted fewer restive Whites. Instead, they focused on denying white privilege to incoming immigrants and to Africans, enslaved or free, hoping to enhance their own status as free men who owned their own labor or as women who served no one but their husbands. Racial "reality" was constructed—and contested—for Mexicans in the conquered Southwest and for each immigrant group arriving from Europe. A hierarchy of white, not-quite-white, not-white, and black was gradually constructed. The workers of the United States were now divided and easier to rule.

RESISTANCE IN BLACK AND WHITE

During the early 1800s, while Whites could still run away, or at least believed they could, and while Whites believed that as Whites they were free, white unrest was fairly muted. The reorganization of the drainage system that had begun in the aftermath of Bacon's Rebellion had indeed succeeded in quelling white protest. Quite the opposite situation prevailed for black workers, however. Slavery had become considerably less flexible than it had been in the 1700s.[1] This resulted partially from the rigidity needed to construct a clear difference between blackness and whiteness, and partially from changes in the plantation economy itself.

Plantation owners now focused less on economic self-sufficiency and more on the production of a single cash crop like cotton or tobacco. Northern financiers provided credit to buy goods from Northern manufacturers, and planters put nearly all of their slaves to work in the fields and purchased the goods that skilled slave craftspeople had previously produced.[2] Consequently there was less opportunity for slaves to work themselves into positions that provided a little autonomy, such as hiring out their own labor. In North County in the early 1800s, however, transportation for Northern goods was still a problem and skilled slaves continued to produce many necessities locally.[3]

Resistance and revolt among enslaved workers

The shift to a single cash crop meant increased slave discontent. Some lost what little autonomy and satisfaction they had had in skilled work. Most suffered from a work speed-up at very hard labor inflicted on them by indebted planters trying to increase profits, or at least stay afloat.[4] Slave fingers, in other words, were becoming bonier, and this was occurring at a time when the tightened control of the latter days of slavery was not yet thoroughly organized.[5] Slaves ran away, but in the early 1800s they also revolted and planned revolts, something bony-fingered industrial white workers didn't do with much regularity until the 1830s.

Plans for major revolts came to light about once every ten years. Some, such as Gabriel's Rebellion of 1800 in Virginia and the conspiracy led by Denmark Vesey in South Carolina in 1822, never got beyond the planning stage. Several thousand slaves were at least peripherally involved in Gabriel's Rebellion, but the combination of a massive storm that threw off the timing of the planned attack on Richmond and leaks to slaveholders at the last minute, led to the arrest of the leaders and ended the rebellion. Vesey, a free Black, likewise led a plan involving thousands, intent on winning Charleston, and was likewise betrayed and executed. However, had these slave revolts been successful they would have overthrown local government and ended slavery. Other revolts did get past the planning stages. A revolt in 1811 on a plantation near New Orleans spread to involve four or five hundred slaves and was put down by U.S. Army and militia forces. Nat Turner led another revolt in Virginia in 1831. The fact that Whites were actually killed—at least fifty-five of them in Turner's revolt—threw white Southerners into a panic.[6]

In fact, these were merely the most dramatic slave acts of rebellion. The first "official" murder in North County—not counting deaths of European-Americans and Native Americans at each other's hands—was a slave killing his master.[7] Such murders were not uncommon, according to Lerone Bennett, who says that in addition slaves "staged more than two hundred revolts and conspiracies."[8] They also engaged in work slowdowns and "disorderly acts," despite knowing about the punishments that were a regular feature of plantation life. Whippings were common, reflecting the frequency of slave resistance and owners' efforts to maintain control; they were generally administered on bare backs of men and women with a bullwhip. White slaveholders had learned to live with all this small-scale revolting, but Turner's Rebellion conjured up visions of the successful Haitian slave revolt in 1791. Consequently, as the enslaved part of the labor force struggled against the consolidation of slavery, Whites tightened the security system, making it far harder for slaves to organize. The repression of Blacks and of Whites who aided or cooperated with rebelling slaves became so severe that open rebellion and formal revolts virtually ceased after 1831. However, slaves fled in ever-greater numbers to the North, where slavery had virtually disappeared by this time.

Resistance and revolt among "free" wage workers

As overt black resistance died down, however, working class Whites began consolidating their own resistance. This was when scientists were beginning to construct clear, supposedly biologically separate, racial categories of humans. The scientific separation of "native Whites" from European immigrants and from free people of color appeared as an immutable fact of nature.[9] This "fact" became an integral part of the struggles between wage earners, all trying to sell themselves piecemeal.

Working class white resistance was at first localized and sporadic. It started in the late 1700s among Northern journeymen as their conditions within the apprenticeship system deteriorated. They were followed by skilled artisans who worked for small employers in workshops outside the factory system. These men owned their own tools but worried about maintaining their independence and wages in the face of spreading industrial production. Organized resistance eventually grew widespread throughout the wage-earning labor force.[10]

From the end of the 1830s until the Civil War there were many riots and strikes.[11] Union organization exploded in the 1820s in the textile industry, where women predominated. The number of female factory workers grew rapidly, so that by 1850 they made up a quarter of all manufacturing workers. Men and women struck jointly and separately, and were later joined by workers in other industries, and by working children, farmers, renters, workers under the "putting out" system, the hungry, and the jobless. Many people's wages were so low they barely fed one person, despite working well over ten hours a day. Regardless of whether a family had one child or ten, such wages meant that everyone over age ten or so tried to find a job, while factory owners grew wealthy off their sweat. But jobs were scarce: in New York City in 1837 one third of workers were without work and hunger was rampant. Outside the city, conditions were scarcely better: huge landowners, the largest with 80,000 tenants, lived in luxury while their tenants struggled to pay the enormous rents that made the landowners wealthy.[12] Conditions were comparable in other parts of the Eastern non-slave states.

For people this poor, going west was nearly impossible, except occasionally for young men who could shed all family encumbrances.[13] So instead of "running away" they tried to improve the conditions of their lives where they were. They rioted and struck, revolted against excessive rent, formed political parties, and in Rhode Island elected an alternative state government. Many were quite clear about the source of their problems. They saw themselves being drained within an inch of their lives, and often beyond—the death rate for their children and for themselves was extremely high—because capitalists and landowners wanted to be richer. They fought for higher wages, lower rents, lower food prices, free public education, the right to a ten-hour day, and improved safety and working conditions. In a word, they fought for the right to a life not entirely dedicated to making someone else richer. These changes were all needed if parents were to see their children, have time to talk to each other, educate their children and expect to see them live to adulthood, even have energy to go to church—to do anything except come home to eat, drop into an exhausted sleep, and drag themselves out of bed to do the same thing all over again the next day, and the day after.

Maintaining Control: Welfare for the Elite

Just as in the South, landowners and employers in the North were dependent on the state to protect their right to drain their workers. Legislators were capitalists themselves or obligated to capitalists for support; in some states a candidate had to meet property qualifications to run for office. These legislators refused to allow the majority of adults to vote. The disenfranchised included all women and many men: those who were enslaved and in some states free Blacks, Native Americans, certain immigrants, paupers, and men without property or who did not pay taxes.[14] In other words, the vote was restricted to that group with the largest percentage of people placed high enough on the drainage system to benefit from the continued existence of the drainage system—or to think they might benefit—and thus to gain from protecting it.

The legislators passed laws that tacitly upheld owners' rights to work people literally to death and to ignore the human needs of their families. They allowed capitalists to organize to improve their position but denied workers the same right. They provided enormous financial help to corporations—free land and advantageous tax laws.[15] Equally important, the state kept angry workers and the hungry in line. Although Northern employers couldn't whip workers who objected, as slaveholders could in the South, they could have them jailed or shot. The legislators agreed to pay for sending in troops to put down riots and to control strikers, just as they did when slaves revolted. They agreed that the many deaths of rioters and strikers at the hands of soldiers were not murder any more than was the killing of revolting slaves by soldiers or the "accidental" death of a slave after a severe whipping. The occasional deaths of soldiers at the hands of rioters, strikers, and revolters, on the other hand, were indeed considered murder, as was the killing of a slaveholder. Paying wages so low that some people would inevitably die, however, was not murder; neither was putting people to work under conditions so unsafe that some were guaranteed to die. Legislators willingly turned a blind eye when employers hired their own militias—security guards—but did not allow workers or the hungry to do the same. The "justice" system sentenced, fined, and jailed strikers. This was the state welfare system provided to the elite.

Growing elite problems

So, in both North and South from the 1830s to 1860s, those who were at the top of the drainage system tried to tighten their control of those at the bottom. However, as industrialization progressed and technology became more complicated and expensive, manufacturers began consolidating production in bigger factories to save costs.[16] And as factories grew, so did the urban population around them. People losing their land went to cities looking for work and immigrants coming into the United States did the same thing. Huge clusters of poor workers and even poorer unemployed built up, facilitating resistance.

Although most antebellum industry was in the North, by the 1840s cotton mills were becoming common in the South. Louisville, like many other Southern cities, developed considerable manufacturing, and large numbers of German immigrants joined unions there in the 1840s. Some skilled craftspeople received relatively high wages, but most Southern industrial jobs were extremely low paid.[17] In North and South County even in 1860 there were very few nonagricultural jobs—a grand total of sixty-two manufacturing jobs in North County and forty-seven in South County, mostly in a single tobacco manufacturing plant. This is a far lower rate of industrialization than that of parts of eastern Kentucky and Southern Appalachia, where the extractive industries—mining, iron, salt, and lumbering—developed early.[18]

As the technology costs of large-scale production increased, so also did industrialists' financial risks. For industrialists, the greater financial risk meant that their stake in a compliant working class was higher. They needed the support of the working class within their factories, but equally they needed working class *political* support for the corporate welfare system on which capitalists depended. Because factory workers were free, the administration of discipline through the daily, piecemeal, individualized violence that slaveholders used was, for the most part, impractical. In industrial settings even slaves often had to be treated somewhat better.[19] Use of violence on a large scale—calling out the troops—worked in the short term: people usually did back down in the face of rifles. But such treatment didn't make them contented, dedicated workers. Furthermore such confrontations were expensive. Money had to be spent on troops and security guards; more money could be lost if machinery was wrecked; and there was the cost of lost production time. Worst of all, people noticed when they or people like them were fired on. And they had an obvious explanation for what was happening: the capitalist class was willing to kill some of them, with starvation or exhaustion if they worked, and with guns if they refused to work. A more subtle form of discipline was needed by the elite, one to which many people would acquiesce without noticing, ideally one that would focus people's anger away from the capitalist class.

At the same time, poor Southern white allegiance to the landed plantation aristocracy was fraying. Renting rather than landowning gradually became more common throughout the South, and its character was changing. For diversified subsistence farmers outside plantation areas, renting was frequently a stepping-stone to ownership. But in plantation areas land was more expensive and the price of the slaves needed to compete in a plantation economy was rising. Just as the bigger planters became enmeshed in Northern commercial empires, debt brought smaller planters and yeomen under the control of local elites. By the 1850s many yeomen even in up-country areas were beginning to worry about "bondage" to planter-merchants, land speculators, and bankers.[20] This dilemma must have presented itself more obviously in South County than in the more diversified subsistence economy of North County. As in other plantation-oriented areas, class differences among free Whites, particularly in the southern part of the county where most of the tobacco was grown, must have been blatant.

THE PSYCHOLOGICAL WAGE

A partial solution from the elite point of view was found in what Du Bois calls the "psychological wage" of whiteness.[21] The initial construction of whiteness had been based on a material benefit for Whites: land, or the apparently realistic hope of land. By the 1830s and 1840s, most families identified by their European descent had had several generations of believing their whiteness was real. But its material benefit had faded. Many Whites were poor, selling their labor either as farm renters or as industrial workers, and they feared wage slavery, no longer certain they were much freer than slaves.[22] But this time, to control unrest, the elite had no material benefits they were willing to part with. Nor were employers willing to raise wages. Instead, politicians and elites emphasized whiteness as a benefit in itself.

The work of particular white intellectuals, who underscored the already existing belief in white superiority and the worries about white slavery, was funded by elites and published in elite-owned printing houses.[23] These intellectuals provided fodder for newspaper discussions, speeches, scientific analysis, novels, sermons, songs, and blackface minstrel shows in which white superiority was phrased as if whiteness in and of itself was naturally a benefit, despite its lack of material advantage. This sense of superiority allowed struggling northern Whites to look down their noses at free Blacks and at recent immigrants, particularly the Irish. This version of whiteness was supposed to make up for their otherwise difficult situation, providing them with a "psychological wage" instead of cash—a bit like being employee of the month and given a special parking place instead of a raise.

Many Whites bought into the psychological wage, expressing their superiority over non-Whites and defining them, rather than the capitalists, as the enemy. They focused, often with trade union help, on excluding

Blacks and immigrants from skilled trades and better-paying jobs. Employers cooperated in confining Blacks and immigrants to manual labor and domestic work, making a clear definition of the work suitable for white men.[24] Native white men began shifting away from defining themselves by their landowning freedom and independence. Instead they accepted their dependence on capitalists and the control employers exercised over their lives, and began to define themselves by their class position as skilled "mechanics" working for better wages under better working conditions than other people. They became proud of their productivity, which grew with the growing efficiency of industrial technology, and began using it to define whiteness—and manhood. The ethic of individual hard work gained far wider currency. Successful competition in the labor marketplace gradually became a mark of manhood, and "white man's work" became the defining characteristic of whiteness.[25] Freedom was equated with the right to own and sell your own labor, as opposed to slavery, which allowed neither right. Independence was now defined not only by property ownership but also by possession of skill and tools that allowed wage-earning men to acquire status as a head of household controlling dependents.[26]

This redefinition of whiteness was built as much on changing gender as on changing class relationships.[27] Many native white men and women, including workers, journalists, scientists, and politicians, began discouraging married women from working for wages, claiming that true women served only their own families. Despite this claim—the cult of domesticity, or of true womanhood—many wives of working class men actually did work outside the home. They were less likely to do so in those cases where native men were able, through strikes and the exclusion of women, immigrants, and free Blacks, to create an artificial labor shortage. Such shortages gave native working class men the leverage to force employers to pay them enough to afford a non-earning wife. Women in the families of such men frequently did "stay home" and frequently helped to promote the idea that people who couldn't do the same were genetically or racially or culturally inferior.

But native Whites whose wages actually weren't sufficient struggled on in poverty. If a native woman worked for wages, particularly in a factory, the family lost status. Many female factory workers were now immigrants rather than native Whites. Many had no husband or had husbands whose wages, when they could get work, came nowhere near supporting a family.[28] It is no wonder immigrant women weren't particularly "domestic." Such families didn't meet the cultural requirements for white privilege—

male "productivity" in "white man's work" and dependent female "domesticity." These supposed white virtues became a bludgeon with which to defend white privilege and to deny it to not-quite-Whites and not-Whites, helping to construct a new working class hierarchy. This new hierarchy reserved managerial and skilled jobs for "productive" native Whites. So, for the price of reserving better jobs for some native Whites, the capitalist class gained native white consent to their own loss of independence and to keeping most of the working class on abysmally low wages.

In the South, where there was less industry, the psychological wage slowly developed an additional role. It was used not only to gain consent to oppressive industrial relations, but also to convince poor farming Whites to support Southern elites in their conflict with Northern elites. Du Bois points out that by the Civil War

> . . . it became the fashion to pat the disenfranchised poor white man on the back and tell him after all he was white and that he and the planters had a common object in keeping the white man superior. This virus increased bitterness and relentless hatred, and after the war it became a chief ingredient in the division of the working class in the Southern States.[29]

THE IRISH STRUGGLE FOR WHITE PRIVILEGE

But even with the psychological wage in place there was still a fly in the ointment: the discontented part of the working class was still large and growing larger. Some went west, but many, particularly Irish immigrants, who had arrived in America in desperate poverty, couldn't afford the trip west and remained in the East. The Irish lived and worked under conditions so awful that their average life expectancy once they arrived in the United States was six years. In the South they were the major group used where slaves were considered too valuable to risk.[30] "No Irish need apply," the exclusionary barrier enforced by native Whites to protect their jobs in North and South, meant that Irish families were desperate enough to take those risky jobs, thus saving capitalists the cost of higher wages or of improving safety conditions. Most Irish were denied "white man's work," a tactic justified by describing them as lazy, unreliable, diseased, bad tempered, promiscuous, overly productive of children and under productive of everything else. Native Whites, particularly in the North, blamed the Irish for the ills of society, an early version of the long American tradition of immigrant bashing.

Many Irish were as poor as free Blacks, and in material terms were little better off than slaves.[31] They were defined as a separate, not-quite-white
race, citizens perhaps, but citizenship in and of itself in the antebellum
United States provided little; "a citizen (or potential citizen) was distinguished by three main privileges: he could sell himself piecemeal; he could
vote; and he could riot."[32] But of course the "right" to riot was limited.
Rioting against the capitalist class was off limits; rioting against non-Whites
was at times encouraged and the rest of the time at least protected by the
blind eye of the law. Native Whites exercised this right by rioting against
the Irish, including the Bloody Monday riot of 1855 in Louisville, when at
least twenty-two people were killed and much property was damaged by
fire in a protest against Irish, and to some extent German, voting rights.[33]

At this point Irish Americans had a choice, and the choice most made
became critical in restructuring whiteness after the Civil War. Daniel
O'Connell, leader of the movement to free Ireland from England, pleaded
with American Irish leaders to make common cause with the rest of the
people in the United States who were in desperate straits, particularly with
free Blacks and slaves. In the 1820s many Irish and black families lived
side-by-side under comparable conditions. At that point the Irish didn't
clearly distinguish themselves from their black neighbors. Intermarriage
and other forms of socializing within the neighborhood were common; in
prison they were treated the same and cooperated in defying the authori-
ties. Making common non-white cause with Blacks against the capitalist
class was not an impossible choice in the face of extreme and equal
exploitation.[34]

For the capitalist class much was hanging in the balance. Free Blacks
and Irish together made up a large proportion of their cheap labor. If they
banded together they could present an extremely dangerous threat to profits. Also, Blacks were the mirror that reflected whiteness, freedom, manhood, and domesticity for the entire nation. If they were joined by poor
Irish, that mirror would reflect differently, perhaps jeopardizing whiteness
and necessitating another reorganization of the drainage system.

But those well-to-do Irish who had been admitted to the buffer class or
who ran local businesses chose not to make common cause with abolitionists. They assumed their bread was buttered on the capitalist side, and
hoping for recognition by white capitalists, opted for whiteness. They
rejected O'Connell's appeal and ignored Frederick Douglass's explanation
of the advantages of joining with Blacks.[35] Oppressed Irish who followed
their leaders in accepting oppression for Blacks but not for themselves
often chose the citizens' right of rioting, targeting Blacks as scapegoats. The

rioters, often lead by local elites, were establishing their difference from Blacks through violence.[36] Employers soon cooperated, allowing Irish workers to replace Blacks in the 1830s in foundries, factories, domestic service, and as laborers in canal and railroad building.[37] Beating and killing Blacks had been a mark of whiteness since whiteness was invented, and Irish rioters followed that pattern, perhaps hoping their acts would serve as admission tickets.[38]

The tide turned when the elite became increasingly worried about stability and law and order problems arising from continuous rioting, and began enlisting Irish police officers. These Irish thus became acceptable citizens by becoming agents of the elite.[39] The Irish position was again reinforced during the Civil War when Irish soldiers shed native white blood in both armies at the command of elites struggling over control of the value produced by southern black and white workers. Real whiteness, however, didn't come until after the war when the Irish joined other Whites in denying Blacks the brief citizenship during Reconstruction that black soldiers, in shedding Confederate blood, had gained for all Blacks.[40]

CIVIL WAR: RESISTANCE AND THE END OF THE OLD DRAINAGE SYSTEM

The Civil War came at a time when the Northern struggle between workers, the unemployed, and the capitalist class was intense.[41] White Southerners were beginning to feel the effects of industrialization, and the pressure cooker that was slavery was threatening to explode, blasting not only slaves but free Blacks and poor Whites as well out of the control of the elite. John Brown's revolt in 1859, which brought together Whites, slaves, and free Blacks to end slavery, illustrated this potential.

When the war broke out, hardly anyone with power intended to free any slaves. The Union at the start of Civil War was not fighting to *end* slavery; if it had been, poor white Southerners would have fought for the Confederacy in far larger numbers, and the Confederacy might have won. Instead, as Frederick Douglass aptly described, the war was fought *for* slavery, with the Union fighting to keep it in the United States by refusing to let the South separate from the Northern states and the Confederacy fighting to take it out by forming a separate nation. Neither Northern nor Southern leaders expected to end slavery. Lincoln eventually abolished slavery only in Confederate territory, and did so only as a last resort. Even most white abolitionists assumed either that freed slaves would continue providing extremely cheap plantation and manual labor under white control, or that they would be sent to Africa. Many Northern politicians and business owners wanted to keep the enormous Southern resources of land and labor—both slave and free—within the Union and were willing to avoid splitting the Union and losing those resources, by placating Southern elites, leaving slavery intact.[42]

Many poor white Southerners believed their whiteness gave them good reason to support white supremacy. The psychological wage, giving them someone to look down on, led them to side with the white elite. Many believed slaveholders who said the war was about property rights in land as well as slaves, and therefore they, as actual or hopeful small landowners, had as great a stake in the outcome as did slaveholders. Others were economically dependent on local planters and thus likely to fight on the side of the Confederacy. Or they saw the plantation system as integral to the patriarchy that gave them control of their families and laborers. But many Southern Whites, like many Northern soldiers, fought for the Union because they wanted to prevent the spread of slavery and to limit their competition with unpaid labor, not because they wanted to end slavery or establish equality with Blacks. Some Southern Whites opposed the Confederacy in order to oppose the growing despotism of the planter elite.[43]

The split was particularly severe in border slave states like Kentucky, where many were at the same time pro-slavery and pro-Union. Kentucky remained in the Union, but also had a provisional Confederate government.[44] There was a tendency in Kentucky for Whites in non-plantation areas to favor the Union, except for those tied by mercantile interests to the South.[45] Approximately 60,000 white Kentuckians fought in Union armies and 35,000 in Confederate armies. South County provided nearly as many recruits per capita for the Union army as did some Northern states, while North County was seriously split in its recruitment patterns.[46] Ambivalence about the Confederacy among white Kentuckians outside the heavily plantation areas of the Bluegrass and western Kentucky may have been critical to the outcome of the war. Louisville had a near monopoly on north-south rail and river travel through the Ohio Valley, and Confederate failure to control this transportation system probably contributed to their military defeat.[47]

Given the ambivalences, the outcome of the war may well have been determined, not by the decisions of politicians and generals, but by what Du Bois calls the "General Strike," the withdrawal of support by those in the North and the South most directly affected by an extremely bloody war.[48] By 1863 Northern volunteers were deserting in droves and recruiters couldn't find enough volunteers to replace the dead, maimed, and long-gone. The Northern white working class had gone on strike, despite the carrot of land the elite held out by passing the Homestead Act of 1862—which in actuality provided land mainly for already wealthy railroad and land speculators; the truly poor couldn't afford to homestead.[49]

In the meantime, slaves were also on strike. Slaves had, whenever possible, already withdrawn their labor from the plantation system that supported the Southern economy, engaging in slowdowns and sabotage, providing information to Northern troops, or running away. A breakdown of the Southern economy would be greatly to the North's advantage. Lincoln and the Northern generals eventually recognized that their best chance of winning the war lay with the slaves.[50] Rather unwillingly, Lincoln declared emancipation for slaves in enemy territory as of January 1, 1863, thus making escape far easier. Also rather unwillingly, the Union increased the army's use of black laborers. But as the Northern strike deepened there were fewer volunteers, and when military conscription was instituted Northerners responded with the Draft Riots of 1863. In New York and elsewhere working class Whites, angered by conscription and a provision in the law which allowed the wealthy to buy their way out of the draft, protested violently. New York's property loss was over one million dollars, and the rioting took on an anti-Union, pro-slavery character, and included attacks on Blacks. It took the military to restore order.[51] In desperation, Blacks were finally admitted to gun-carrying status. Allowing Blacks to fight reduced the number of Whites who had to be drafted, but it also ended any real possibility of maintaining the fiction that black men were not real men, and thus made the abolition of slavery almost inevitable. Because military service, particularly on the front lines, is a male initiation rite, bringing rights with it, many Whites were reluctant to admit Blacks to the fraternity of soldiers.[52] Once admitted, black soldiers were often used on the frontlines in particularly dangerous or hopeless situations, and performed extremely well.[53] By the end of the war the Northern army was one-tenth black; about 180,000 black men had fought with the Union army, 25,000 of them from Kentucky.[54]

Southern Whites struck too. As the war dragged on, Southern farmers were desperately needed at home. Like their Northern counterparts, many deserted—about one-third of the Confederate army at any one time. Volunteers became scarce. Apparently they saw little point in dying to save the plantation aristocracy, especially after conscription began with slaveholders exempted.[55] Women, particularly yeoman women, joined the strike. They encouraged their men to desert and return home to help save the family from starvation and protect it from marauding soldiers of both armies. They instigated riots, smashing windows and stealing bread and other provisions, and as the war continued and conditions became worse these bread riots spread.[56] Draft riots broke out in the South. Some white Southerners began to argue that *their* only hope of winning the war lay now with promising freedom to slaves if they would just fight for the Confederacy.[57] But agreeing to let slaves be soldiers, not just impressed laborers, and therefore true men, was too high a price for winning the war, and it was not done. Du Bois describes the South's sudden decision to surrender at Appomattox as a decision to surrender to the North, rather than to Blacks.[58] Southern elites may have hoped to save some form of slavery through the terms of surrender, but if not, at least to avoid disruption of their authority over the system of social control of Blacks and poor Whites.[59]

In this last they proved to be correct, but in the meantime the General Strike was successful. The war between capitalists over the control of black and white labor, North and South, and over the distribution of the fruits of that labor, had been stopped. Those who provided that labor had stopped it by the only means available: they just said "no." They voted with their feet by deserting; they rioted; or they proved that they, like other "real men," could kill. As chaos increased and the supply of human cannon fodder decreased, the elite had to capitulate and the drainage system had to be reorganized yet again. In a now-familiar pattern, whiteness also had to be reconstructed to accommodate the new system, this time depending on that partial solution, the psychological wage, but also on new relationships of force.

5

FORKS IN THE ROAD

For a brief period after the Civil War there was a possibility that bony-fingered people could have won a social structure that would allow Southerners, both black and white, to keep more of the value of their own sweat. They might have owned their own bodies and their own labor as well as the land they needed for real freedom. Those who were not farming, but selling themselves piecemeal in North and South, would have received higher wages. That this road was not taken is testimony to the power of an elite determined to protect its right to wring as much sweat out of "little guys" as it can get away with. It is equally testimony to the power of racism to blind those who are suffering, so that they support the social structure that causes their pain.

After the Civil War local Southern elites continued to preside over the new system at the local level, but they were more tightly tied into the national drainage system. They were utterly dependent on the ideology of white supremacy and the psychological wage to maintain control of the Blacks and Whites whose sweat they drained. They played on white fears of black reprisals for slavery, and on the unsupported fear that black men would start raping white women just as generations of white men had raped black women. Most southern Whites, regardless of class, readily agreed that Blacks were dangerous, and that they wouldn't work except when forced. The legal divisions of free or enslaved had disappeared with emancipation, leaving the now widely accepted belief in the biological reality of race to bear the entire burden of making these claims appear plausible.[1] Poorer Whites, blinded by their belief in their own whiteness, thus agreed to a reorganization of the drainage system which they soon found trapped them, as well as Blacks, in the desperation of unfree sharecropping. The consequences of poor white failure to protest would quickly come back to haunt them.

Despite the power of racist ideology, however, there continued to be historical moments when cross-racial coalitions seemed imminent, when many bony-fingered Whites saw the psychological wage for what it was, and threatened to join Blacks in mounting a genuine challenge to the rule of the elite. The elite, in danger of dispossession, moved quickly each time to restore the power of race, to get Whites to "settle for being white."[2] These were the moments when the road forked, when there was a brief possibility that history could have taken a different course and the mighty river that was sweat flowing up could have been dammed.

REORGANIZING UNFREE LABOR

The first of those forks came during and immediately after the Civil War, when the federal government seriously considered confiscating land from the conquered Confederate elite. The land would have been redistributed to the landless former slaves who had made the planters' wealth, and to landless white war refugees. Former slaves were demanding this redistribution, maintaining that the country they had enriched had an obligation to them beyond simply turning four million of them loose with nothing but the clothes on their backs. Blacks asked for forty acres, a small piece of the land they had worked as slaves. They asked no further recompense out of the profits they, their children, their parents and grandparents, and earlier generations had made for their owners. Nonetheless, any land redistribution would have violated the sanctity of private property and threatened Northern and Southern elite plans for the region.

Rejecting equality

Radical Republican leader Thaddeus Stevens proposed taking the land of the "chief Rebels," owners of thousands of acres. According to his calculations, this would provide forty acres for all adult male freedmen with plenty left for landless Whites to buy. He proposed indemnifying loyal Southern Whites, whose indemnity money could have gone toward the purchase of land. He assumed the land would sell at an average of ten dollars an acre.[3] However, in all likelihood, the glut on the market resulting from the sale of more than three-quarters of the South's agricultural land would have rapidly lowered the price. Even poor Confederates could have bought land. Presumably also, many of those whose land had been confiscated could have bought enough for successful diversified subsistence farming or for commercial family farming. Stevens assumed that those who couldn't stand the loss of their elite status would go into voluntary exile.

For several years the federal government had taken steps in conquered Confederate territories that made Stevens's proposal look politically feasible.[4] The Second Confiscation Act of 1862, although never really enforced, provided that land be taken from disloyal Confederates, those who didn't pay their taxes, or who had fled. Congress authorized the Freedmen's Bureau in 1865 to divide abandoned and confiscated land into forty-acre tracts with rent-to-buy arrangements, allowing freed slaves and loyal white refugees a real chance to acquire land. Even during the war the Freedmen's Bureau and some Union generals had experimented with land redistribution as a way of dealing with slaves who had freed themselves by crossing into Union territory.

But from the point of view of Northern capitalists wanting Southern raw materials, and of Southern capitalists wanting labor in Southern industry and agriculture, these experiments merely proved that redistribution of land was an extremely bad idea.[5] When freed slaves on their own farms rapidly moved toward diversified subsistence farming, rejecting exclusive cash crop production, Northern industrialists worried that the production of raw materials might drop.[6] And if Blacks and Whites had received land as proposed, the South's landless class—those "willing" to work for a pittance—would have shrunk remarkably. Northern manufacturers worried that without competition from cheaper Southern wages, Northern workers would insist on higher wages. In fact, the Northern appetite for raw materials could have been met without denying land to Blacks. For example, Blacks ran their former plantation at Davis Bend as a co-op, producing cotton efficiently for sale and keeping the profits for themselves.[7]

Elite concerns were compounded by the growing Southern split between the white elite on one hand and white working class and yeomen on the other. This split had been at the heart of the Southern white version of the General Strike, when many Whites stopped supporting the elite during the Civil War. Since land is the basis of power in a slaveless agrarian economy, redistribution would have made control of the working class and yeomen even more difficult.

While all this was going on, the Republican federal administration also faced the problems of reuniting a shattered country. Northern industrialists who formed the backbone of the Republican Party wanted social and political stability so they could take advantage of this opportunity to increase their control of the Southern drainage system.[8] The South, as a conquered territory, became in many senses a colony of the North. Like other colonies it would produce cheap raw materials for industry and supply workers at extremely low wages. As in other colonies, this would be done under the direction of local elites who were themselves controlled directly by the dominant national industrial elites. Thus the interests of both planters and industrialists coincided in their need to reorganize a cheap labor force to replace slavery. Both realized that if the land of conquered wealthy Confederates were appropriated, there would be no hope of organizing the South under colonial conditions, with cooperative Southern elites serving as links to the Northern drainage system.

Reestablishing elite power without slavery

In a sense, giving Blacks the vote was a substitute for land redistribution. Many Southerners, as well as Northerners, argued that with the vote Blacks should be able to protect themselves from white violence, relieving the army of that expensive operation, and could be held responsible for their own economic fate.[9] After months of indecision, the federal government voted to require former Confederate states to end slavery except in prisons and to make enfranchisement of Blacks a condition of readmission to the Union.[10]

Serious consideration of land redistribution for the poor ended with President Johnson's Amnesty Proclamation in May 1865, which promised Confederates declaring loyalty to the Union the right to recover their land. He then vetoed an act in 1866 that would have strengthened the Freedmen's Bureau's ability to redistribute land.[11] Blacks who had established homes and had become self-supporting in the experimental programs, who had tasted what generations of Blacks had dreamed of, the right to control their own lives and labor, were told to leave their forty acres and return to landless servitude. When they refused, as many did, they were driven out at federal gunpoint by the troops who presumably had fought to free them. Within a year after the end of the war, most planters had regained their land.[12]

In failing to protest when Johnson gutted land redistribution, poor Whites hurt themselves as well as Blacks. Perhaps the fact that they were included in redistribution and rent-to-buy plans was a well-kept secret. Johnson justified his veto by asking why Blacks should be helped when Whites had never been helped. This was a rather remarkable justification, since Whites had been helped regularly.[13] The bureau gave rations to destitute Whites as well as Blacks, and could have helped both races to landowning, yet white elites in the Democratic party described the bureau as "an agency to keep the Negro in idleness at the expense of the white man."[14] That this tactic has a modern ring to it shouldn't be too surprising, considering that the Freedmen's Bureau was the first large-scale welfare program for the poor undertaken by the U.S. government. Like modern welfare programs, it regulated the labor supply.[15] It provided just enough financial help to prevent rioting on the part of the desperately poor, and put a very low lower limit on employers' ability to exploit people at the bottom of the drainage system.

Once land redistribution had been rejected, the Freedman's Bureau became the agency overseeing the transition from slavery to landless freedom in conquered Confederate territory. Kentucky was also placed under the bureau, despite its Union status, because of its recalcitrance in freeing its slaves.[16] The bureau played a double-edged role in the conflict between landowners and workers, by protecting Blacks from the worst excesses of landowners, but also organizing the black labor supply for those same landowners. Anti-vagrancy laws, now making unemployment a crime for Blacks as well as Whites, forced people to accept even gang labor contracts if they couldn't find a better situation. Kentucky laws required officials to "'sell into servitude' (or apprentice if the defendant was a minor) all 'able-bodied persons . . . found loitering or rambling about, not having the means to maintain himself, by some visible property' or who does not work or make an honest effort to find work."[17] Anti-enticement laws made it illegal for Whites to persuade Blacks to leave an employer, even for higher wages. At the same time, most Whites refused to rent or sell land to Blacks; Blacks who did rent or buy were in danger of being lynched.[18] Whites who rented or sold to Blacks, or who hired them as laborers, might be ostracized and ran some risk, either to their property or to themselves. During Reconstruction, Kentucky was the only Union state in which the Ku Klux Klan gained much power; it committed as many acts of violence there, and the legal system turned just as deaf an ear there, as anywhere in the South.[19] The result was, at least for Blacks, a "compulsory system of free labor" enforced by the legal system and by the illegal wave of Klan and other organized violence that swept the South after the war.[20]

Plantation owners and the Northern elites who were commercially allied with them advocated going back to gang labor under conditions very similar to slavery, and Blacks put up a determined resistance. They pushed for their own farms, and frequently refused to work under the conditions landowners proposed. Meanwhile landowners in Kentucky and throughout the South pursued the possibility of bringing in immigrant labor. However, they had to abandon that plan when they found that European immigrants now expected to benefit from white privilege, found plantation conditions unacceptable, and left as quickly as they could. Planters discussed importing Chinese labor, but were foiled by the state of international relations at the time.[21] Landowners hesitated to turn to native white gang labor for fear of provoking a rebellion by reducing Whites to conditions comparable to Blacks. After all, elites had mustered poor white allegiance during the Civil War by claiming the war would maintain white privilege. Gang-laboring Whites, former soldiers and their families, might conclude they had endured the bloody Civil War for nothing and change their minds about the value of following the elite. [22]

By the end of Reconstruction the conflict over labor control was settled through the sharecropping system, which in many cases drained the family as a unit as thoroughly as the individuals in it had been drained during slavery. Still, in Kentucky and elsewhere, freed slaves continued to resist. They withdrew their labor either by joining the flood of freed slaves going North or by insisting that black women had the same right to spend time taking care of their children that white women had, causing landowners to complain of a labor shortage.[23] Initially this reorganization of the drainage system applied only to Blacks, but by the end of Reconstruction the elite lost their fear that they might instigate revolt if they treated Whites like Blacks, since white anger had been successfully refocused on Blacks rather than on the elite. Hunger and lack of options—often the consequence of the death and destruction of a devastating war for people who are already economically vulnerable—drove more and more Whites to sharecropping.[24]

The consequences of this shift to sharecropping were horrendous for black and white families who saw their hopes of real freedom evaporate. Many white families were now caught in a vicious landless circle similar to that of black sharecroppers. They had acquiesced in the elite's choice of roads at the fork of Reconstruction, and their only comfort now was the psychological wage: "At least I'm white."[25]

The Drainage Continuum: Degrees of "Freedom"

In Kentucky and elsewhere after Reconstruction a wide range of free, fairly free, and unfree labor gradually evolved.[26] Each form, ranging from convict labor to forced apprenticeship, sharecropping, hired farm labor, renting, industrial labor, and farm-owning debt peonage, was organized by laws and enforced by the "justice" system. During Reconstruction Blacks had gained the right to testify against Whites in court and to vote, and in some areas held elected office, and masked terrorism was criminalized. But with the discontinuation of the Freedmen's Bureau and the Republican defeat at the polls, it became easier and easier to disregard the rights of all Blacks and many of the rights of poor people generally. The interests of employers and big landowners, who made up the majority of elected officials, lawmakers, and judges, rapidly regained uncontested priority over the interests of employees, small landowners, and landless farmers. During the last decades of the 1800s the elite passed and enforced the new laws that made the new drainage system work.

Unfree labor: continued slavery

In the new drainage continuum slavery did exist, although including fewer people than formerly. The "justice" system processed some real and many trumped up charges against mostly young black men who became legally "slaves of the state," providing slave labor for plantations, railroads, and businessmen through convict leasing.[27] Anti-vagrancy laws were particularly helpful in this endeavor, as was lengthening the sentences for minor offenses. As a result, the number of convicts tripled or quadrupled within just a few years.[28] Convict leasing rapidly became a major source of labor and profit. In 1890 alone, 27,000 convicts were leased at low cost from local and state governments throughout the South. Most of those convicted were black because the laws were written to make Blacks more vulnerable than Whites, and because laws were far more strictly enforced against Blacks than Whites. In some states only black convicts were leased; many of them were children and adolescents. Potential profits were vast and "some of the wealthiest capitalists benefited enormously from it."[29] In Kentucky until 1880 prisons themselves were leased to the highest bidder. The successful entrepreneur then set the prisoners to work making salable merchandise under conditions so awful that in 1875 20 percent of the prisoners had tuberculosis. "Reforms" in 1880 allowed convicts to be leased outside the prison where they worked as miners or built railroads or reservoirs while living in "virtual death camps."[30]

Whites were afraid of Blacks, were convinced of their criminal tendencies, and often blamed Blacks for white poverty. They applauded this use of the courts and believed convict labor and the chain gang were well-deserved punishments that protected Whites against black lawlessness. What convict slavery provided, however, was not protection of Whites, but protection of the profits of big landowners and business contractors. Just as slavery had done earlier, prison slavery meant even lower wages for those outside of prisons.[31] Every employer using prison slaves was an employer who didn't have to hire free workers. With fewer jobs available, employers could reject anyone demanding a living wage, knowing that someone desperate enough to take starvation wages would soon show up. So employers using prison labor benefited from the low cost of leasing. They also recognized that safety standards could be substantially lower for convict laborers; there was little public outcry over the high convict death rate. Those who didn't lease convicts themselves also benefited, through the increased desperation of those outside the prison without jobs or land. Convict labor was thus a part of the social and legal structure that trapped most Blacks and many Whites in other bony-fingered positions at or near the bottom of the new drainage system.

Unfree labor: debt peonage, indenture, and apprenticeship

The unfree labor system underwent changes of emphasis after the war. Involuntary indenture and apprenticeship continued to turn many black children and "vagrant" black adults in Kentucky into virtual slaves. County officials resisted Federal attempts to regulate this system.[32] Like sharecropping and renting, which had also existed before the war, debt peonage escalated. Much of Southern industry depended on debt peonage to provide an additional unfree labor force, particularly in extractive industries like lumbering, turpentine, and mining. These industries were so dangerous and paid so little that people with any choice avoided them. Debt to the employer was legally organized to prevent workers from leaving until they had paid the employer back in full. Debt was often orchestrated through a company store system and wages were paid in scrip—coupons that could be redeemed only at the company store—instead of money. While not slavery and not indenture, this system was certainly a close relative of both, and was used to control industrial workers as well as sharecroppers. It created a bound labor force within what was technically a system of free wage labor.[33]

THE SHARECROPPING TRAP

Next on the continuum of unfree labor was sharecropping. The combined effects of legal and illegal "justice" made sharecropping for Blacks nearly as tight a system of control as slavery had been—resistance was often suicidally dangerous. The legal "justice" system operated through courts enforcing laws written to benefit landowners and merchants. The illegal "justice" system operated through white violence enforcing the unwritten laws of deference, obedience, and white male rights to black and white women. For Whites sharecropping was somewhat more flexible, but nevertheless gave landowners immense power over every aspect of their lives.

The sharecropping contract legally created unequal power between sharecroppers and landlords. It also forced sharecropping families into commercial agriculture and away from the diversified subsistence farming that many preferred.[34] The usual contract stated that the sharecropping family would provide the labor to grow a crop. In cotton farming, most families worked between ten and twenty acres; in tobacco the average was about five. In either case farm work absorbed the labor of the entire family. The landlord in return would give them half the crop and generally provided mules, equipment, and a "house," often a leaking, windy, falling-down shed. A generous landowner might allow sharecroppers to cut firewood and grow a garden. Labor contract laws gave landlords the right to regulate all aspects of the behavior of an entire sharecropper family. The landlord had the right to terminate the contract for any breach, including "bad or immoral conduct." Needless to say, the sharecropper didn't have a reciprocal right to terminate the contract for the immoral or bad behavior of the landowner. The contract could legally require that the entire sharecropping family be suitably deferential. It could specify the landlord's right to make all decisions about what crops to grow and how to grow them. It could require that the entire family be ready at any time of day or night to do the landowner's bidding, which often included cooking, cleaning, and running errands, as well as fencing and other farm maintenance work. Terminated families forfeited any rights in the crop on which they had worked. This was somewhat easier to do to black than to white families, since the justice system frequently ignored black testimony about what had really happened.

Once the crop was harvested the second law controlling sharecropping came into play. The crop-lien law gave creditors prior rights to the crop grown by their debtors, and sharecroppers were almost always in debt, usually to the landlord, sometimes to local merchants. Since the family wouldn't be paid until the crop was sold, and had to eat in the meantime, the landlord "furnished" the family, giving either supplies or credit at a very minimal level of subsistence, all to be paid back after the harvest. Often at the final reckoning the landlord added other deductions. Most sharecropping families eventually were unable to "pay out" their debt and could be made to agree to stay on until the debt was paid. Laws against enticing away another landowner's workers facilitated this control, making it difficult for indebted families to look for a landlord who might give them a better deal. As each year's debt added to that of the previous year, the family became less and less likely to pay out.

The family couldn't avoid the furnishing system and thereby stay out of debt to the landlord because there was no alternative source of credit for people with no collateral.[35] Sharecroppers needed furnishing because the landlord didn't permit diversified subsistence farming, and often didn't even permit a garden, since land and time devoted to growing food for the sharecropping family didn't make profits for the landlord.[36] Even worse from the landlord's point of view, a family out of debt was a family free to leave. Once in debt the whole family belonged, for all intents and purposes, to the landlord for as long as he continued to want them.

Sharecropping parents seeing themselves and their children being worn down or dying from malnutrition or overwork sometimes tried to resist this system. If they became too vocal, or tried to use the legal system to question the landlord's bookkeeping, they generally found little help from local officials. If they persisted they could expect a visit from the Ku Klux Klan or other terrorist organization. Frequently they were blacklisted so that they would never find another landowner who would allow them to sharecrop. Runaway sharecroppers were legally returned to their landlords.[37] In reality, in rural Kentucky and much of the rest of the South, running off or leaving to find a job wouldn't help very much. Working for wages for a farmer, especially if room and board were provided, might work for single men and women. However, the seventy-five cents a day—when there was work—paid in South County in 1880 left the day-laborer as vulnerable to the employer as did sharecropping.[38] North County had a few town jobs, but was cash poor.[39]

In addition to the legal structures that controlled sharecropping for both Blacks and Whites, there were de facto laws, which applied only to Blacks. Some of these laws, although unwritten, nevertheless clearly operated within the legal "justice" system. Whites understood that the vagrancy laws applied primarily to Blacks. They acted on the assumption that the glance of a black man toward a white woman could signal his intention to rape her, and that a touch could be defined as attempted rape. To this was added a general white agreement that black self-assertion was "uppity" and black success was aggression. Consequently black entrepreneurs, craftsmen, and professionals were in danger of being defined as "out of line." These unspoken agreements influenced arrests, indictments, and jury verdicts within the legal "justice" system.[40]

The illegal "justice" system of mob and Klan violence often came into play when these de facto laws were violated by Blacks or by white "nigger-lovers," filling in where the legal system couldn't or wouldn't tread.[41] This was particularly common when the victim had done nothing punishable legally, when Whites were worried about a "miscarriage of justice," or when Whites were particularly enraged and wanted a swift reprisal for alleged black crimes. Beatings were common, as were lynchings—murders by groups without legal sanction, ranging from hanging to torture and dismemberment to burning alive. Although newspapers frequently cited rape as the reason for lynching, analysis of lynch victims shows that most weren't even accused of rape. Instead, they appear to have violated the "law" against black success. After the Civil War, lynchings were carried out in the South at the rate of two or three a week until 1900, mostly, but far from exclusively, of Blacks. Their effect was not simply to punish offenders, but to implement a terrorist campaign that sent a message to the entire black and white population, warning of the consequences of challenging the status quo.

Even after sharecropping became common, White people outside former plantation areas were often able to insist on renting rather than sharecropping. Sharecropping rates were fairly low in both North and South County, since a good many Whites owned their own farms and because with relatively low enslavement there were relatively few freed people looking for land to farm after the war. Thus those looking for farms, particularly Whites, were more likely to be able to negotiate a rental contract. In addition, Whites were more likely than Blacks to be in a position to rent, since renters were usually required to provide their own mule and equipment and white mule ownership wasn't likely to be defined as "uppity."[42] Despite the advantage of renting over sharecropping, including direct ownership of the crop, many renters remained mired in debt. The prices they got for their crops were low and the interest rates charged by merchants or landowners were high for the furnishing the family needed until the crop sold.

THE LANDLORD AND THE TRAP

The flip side of sharecropping and renter poverty was wealth for landlords. Prices for crops did vary tremendously from year to year, but even in a bad year most large Kentucky landowners came out ahead, receiving income from half the crop of as many as fifty families, with comparatively light expenses against that income.[43] Those with many families to furnish often set up their own plantation store, buying in bulk and adding a huge markup. Many used vouchers that would be honored only at the store owned by the landlord, similar to the scrip that miners were later paid. Like scrip, the voucher system insured that any cash a landlord paid out or that renters received when they sold the crop would be cycled back into the landlord's pocket. Should a sharecropping family do well, landlords sometimes manipulated the books to make sure they received no cash.[44] This system of unfree labor–debt peonage–legally ended in 1911. However, on a de facto basis it continued to operate into the 1960s, although the jaws of the trap became somewhat looser in both the legal and illegal justice systems.[45]

Landlords, having constructed legally and socially the trap that was debt peonage, indulged themselves in the belief that sharecroppers were poor because they were lazy, wasteful, or inefficient. Stereotypes about childlike or irresponsible Blacks and lazy "white trash" disguised the reality of the trap. Landlords discussed among themselves and for various inquiring outsiders their difficulties in finding good, loyal, hardworking "hands."[46] This discussion allowed them to believe their hard work–and some did work hard–was the source of their comparative or actual wealth. In reality, their position was built, just as the Rowans' had been, on welfare and on the unrequited and unremitting labor of generations of men, women, and children, first slaves and later black or white sharecroppers and tenants. Most landlords, particularly those with enormous holdings, had inherited their land, and as a group had successfully refused to permit redistribution. They had persuaded the federal government to readmit them to the Union and to forgive their disloyalty without forcing them to give up their land. Once readmitted and back in local, state, and national government, they voted for laws guaranteeing their right to their property and to pay starvation wages and to use enslaved convict labor. And, should sharecroppers or tenants have the nerve to challenge their illegal behavior as Klan leaders or as landlords manipulating the books, they could count on their control of the legal system, on deference, or on white supremacy to avoid conviction.

THE ROUTE CHOSEN

By the end of Reconstruction this system was thoroughly in place. The elite had responded to emancipation with organized and unorganized, legal and illegal, violence against Blacks. They justified the new system by playing on white fears of Blacks returning to their "natural" state of bestiality without the restraint of the whip in the hand of master or overseer. Black demands for land were seen as proof that they were about to overthrow the "natural" social order. Because of all the mythology to the contrary, it is important to emphasize that former slaves were not threatening organized group violence to gain land, and there were almost no instances of individualized violence against Whites. There was nothing in terms of black criminal behavior after emancipation to justify the vicious system of control that eventually replaced slavery. Landowners instituted "state-sanctioned neo-slavery" in order to regain their control of profitable black labor, not in order to protect Whites from actual danger posed by Blacks.[47]

Although the system was initially designed to control Blacks, it was quickly applied to poor Whites as well, giving elites the opportunity to increase their drainage from white families. However, fear of Blacks induced many poorer Whites to direct their violence against Blacks rather than against oppressive landlords. They joined the Ku Klux Klan, the illegal enforcement system led by local elites, believing that they were upholding white womanhood and white honor by keeping Blacks "in line." They were paying themselves in the coin of the psychological wage. But that same Klan could be turned against poor Whites if they protested, or if they tried to unite with Blacks. Just as the initial consolidation of slavery and of whiteness had been built with violence and blood, this consolidation of "neo-slavery" for Blacks and many Whites required a reconstruction of whiteness and was built with blood and violence, with the lynching, burning, and beating of many Blacks and of some Whites. As Eric Foner emphasizes, Reconstruction ended because of violence and fraud, not because landless Blacks succumbed to economic coercion.[48]

Unfree labor now included both Blacks and Whites for the first time since the original construction of whiteness had separated unfree African and European laborers, freeing Whites and enslaving Blacks. Once Whites "agreed" to this reconstruction, siding with those who drained both Blacks and Whites as sharecroppers, renters, or day labor, the balance of power again tipped safely toward the elite. The road had forked; the route of continued oppression had been chosen.

6

GENDER, WHITENESS, AND THE PSYCHOLOGICAL WAGE

Sharecropping neo-slavery now controlled the lives of thousands of black and white families throughout the South. Others were much closer to freedom, but even they found their position eroding. Small landowners gradually came under the thumbs of local merchants and of an increasingly powerful class of national capitalists. This process accelerated in Kentucky as more and more landowning families shifted from diversified subsistence farming to commercial family farming, with its greater dependence on markets and cash. Ties to the national drainage system tightened as families bought more from merchants. They paid high prices for food, clothing, and farming necessities produced by national corporations, and received low prices from the national corporations that bought the commodities they produced. The result was poverty for many and a debt peonage, which, while not as extreme, bore some resemblance to sharecropping.

CLOSER TO FREEDOM

In yeoman areas, like much of North and South County, the drainage system was not as dependent on sharecropping and renting as it was in plantation areas. Here, although there were some sharecroppers and a few renters, many more white families than in plantation areas owned and worked their own farms, as did occasional black families. Some families, those close to streams and rivers, who still had timber on their farms, turned to logging as a source of cash and a way to avoid debt.[1] Logging could be carried on during the winter when agricultural work eased off. Then early in the spring, as streams rose, young men in the family, or hired hands, joined the logs into rafts and set out for Evansville, Indiana, the hardwood capital of the United States. Lives and limbs were often lost as rafters rode the high water to "jump" the numerous milldams that blocked the streams and smaller rivers, and then negotiated the logging traffic on the Green and Ohio Rivers. The cash they earned sometimes survived the temptations of the city and the long trip home, and sometimes didn't; in either case, the young men involved apparently regarded the trip as an adventure. However, this was a route open only to farm owners and to those close to water, and since the risk of death or disablement was high, it could lead to the impoverishment of the family. A safer but less lucrative source of income was found in crafts, such as South County's basket-making tradition.[2]

In 1890 most farming families in North and South County cultivated their own farms—84 percent in North County, 79 percent in South County. Farms in South County were somewhat smaller, and in both counties there was more sharecropping than renting.[3] However, farm ownership was probably more concentrated than this would indicate. Big landowners now, as they probably did in 1890, own many farms scattered over a wide area, with a renting or sharecropping family on each, rather than the consolidated holdings typical of a plantation economy. Working a family-owned farm in North or South County didn't necessarily mean the family provided all the labor, particularly for tobacco growing. Some growers kept the women in their families out of the fields and hired black laborers by the year, with board and rations, and hired additional help as needed by the day. In 1880 South County produced twice as much burley tobacco as did North County, and continues to this day to depend far more on tobacco than does North County. Burley's introduction in South County in the 1880s was described by the local newspaper editor as a "New Era" for a county with the best burley soil in the region.[4] The county also had the right kind of soil for tobacco for cigar wrappers, which were grown by a "small class of planters" who had the necessary "fixtures" and "much personal reputation."[5]

Tobacco as a cash crop gradually became feasible in areas without rivers for transportation as railroads spread and roads that were passable at least part of the year penetrated further into the countryside. At the same time a new cigarette-rolling machine made large-scale cigarette manufacturing feasible, and as burley's main use is in cigarettes, it suddenly became extremely lucrative—for merchants. In areas like North and South

County, dominated by family farmers owning their own land, merchants joined landlords in controlling commercial production and commercial farm families through debt.[6] Some merchants refused to accept the products of diversified subsistence farming, requiring farmers to use tobacco for repayment of debts, although in many areas they could still bring in corn and country produce for smaller purchases. One South County merchant lists 31 acceptable items, many of which, from eggs to dried apples to candles, were probably produced by women, and at least in many cases the resulting income was apparently controlled by women.[7] But small farms couldn't produce both tobacco and subsistence goods, so debt forced them into greater commercial production and into more debt for necessities. Other families, not driven by debt, undoubtedly saw burley as an opportunity to get cash for the purchase of more consumer goods, and voluntarily entered commercial family farming.

Despite the lure of burley and the cash it could bring, anti-consumerism was common. A South County editorial in 1887 identified the failure to use home manufactures as a cause of poverty. The editor then summed up the anti–big guy, anti–consumerist philosophy:

> Well, I'm poor and I don't want to be rich. I don't believe a man can get rich without using unfair and dishonest methods, wronging his fellow man in some way. My wealth is my own self-respect, and the hope of a better condition in the great hereafter.[8]

Even today some in my area avoid consumerism. They do this partly out of the religious belief that materialism is wrong. They are aware of the problems arising from giving in to the pressure to buy unnecessary items, including televisions, telephones, women's and children's clothing, and prepared foods that they could instead raise or make at home. Consumerism, they believe, would ultimately lead to women working outside the home and farm. Both men and women would work harder, have less time for family and God, and no time at all for fishing and mushroom hunting in the woods. They claim that this attitude came from the culture of their parents and grandparents. If so, and taking into account the common resistance to elite plans to bring in roads and railroads, the likelihood is that many families were driven into commercial farming by debt rather than choosing it voluntarily.

In any case, tobacco production in yeoman areas increased rapidly after the Civil War. Once involved in commercial farming, many landowning families found themselves caught in a vicious cycle. Both men and women eventually did have to work harder just to stay even. For diversified subsistence families being poor may have meant a shortage of cash, but they usually ate well, secure under a solid roof. Poverty for commercial farming families, by contrast, often meant a shortage of basic necessities. This type of poverty has regularly accompanied shifts to commercial family farming all over the world, not just in Kentucky.[9]

Tobacco prices being what they were, unpredictable and often very low, families in Kentucky frequently didn't make enough to cover the costs of tobacco production or to pay their taxes. Tobacco prices dropped from six and a half cents a pound in 1876 to five cents in 1879, while the cost of raising tobacco was at least five cents a pound.[10] When families couldn't survive such prices, merchants would extend credit. If the family was unable to pay out after several years, the merchant could foreclose, and that family or another became tenants or sharecroppers on the farm. Alternatively, although there was little practical difference, the merchant could continue carrying the family from year to year. Merchants in this case took a significant proportion of the crop to service the debt, as provided by the crop-lien law. They could even refuse to take crops other than the region's cash crop as collateral. Such limitations forced the family's time away from subsistence crops and made them more dependent on store credit for basic necessities. Although landowning families caught in this trap had more control over their lives and what they did with their land than did sharecroppers, they nevertheless were not truly free.

THE RIGHT OF PATRIARCHY, FREEDOM, AND THE LABOR CONTINUUM

Merchant, landlord, and jailer together controlled a continuum of labor, ranging from slave to nearly free, and freedom was not as clearly racially defined as previously. Those toward the unfree end of the continuum were more likely to be black, and the continuum got whiter and whiter toward the free end. Convict slaves belonged to the state and by the 1880s could be leased, but not sold, and this form of slavery was no longer exclusively black; there were now a few white convicts. At the other end of the continuum there were more black landowners than previously and a few well-to-do black entrepreneurs and professionals. This shift in the relationship between race and freedom, combined with the shift from diversified subsistence farming to commercial family farming, led to corresponding redefinitions of gender and of whiteness. Freedom could no longer be equated with whiteness. Both women and men lost autonomy as the value of the labor of the whole household now flowed through a valve—the head of household—into the wider drainage system. Patriarchal white supremacy was revised to reflect these new conditions. It affected people differently according to their class and became the organizing principle of the entire social structure, much to the detriment of black men and women, white women, and most white men.

The patriarchal "head of household" and commercial family farming

Gender roles changed with the shift to emphasizing commercial tobacco production.[11] In diversified subsistence farming, production for sale had brought in only a trickle of money. Part of this income came from women's independent endeavors, selling cloth, butter, and eggs. Part of it came from men's comparable independent endeavors, for instance in lumbering or whiskey or corn, with perhaps some tobacco. But a large part of the labor of men, women, and children went into production for their own use within the family, with men in charge of field crops and women in charge of dairying and much home manufacturing.

By contrast, a commercial family farm devoted far more labor to growing cash crops and far more money was involved. Field crops had always been under male control, so the position of patriarchal "head of household," which had existed in the background all along, began to move to the forefront as commercial crops took priority.[12] On commercial family farms the husband/father directed tobacco production. Tobacco absorbed most of the family's labor. It was sold in one transaction that provided most of the family's yearly income; payment was made to the husband/father. This enhanced significance of the patriarchal head of household obviously mattered to relationships within the family; women came more directly under the control of the men in their families. But at the same time men were more directly under the control of other men further up the drainage system. Manhood could no longer be defined as Whites previously had done, as being independent, making your own decisions, and keeping the labor of women in your family from flowing to outsiders. Much that had made up manhood had been appropriated by those further up the drainage system.

It is in this loss of male independence that the other side of patriarchy kicks in. Patriarchy actually implies more than just the power of men over women and children and bound or hired labor in their households, or even over women in general. It also implies the power of men in authority over men with less power.[13] Commercial production connected whole families to the drainage system through men *as heads of households* who managed an entire family's labor. In diversified subsistence farming, by contrast, the connection to the drainage system wasn't as tight, since less labor was devoted to cash production. At least to some extent, both men and women in diversified subsistence farming were connected to the drainage system not through a head of household, but *as individuals*, managing their own time and labor.

As black families began commercial family farming, sometimes as landowners but much more often as sharecroppers, they too underwent a redefinition of gender to construct families built around the male head of household drainage system rather than the individualized drainage of slavery.[14] In slavery the overseer or driver, not the husband or father, controlled workers and directed production. Slave husbands had no property rights in the sexuality of wives, nor in the labor of wives and children. A man who abused a slave woman enough to interfere with her ability to bear children or to work was himself liable to be punished for damaging her owner's property. White men, on the other hand, had the right to abuse their wives with impunity—as long as they used nothing thicker than their thumb to beat her with. A slave husband had no right either to protect his wife from rape or other forms of sexual coercion by Whites or to control his wife's sexual behavior, but white husbands did.[15] A white husband had the right to demand that his wife have sex only with him, and could punish her if she disobeyed. White husbands theoretically had the right to demand service from wives and children and to deny to other people the labor of their wives and children. In practice, however, only women in the middle and upper classes were able to avoid "public work" outside the family for their entire lives. These were the "ladies" "honored" in the glorification of white womanhood and held up as the white standard, part of the system of both race and class control.[16] All of these white rights were part of the in-family patriarchal organization that gave men the power, often overlaid by love and mutual responsibility and supported by the cult of domesticity, to control their households. With this power they could organize commercial family farm production and become the valve through which the family's labor is drained.

Black families shifting from slavery to sharecropping tried to claim the white right to in-family patriarchy, with the same rights to household autonomy and the same male right to administer his family. This was a double-edged sword. On the one hand it protected black families, in theory at least, from direct interference by Whites, but it also gave black men the power over family members that white men already had. If sharecropping was to work, white landowners had to hand over to black men the control of family labor; black men instead of overseers now set tasks for women and children. They themselves were the only members of the family—theoretically—under the direct control of the landlord. The Freedmen's Bureau formally established the man as head of household; the bureau designated him to sign and be responsible for the labor contract covering the whole family. Black families, having been denied land and the right to diversified subsistence farming, were told that their only route to economic success was to imitate the structure of white commercial farming families, in which women were to support and obey their husbands.[17] For white women and children coming from diversified subsistence, the new system with its tightened patriarchy promised no improvement and frequently meant a loss of their former degree of freedom. But for black women and children coming from slavery, as well as for men, family patriarchy, despite its double edge, was potentially an improvement in their lives, simply because their lives under slavery had been so much worse.

Because the patriarchal form did promise some protection, black families struggled for it in the legal arena and in daily encounters with Whites and with spouses and children. First, however, they had to fight even for the right to legal marriage. This they accomplished, but in the process marriage laws, by defining whose marriages were legal, also codified race. The idea that race was biological was enhanced by assigning all people with any (recognized) African ancestry to the black race. All *marriages* had to be between members of the same category; interracial *sex*, however, continued unabated. There was a taken-for-granted white assumption that black women were promiscuous and couldn't be raped because they were always willing. In practice this meant that black women had no right to their own bodies and that black women and men had no right to protest rape or sexual coercion by Whites. Offspring of interracial sex were defined as black. Thus, as Cott points out, marriage constructed race, and vice versa.[18] Scientists at the same time were still engaged in the construction of racial categories, undeterred by their failure to find clearly differentiated categories of humans.

Once marriage for Blacks was established as a legal right they fought for the patriarchal family form. They struggled, for instance, for the right to whip their own children, rather than letting landlords do it. They objected to laws allowing their children to be forcibly apprenticed if the parents were deemed "morally unfit" or unable to support them. Such laws meant that the right to be a parent depended on white approval and on whether, and how much, Whites were willing to pay them for their labor. Black women were accused by Whites of "female loaferism" when they tried to withdraw from field work; female domesticity was a white right only. Women were in less contact with white men if fathers and husbands directed their work, particularly if they could stay out of sight indoors rather than working in the fields. They were therefore somewhat less subject to rape and harassment by Whites. However, many black women had to supplement family income by working in white homes and continued to be under the direct control of white women and men. White families with black servants generally continued to assume that their own needs took unquestioned priority over the needs of their servants and their servants' families.

Blacks who objected to any of this ran the risk of losing the "protection" of their employers and receiving a visit from white terrorists. Maintaining black patriarchy, in other words, was an area of continual struggle between Blacks and Whites. It was also an area of continual struggle between men and women, since black women, like white ones, found that patriarchy meant abuse and control by husbands and fathers despite its promise of protection from Whites. Patriarchy thus carried quite different meanings for black and white women.

Losing freedom, gaining the psychological wage

The postbellum reorganization of the drainage system tightened patriarchy within the family, buttressed class and gender inequality, and redefined racial inequality. Many Southern poor Whites were less free as sharecroppers than they had been before the Civil War.[19] Like slaves, white sharecropping women had to work in the fields to enrich someone else. White men's formal control of women had increased, but their control of the value produced by themselves and their families had decreased. Whiteness therefore needed reconstruction, this time to accommodate the new social relations of sharecropping. Many Whites' primary identification now became race *in and of itself*, rather than as a *symbol* representing class considerations such as freedom, the hope of slave ownership, and supposed skill and productivity.

In this new construction, the fact that many people identified by European descent were now, as sharecroppers, in almost identical material conditions with people identified by their African descent was defined as irrelevant: they were white and that was all that mattered. Many newly-white and native white factory workers now defined their right to those factory, mining and timbering jobs that were reserved for Whites–that is, to child factory labor, to working conditions that sickened or killed, and to abysmally low wages—as a piece of white privilege.[20] Recent immigrants, not yet fully white, were subjected to angry diatribes in the South County paper for threatening the value of such jobs. Such immigrants "underbid respectable workmen and live in conditions of beastliness. We do not want crack-brained anarchists who come here to preach defiance to the laws and institutions of our country . . . ."[21] It was largely these jobs, denied to non-Whites, that proved to the Irish and other new Whites that they were, in fact, white, and thus superior to blacks who were servants or manual laborers.

The right to claim racial superiority—the psychological wage—had to substitute for the cash wages withheld from poorer Whites by the capitalist class in the newly reorganized drainage system. Whiteness had become its own reward. Its lack of material content for Whites at the bottom of the drainage system was disguised by the fact that those further up the drainage system were almost entirely white. Whiteness *appeared* to provide a realistic hope for material gain, a hope that for most poor Whites was entirely illusion. Poorer Whites, both North and South, in other words, adjusted to their increasing dependence and loss of autonomy as they shifted to sharecropping and industrial labor, particularly after slavery was abolished, by claiming the right to put Blacks down.[22] In this they were encouraged by representatives of the local elite. The editor of the South County paper, for instance, declared that Whites should take "a commendable pride in the fact that a Caucasian, though born and bred in the South, is superior to the African in every element of character, either by nature or acquisition, that go to make life worth living."[23] Poor Whites' allies in maintaining the right to put Blacks down, helping them to keep Blacks "in their place," were those Whites who ran the justice system and legislature, led the Klan, or agreed to hire on the basis of race but not to pay a living wage. But this meant that their allies were the same class that was profiting from their unsafe and underpaid labor—they were allying themselves with the very people who were the cause of their bony fingers.

But even as the psychological wage became thoroughly entrenched, it was never more than a partial solution to white unrest, North or South. Strikes and revolts didn't end with the invention of the psychological wage. However, they *were* easier to control and contain when white unrest focused on excluding Blacks or not-quite-white immigrants from "white" jobs. They thus defined those below them in the drainage system as the source of their problems, rather than those at the top of the drainage system. However, among Southern farmers, black and white, desperation rapidly led to another fork in the road when interracial organizing nearly succeeded in challenging not just elite control, but class and race relations within capitalism itself.

7

JIM CROW, UNDERDEVELOPMENT, AND REINFORCEMENT OF THE TOTTERING DRAINAGE SYSTEM

As Reconstruction came to an end in the last half of the 1870s, the hope of land ownership for most Blacks and poorer Whites went with it. First there had been the demise of the Freedmen's Bureau mandate to redistribute land. Then there was the construction of sharecropping which made it almost impossible to earn enough to buy land. Then even many small landowners found themselves no longer fully free. But those who were desperate didn't simply roll over and play dead. The result, as this chapter describes, was revolt. Despite the influence of the psychological wage, black and white farmers in the last two decades of the 1800s formed the Farmers' Alliance and its political wing, the Populist Party, to fight back. However, this was nothing new. Poorer Southerners, both black and white, had regularly opposed the entrenched power of the elite.[1]

Jim Crow eventually solved this problem for the elite around the turn of the century. It established a caste system, dividing the working class into two groups based on ancestry, and in most Southern states it eliminated the votes of many, both black and white, who opposed elite rule. New South "progressivism" depended upon massive disenfranchisement of those who might object to it.[2]

NEW SOUTH ELITES AND THE INCREASING POWER OF NATIONAL CAPITAL

Many Kentucky tobacco growers, like farmers throughout the South, explained their economic problems by pointing to the role of Northern financial elites. As one put it, "[W]hen New York takes snuff, the rest of the country is compelled to sneeze."[3] This description reflected the increased control of the Southern economy by Northern corporations after the Civil War. To a large extent, the Civil War had been a fight between Northern and Southern elites over control of the drainage system, over which set of elites would benefit the most from Southern sweat. With the Union victory, the South entered into a more tightly colonial relationship with the North, built on military and then political control of the South.

Eric Foner describes this process, adding up to vastly increased federal power over the states and the economy, as the "birth of the modern American state."[4] With increased federal power the South could be "developed" and "civilized."[5] Such ideas justified connecting the Southern drainage system more tightly to the Northern system and underdeveloping it in relation to the North for the benefit of large corporations operating on a national level. By the 1880s outside capital controlled Kentucky's economy and most of the profits from the use of Kentucky's resources therefore left the state. As time went on this control tightened.

At the same time, wealth was concentrated into fewer and fewer hands. James Duke controlled almost the entire tobacco industry, for instance. J. P. Morgan controlled half of all the railroad mileage in the United States. This concentration of control and of wealth resulting from massive ownership of resources gave men like Duke and Morgan the power to influence government policy in their own interests. They arranged for policies that gave them control over the resources that had become available after the Civil War, both in the South and in frontier areas. Class differences sharpened throughout the United States as the wealthy became wealthier through this welfare system they had devised for themselves. In Kentucky, as in the rest of the South, colonial status enriched corporate owners but left many other people even poorer than they had been.

As is common all over the world when underdevelopment is being orchestrated—when drainage is being reorganized so that the value of local labor and resources flows to people outside the region—some local people in the South benefited by taking an intermediate position on the reorganized drainage system. They became members of the buffer social control class with jobs in various branches of the legal system controlling the Blacks and poorer Whites whose sweat trickled up that drainage system. They also took managerial positions in financial, industrial, and exporting firms owned mostly by Northern elites.[6] The "New South" movement represented the interests of those in the managerial group promoting development through the use of cheap Southern labor for Northern-owned industry.

The South thus became a labor reserve, where corporations could find cheaper labor than in the North. Labor remained cheap because of the vicious labor control system orchestrated legally and illegally by local elites, landlords, merchants, and employers as well as those working within the justice system. Employers often used part-time labor, debt peonage, scrip, and credit in place of cash wages for both Blacks and Whites. Consequently most landless Southerners, black and white, working for wages were desperately poor and, like sharecroppers, only semi-free.[7] People with enough land for even a garden were better off than those without, and frequently were able to avoid debt peonage by supplementing low wages with food they raised themselves. Others, without such ties to land or forced to break them out of desperation, moved frequently in hope of better conditions. Employers and those who could stay put disparaged them as "shiftless."[8]

New south elites and underdevelopment

Before national capital could penetrate a region it needed a transportation system to tie it into the national marketing network.[9] In places like Kentucky, where becoming part of the national system led to internal colonial status within the United States, the transportation system was used to ship raw materials out and to ship manufactured goods in. As Northern capitalists gained power in the South they connected the Northern and Southern rail systems, tearing up Southern tracks and adjusting them to the Northern gauge. When the Northern and Southern railroad systems were connected, new policies facilitated the South's role as an area to be drained for the benefit of Northern industrial capital. Railroad shipping prices were organized so that goods and raw materials would flow between North and South, and from Kentucky to Northern industrial centers, more easily and more cheaply than from one part of the South to another, or from one part of Kentucky to another. At the same time, however, aspects of the older transportation systems remained in effect well into the twentieth century: logs still floated to market on Kentucky rivers; tobacco went to market in horse-drawn wagons; and cattle, hogs, turkeys, and geese went to market, sometimes several days' journey, on their own legs.

Despite the continuation of earlier systems of transportation, and despite the persistence of local businesses, once the country was joined by rail the *potential* market for centrally produced goods made using raw materials shipped in from all over the country was vastly increased. Around 1900, laws were passed that allowed corporations to take advantage of this opportunity. Corporations were given the right to private property and private profits that formerly had belonged only to individuals, and corporate owners were granted immunity from liability as individuals. These laws made it easier to concentrate wealth in corporations. Corporations began forming monopolies, and like Duke's American Tobacco, pushed smaller businesses out, controlling the entire production process from raw material to finished product.[10]

New South elites stood to gain from development. They saw opportunities for themselves as railroads penetrated deeper and deeper into the countryside, with industry following in their wake. Hard-surface roads provided one such opportunity, so some of them formed private companies to surface roads and charge tolls on the more traveled routes. These turnpikes aided in the distribution of goods to local stores and helped buyers get to town to buy regularly, but they were deeply resented by people who couldn't afford to use them.[11] New South elites, however, saw the need for lawyers and bankers escalating with roads and development. They envisioned huge increases in the value of their land, or of the timber and mineral resources on it. The value of their town lots and buildings would likewise skyrocket. And they were quite correct in their calculations.

Because it was obvious to many farming families who were still making it through diversified subsistence farming that those calculations were indeed correct, they opposed bringing in railroads.[12] They believed, also quite correctly, that their independence would leave with the arrival of the railroads. Merchants would insist on payment in cash rather than accepting home manufactures, or would pay less as competition from factory-produced goods grew. As the value of land increased, creditors would have greater incentive to foreclose, and those teetering on the brink would be pushed into growing more and more commercial crops. Many would eventually lose their farms. As the railroads made the development of timber or mineral resources feasible, corporations had enormous incentives to drive people off their land or into wage labor in mining, textile mills, and the timber industry. Even some planters opposed railroads and the New South elites because they worried that they would have to pay higher wages if people had the alternative of employment in industry. Local business owners objected as people began buying directly by mail order catalogs from national corporations. These orders were delivered by train, bypassing and destroying local businesses. The West County newspaper during this time is full of pleas to readers to buy locally and ignore the mail order catalogs. In fact, local businesses did die and sharecropping increased when railroads, the initial tentacle of Northern and national capital, entered a region.

RESISTING UNDERDEVELOPMENT: THE FARMERS' ALLIANCE

Blacks, poorer Whites, and small farmers were all caught now in a vise between national and local New South industrial elites orchestrating underdevelopment, and agricultural elites orchestrating biracial sharecropping. This new system had taken a decade to force into place after the Civil War, and once established led almost immediately into the Populist revolt.

The Farmers' Alliance, founded in 1878 in Texas, planned to reorganize the drainage system to the advantage of producers, both small commercial family farmers and big landowners. The People's Party was organized to push politically for the economic aims of the Alliance, and gained some support even outside the farming sector. It became the biggest third party movement the United States has ever seen, controlling seven Southern state legislatures and winning congressional seats. By 1892, the Alliance had reached into 43 states and territories, with a membership perhaps as high as 1,200,000 Blacks and 3 million Whites. Kentucky had over 1000 suballiances.[13] Both politically and economically these organizations challenged the power of the national elite and of local financial and mercantile elites to drain farmers. To some extent they challenged the right of capitalist profiteering itself.

Alliance strength was built on organizing across racial and gender lines. It wouldn't be accurate to say that Whites in the Alliance rejected whiteness, or even wanted racial equality. However, many members did reject much of the racial rhetoric of white supremacy, which they realized fooled people into siding with the elite who were damaging them. Others did believe in white supremacy, and insisted on separate black and white Alliance chapters, but agreed that cooperation between black and white chapters was necessary to prevent being divided and ruled. Black and white Alliance leaders agreed they needed both black and white farmers acting together to create economic power, and Populist politicians needed both black and white votes to create a huge class-based voting bloc. Jim Crow legislation didn't exist yet, so black men could still vote. Some Alliance leaders were black. They led black suballiances and met regularly with the white leaders of white suballiances. In Kentucky and elsewhere, black suballiances tended to take more radical positions, and their opinions at least occasionally were reported in Alliance newspapers.[14]

Women also influenced the Alliance: they were admitted as equal members and could, and sometimes did, become leaders. Women in the Alliance emphasized household production and opposed dependence on a single crop in order to avoid debt. They opposed the growing consumer ethic and women's withdrawal from production into domestic gentility. In agreeing on the importance of women's roles and household production as part of Alliance strategy, both women and men in the Alliance gave at least lip service to women's equality.[15] With economic cooperation across race and gender lines and consequently a huge interracial male voting bloc, they had the power they needed to take on the elite. And they very nearly succeeded.

Smaller farmers in the Alliance wanted to raise farm income; some also wanted to dismantle the system of debt peonage that controlled the lives of millions of Southerners. They were joined by large landowners, who, while not poor, were angered at the underdevelopment which increased Northern financial and commercial control. They felt that they were being drained of an unacceptable proportion of the profits they had expected to realize from the sweat of their farm labor. They objected to the consolidation of power and wealth in the hands of big businesses that controlled the buying of agricultural products and the selling of agricultural inputs. At the same time labor unrest escalated as wage workers, like farmers, objected to having their labor drained in unacceptable proportions. They demanded higher wages, but also an end to the use of convict labor, scrip, child labor, and to the company store system—all mainstays of corporate profits.[16]

The Alliance organized cooperative crop marketing and temporarily succeeded in forcing buyers to pay higher prices. It set up Alliance cooperative stores buying in bulk and selling at much lower prices so that farmers could avoid the high-priced and high-interest merchants. Alliance co-ops were service organizations owned by all members to provide necessary supplies rather than profit-making organizations designed to enrich individuals. Both buying and selling cooperatives distributed any excess cash beyond the costs of operation evenly among all members. Alliance stores experimented, at times successfully, with providing low-cost credit, trying to circumvent debt peonage. The Alliance also advocated the Subtreasury Plan. Under this system the U.S. Treasury would back loans to the Alliance, using crops stored in co-op warehouses as collateral and bypassing local creditors. Not surprisingly, western Kentucky, with its relatively large black farming population, gave most support in Kentucky to the Subtreasury Plan.[17]

But in 1896 the People's Party was beaten in the presidential race. Thereafter the Alliance itself succumbed to the sheer power exercised by those bent on destroying it, combined with pressures exerted along its own internal fault lines.

Fault Lines within the Alliance

The Alliance was weakened by the conflicting class interests of its members, who, although they all farmed, were not all in the same class. The Alliance included large landowners, who, as a class, benefited from the labor of other members who were tenants and sharecroppers. It also included some smaller landowning farmers who, like big landowners, benefited from the labor of hired hands. Most of the leaders were large landowners, and generally speaking, they had no interest in improving the lot of their own labor force. Alliance leaders, therefore, generally didn't support measures proposed by the poorer members that would destroy debt peonage. This class-based fault line intersected with another caused by Whites' belief in white privilege. Black Alliance leaders, more frequently than white leaders, advocated policies that aimed directly at the roots of Southern black and white poverty—sharecropping, low wages, and debt. White leaders were able to thwart these more radical policies, making it impossible for the Alliance to reach the goals of the poorer members. For example, black cotton-pickers organized to strike for higher wages. Black Alliance chapters supported the cotton-pickers, and white pickers as well as black would have benefited from a successful strike, but the large white landowners, those who would have to pay the higher wages, prevented the strike.[18]

White leaders could get away with such behavior partially because of their economic power and membership in local elite networks and partially because of the strength of poor Whites' belief in whiteness. Many Whites who actually wanted to end debt peonage and poverty were fooled into believing that their whiteness placed them on the same side as the white leadership, not on the side of the black leaders who supported the strike. Even if the Alliance had successfully met the goals of its well-to-do white leaders, poorer white and black farmers would still have been at the mercy of larger ones and laborers at the mercy of landowners. But if the goals of poorer and more radical members had been met, the drainage system would have undergone significant changes.

Presiding over the Death of the Alliance

The Alliance and People's Party didn't simply die. Instead they were carefully and consciously murdered by political and economic sabotage on the part of both the local non-planter elite and the Northern elite. The Populist revolt threatened the profits and control of both sets of elites. The threat was not to capitalism itself, but to the enormous inequality within it that created untold luxury for some and starvation, child labor, and exhaustion for others.[19] That threat brought forth an impressive panoply of power against the Alliance.

Killing the Alliance and breaking the interracial alliance on which it was based required careful work and compromises between elites with differing interests. In contrast to earlier periods of threat to the drainage system, there were now several different and powerful elites involved, each competing for its own stake in the outcome. Northern elites were more directly tied to Southern agriculture through increased financing and the sale of manufactured goods. They were no longer simply buyers of Southern products. Southern planters and landlords wanted cheap labor and high prices for agricultural products. Southern industrialists likewise wanted cheap labor, but they also wanted cheap prices for the tobacco, cotton, and other products they bought from planters and landlords. And they all wanted high prices for the products they sold back to those who had produced the raw materials, as well as for the agricultural inputs they sold to Southern farming families.

The Democratic white power structure, controlled by local New South elites, manipulated elections and rigged them if necessary to keep the third party Alliance candidates out of office. Fraud, votebuying, and intimidation were common. In Alabama, when these tactics failed and a Populist was elected governor, they actually called out the troops and installed the Democratic candidate at gunpoint.[20] Local merchants, worried that they might lose the use of debt peonage, quickly organized to use their greater financial reserves to undercut Alliance stores and buying co-ops.[21] Newspapers promoted local merchants and politicians rather than Alliance cooperatives and candidates. The West County newspaper regularly described Alliance policies as absurd, irrational, counterproductive, or irresponsible.[22]

Northern banks were the source of most funding for the South, and they cooperated in refusing loans to the Alliance, making it difficult for the Alliance to offer credit to its members. This concerted move by Northern banks broke the brief stranglehold the Alliance had on agricultural raw materials; creditors could simply use the crop-lien law giving them first rights on the crop to prevent sales through the Alliance. Likewise, Northern manufacturing companies cooperated in refusing to sell to the Alliance, destroying Alliance stores and co-ops. Newspaper editorials, however, blamed the failure of Alliance stores and co-ops on financial mismanagement, as do some historians today.

Playing the race card to break the Alliance

The Alliance and People's Party were powerful partly because the protesters understood that elites generally make policies in their own interests and that it was these policies, not inscrutable and inevitable and uncontrollable "market forces," that were causing their bony fingers. Equally important, many Whites who were suffering were willing, despite their belief in whiteness, to ally themselves for practical purposes with Blacks in the same economic condition. Blacks apparently joined the Alliance in greater proportion than Whites, so that the total membership was a quarter to a third black. Its strength depended on black-white cooperation in controlling the market. Therefore, to break the Alliance it was first necessary to break the interracial alliance.

Politicians and the media worked to decrease white Alliance membership by describing the Alliance and Populists as a threat to white supremacy, fanning the flames of racial hatred. They referred repeatedly to the danger insatiable black rapists supposedly posed to "pure white womanhood." Like many others, the editor of the West County newspaper published predictions of the death of white supremacy if the Alliance got its way. Giving a vote to the People's Party, rather than to the Democratic Party with its commitment to white supremacy, was described as weakening the only party that protected Whites against a supposed rising tide of black power. The effect was to define the issue as racial rather than economic, and it shifted power to the Democrats.[23]

This attempt to remove white support was one prong of the racially based effort to stop the Alliance. The other was to remove black support. A wave of violence swept the South during the 1890s establishing the racial divide in blood and terror. The Klan and other terrorists, generally led by local elites but including a broad white membership, executed physical attacks on black Alliance members and on other Blacks.[24] Newspapers described lynchings and other attacks in graphic detail, making it perfectly clear to Blacks what happened to those who got "out of line." Even when editors objected to lynching, as they did locally, they didn't question the need to kill Blacks. They merely emphasized the need to do it legally, under the direction of the buffer social control class.[25]

RENEGING ON THE CONTRACT: NO VOTE AND NO LAND

Universal manhood suffrage, now that it included both black and white men, had, from the elite perspective, become too dangerous, as the Populist revolt made clear. The solution was to limit voting, not so much by race as by class. In instituting Jim Crow the elite broke the earlier "contract" that had been struck with poorer Whites as they entered Kentucky–the right to vote instead of land, political equality within an otherwise extremely unequal social structure. In establishing Jim Crow the elite were also reneging on their contract with Blacks, who as freedmen had also been promised the vote instead of land. With Jim Crow many poor Whites as well as most Blacks lost the vote, and by the turn of the century universal white manhood suffrage was gone. And what couldn't be completely accomplished legally could be finished illegally through terrorism.

Jim Crow legislation, riding on a crest of racial hatred, was publicly and obviously supposed to prevent Blacks from voting, and it did. But it was also designed to reduce the power of the Alliance and the People's Party. Privately, many legislators made it perfectly clear that their intention was to disenfranchise poor Whites as well, people they described as "ignorant," "unfit," or "vicious." Such Whites, together with large numbers of Blacks, made up an opposition block of one-third to one-half of all Southerners.[26]

In fact, Blacks *as Blacks* were nowhere specifically denied the vote: Jim Crow laws applied to poor Whites as well. For instance, some states used poll taxes of $1 or $2 annually when the annual income of 75 percent of all Southerners was about $55 in 1880 and $64 in 1900. This would be equivalent to asking us now to pay something like $250 out of a full-time minimum wage salary each time we voted.[27] Other ways of eliminating poor white as well as poor black votes included literacy requirements, prior registration requirements, or other convoluted processes. Some poor Whites, mesmerized by race, supported restrictive voting legislation without realizing it would restrict their own right to vote as well. Some Whites, however, mainly from poor white smallholding sections, objected strenuously, not necessarily because they were supporting Blacks, but because they foresaw the elimination of their own political strength.

Until the passage in each Southern state of voting restrictions, voter turnout had been enormous. During the 1880s, 60 to 75 percent of adult white men voted, as did a majority of black men. Voter turnout, both black and white, remained exceedingly high in the 1890s in those states that hadn't yet restricted voting.[28] Opposition candidates, including Populists in many areas, did well in these elections. The South was definitely not solidly Democratic and the elite definitely didn't have a lock on the political process. After restrictive legislation was passed things changed dramatically. Voter turnout dropped to 30 percent, and in most Southern states support for opposition candidates dropped into the single digits by the first decade of the twentieth century. Most black voting was eliminated and the white voter turnout was reduced by an average of 25 percent, but by over 40 percent in some states. Kentucky depended on terrorism rather than on legal measures to control and partially disenfranchise Blacks, perhaps because Kentucky was not an Alliance stronghold, and Kentucky Whites did continue to vote.[29]

Much of the Alliance was now either disenfranchised or seriously discouraged from voting. Needless to say, the People's Party stopped winning and the Alliance eventually faded away. Once again, voting rights had been manipulated to prevent voting by those most likely to be damaged by the way the elite were exercising their power. Voting became a privilege rather than a right, granted only to those most likely to support the elite.

JIM CROW SEGREGATION AND STATE VALIDATION OF THE PSYCHOLOGICAL WAGE

Segregation, the American system of apartheid, legally institutionalized the racial gulf that had resulted as white terrorism caused rivers of blood to flow during the demise of the Populist revolt. It formalized the racialized economy that already existed in much of the South. Lawmakers removed the right of legal, peaceful protest by disenfranchising most Blacks and many of the Whites who were near the unfree end of the continuum. But suffrage restriction was just one edge of the Jim Crow sword. The other edge was validation of white supremacy. It beefed up the psychological wage as "compensation" for the destruction of the earlier contract. It helped gain "consent" to the loss of the vote, to white sharecropping, and to the consolidation of capital in the hands of the "trusts," and it enlisted poor white cooperation in keeping Blacks "in their place" as an extremely cheap labor force for the elite. Many poor Whites acquiesced or participated in terrorism to keep Blacks quiet in the face of massive injustice. In helping to police U.S. apartheid they followed the pattern of Irish rioters and participated in their own oppression as sharecroppers and wage earners as well as that of Blacks.

Jim Crow validated the racial lens through which most Whites now viewed the world. It backed white supremacy with the power of the state and thereby reinvested whiteness with the *legalized* material benefit that it had lost when emancipation destroyed the racial distinction between free and slave. Elites participated in validating the psychological wage through editorials, speeches, and sermons proclaiming white superiority, and led poor Whites in the blood rituals of lynching. They proclaimed that all Whites were members of a supposed biological and social category that superseded the petty differences of class, of white exploiter and white exploited.[30] But without government sanction the poor white recipients of the psychological wage had had to maintain its validity in the face of considerable evidence to the contrary as a few Blacks became well-to-do landowners and professionals. Jim Crow eliminated the need for constant validation.

Loss of independence and the shift to the psychological wage

Despite their belief in white supremacy many independent farmers and craftspeople hadn't felt the need to fall back on using the fact that they were white to make up for the "shame" of working to enrich someone else, even after the Civil War. But as more and more Whites faced the prospect of lifelong industrial jobs or sharecropping, it became important to more and more of them to be able to say, "I'm better than they are, even if I don't have a cent more than they do and have to work like a slave to survive."

White supremacy and male supremacy reinforced each other. Men and women alike could believe that protection of white women justified men's relative power and privilege, since their protection preserved the "race" from biological impurity and saved white women from supposedly dangerous black men. Women who refused to accept the control of a husband or father, or didn't serve him properly, forfeited their right to protection and were abandoned to their fate. White supremacy and male supremacy together constituted the psychological wage for men who in Kentucky did "fealty in money and manhood to James B. Duke."[31] These were men who acted as valves through which drained their family's sweat and who worked, like women and slaves, from dawn to dusk with nothing but bony fingers to show for it.

With the state now backing apartheid as it had earlier backed slavery, white supremacy gained a taken-for-granted aspect that it had lacked since the Civil War. Now government, the media, schools, churches, the "justice" system, white neighbors, social scientists and biologists all, with occasional exceptions, acted on the belief that whiteness was part of God's plan. Black and white politicians who had tended toward equality had been voted out of office and had never been replaced; too many of their supporters had been disenfranchised. Consequently, it was a rare politician who attempted to win office on a platform of economic justice.[32] Generally speaking only black leaders provided any alternative viewpoint, and few Whites heard what they had to say. Most Whites heard that white supremacy was natural, based on both genetic and cultural superiority. This theory presumed that a racialized state was a natural, inevitable, and benign result of that superiority.

Jim Crow segregation also resolved the conflict between elites wanting cheap industrial labor and those wanting cheap agricultural labor. It reserved many industrial jobs, particularly skilled jobs, for Whites. What social mobility there was would be reserved for Whites, particularly for native Whites, a fairly small segment of the population. This limited social mobility didn't threaten the supply of cheap labor and at the same time made it possible for Whites to pretend that the United States was classless by referring only to a white segment of the population.[33] With apartheid in place, employers dealt with separate labor pools and avoided competing for each other's workers.[34] Blacks and Whites both faced limited employment opportunities: landlords tried to take only black sharecroppers and domestic workers, and factory owners tried to take only white laborers. Even for the Irish, still the lowest ranking Euro-Americans, there were significantly more skilled jobs than for Blacks.[35]

The road had forked again, and once again the route of continued oppression had been chosen, and the tottering drainage system had been reinforced. The benefits of apartheid for the elite were clear, and although the basics of segregation were in place by the turn of the century, legislators continued to fine-tune the system over the next fifty years, protecting the elite right to drain families dry and the white right to their psychological wage of superiority.

8

CRITIQUING CAPITAL:
THE WANNABES

Jim Crow social engineering now shaped Whites' conception of the world. Every aspect of white lives was governed by it, and countless numbers of Whites bought into the psychological wage of superiority. Nevertheless, some Whites at the very bottom of the drainage system, experiencing exploitation more directly and more severely, realized that they had little in common with the elite Whites who exploited them. Occasionally they saw that they had much more in common with exploited Blacks. But most Whites were isolated from black members of their own class and were able to remain unaware of their common economic plight. They saw the world and interpreted their continuing struggles through the lens of the dominant perspective of white male supremacy, which replaced or modified any remaining class-consciousness. The lens made it almost impossible for them to consider alliance with Blacks, as people in their position had done at intervals since the 1600s, and as some of them or their parents had done in the Alliance.

Rather than forcing their exploiters to change their ways—they had tried that and lost—many non-elite Whites turned to another old tactic. They began denying those weaker than themselves the right to compete with them for a decent livelihood. This time they were backed by the power of the state's support of Jim Crow and had the active or tacit encouragement of the local elite. They therefore enjoyed a legitimacy that earlier attempts had lacked. Blacks were driven out of neighborhoods, jobs, farm ownership and sharecropping positions, and in the process poorer white farmers were tied more tightly to the big growers or lost their farms. This transition from inclusive to exclusive tactics is evident in the tobacco growers' revolt in Kentucky and Tennessee following the defeat of the more inclusivist Alliance. During these Tobacco Wars, tobacco growers revolted against the exploitative practices of the American Tobacco Company, which had gained a monopoly on tobacco buying and processing.[1] Although the growers protested against the system of *monopoly* capitalism that kept control in the hands of national elites, they did not reject the basic structure of capitalism itself. They too wanted what they saw as their white male right to independence, entrepreneurship, property ownership, and the ability to profit from the sweat of others. The tobacco growers proved themselves to be "wannabes"—they wanted to become successful small capitalist producers, and so didn't question capitalism itself. And because they took that route, they ultimately lost their war to improve their lot. Others, as the next chapter will describe, did question capitalism itself.

THE TOBACCO WARS

In Kentucky, unrest among tobacco growers after the defeat of the Alliance coalesced into a number of tobacco grower "associations," based on the belief that farmers were "oppressed beyond financial endurance."[2] The problem for tobacco growers lay in the fact that James Duke's New York–based American Tobacco Company had gained a monopoly on tobacco, both nationally and internationally.[3] Initially American Tobacco had paid farmers slightly more for their tobacco than did other companies, driving smaller companies out of business or buying them up. Once the other buyers were gone and farmers could no longer shop around for better prices, the company changed its strategy, and began to push prices below the cost of production and keep them there. They paid black farmers even less than white farmers for their tobacco crops.[4] Farming families felt they were paying for the privilege of raising tobacco and giving it to the American Tobacco Company. As a result American Tobacco became one of the largest and most powerful corporations in the United States, paying huge dividends to its wealthy owners.

The flip side of the tobacco company owners' wealth was the poverty of those at the bottom of the drainage system. Big landowners, midway on the drainage system, had to pass much of their potential wealth on to American Tobacco. While they resented this situation, they remained well-to-do. For those who did the actual work on big landowners' farms, how-

ever, malnutrition was widespread, particularly among those sharecroppers who were not allowed a garden and among farm laborers who were
paid almost nothing.[5] Not only were they oppressed beyond financial
endurance; they were oppressed beyond the physical endurance of their
children. During much of the growing season children worked ten-hour
days. They suffered high rates of malnutrition-related diseases and deaths.
Small landowners were somewhat better off since they often were able to
continue some subsistence farming. But if they became indebted that
option might disappear, since creditors often accepted only tobacco in
payment for debts.

Situating North and South County

South County as a whole was one of the biggest burley producers in the
state, producing far more than North County, and, unlike North County,
nearly all white men farmed. Southern South County was part of the "best
burley tobacco belt in the state" and maintained its commercial single crop
emphasis.[6] North County and northern South County, however, appear to
have followed more closely the pattern of diversified subsistence farming
well into the twentieth century. North County farms in 1910 averaged thirty acres larger than in South County, far above the state average, having
relatively few plantations to break up into small sharecropping units after
the Civil War. Agricultural statistics show less sharecropping and continued crop diversity in North County. Farm values were higher in North
County and farms were less likely to be mortgaged.[7]

The black population of North County had dropped rapidly after the
Civil War, while remaining stable in South County, so that by 1910 the
number of black men of voting age in the two counties was about equal.
But farming in North County had become a white preserve. North County
had about fifty black landowners and almost no tenants and sharecroppers, while in South County about half of all black men farmed; well over
one hundred were landowners and a nearly equal number were tenants
and sharecroppers.[8]

Association strategy

Former Alliance leaders and other "prominent tobacco growers," building
on earlier experience in the Alliance, spent several years developing a new
plan of action. In 1904 the leaders of the growers' associations, all part of
a recently formed American Society of Equity, called a mass meeting in

western Kentucky, at which they presented their plan to 5,000 tobacco farmers. By the end of the day organized resistance in Kentucky and Tennessee was off and running.

The Association's aim was to force American Tobacco to raise the prices it paid to growers. The American Society of Equity and the various grower associations that comprised it didn't pose the kind of threat to the local drainage system and to the local elite that had been posed by the Alliance. Therefore it wasn't met by the marshalling of local elite opposition that had met the Alliance. However, the Association did threaten to cut off some of the profit flowing north. Needless to say, this appealed to many local landowners and merchants. They stood to gain if the profits that formerly went north stayed in local hands to be used locally, in buying more, or servicing bigger debts, or in enriching bigger growers. Consequently, landowners, bankers, merchants, local media, big farmers and little farmers, all rallied behind these tobacco associations.

The Planters Protective Association, in the Black Patch (named for its dark tobacco) of western Kentucky and Tennessee, and the Burley Tobacco Society, in the burley region of central Kentucky, became the dominant organizations. They advocated cooperative marketing through a growers' co-op that would not sell its tobacco until American Tobacco Company agreed to the minimum prices set by the co-op. The trick was to persuade farmers in Kentucky and northern Tennessee first to join and then to continue supporting the strike against American Tobacco, which required growing less tobacco and selling it only through the association. Farmers consigned about 65 percent of the crop for cooperative marketing in 1907, but American Tobacco refused to buy from the cooperative.[9] Association members began discussing the possibility of starting grower-owned tobacco factories if American Tobacco wouldn't give in. In 1908, farmers successfully went on strike to increase crop prices through the operation of supply and demand, growing almost no burley at all.

Despite these successes, however, there were two problems. One was that some farmers didn't sign up. The other was that American Tobacco already had a lot of tobacco stockpiled in its warehouses. It added to that stockpile whenever it could persuade a grower to break the strike and sell directly to the company. Together these two problems created the danger that American Tobacco could outlast the association, and the choices the growers made in response to this danger reflected the limitations of their vision through the lens of white male supremacy.

Role of Class, Race, and Gender in Limiting the Wannabe Critique

The Tobacco Wars were largely the result of underdevelopment and the fights it engendered between people in differing class positions on the drainage system as national capital tightened its grip on local growers. The revolt ultimately failed, largely because the interests of some association members were diametrically opposed to those of others, despite their agreement in opposing national capital.

The leaders in both the Black Patch and the burley region were among the wealthiest landowners, and they became increasingly autocratic in running the association.[10] Felix Ewing, for instance, "raised" 260 acres of tobacco. He owned the land and administered approximately fifty families who worked about five acres each. Such planters had no interest in eliminating the debt peonage that controlled sharecroppers, and big farmers had no interest in improving the wages of farm laborers. Big landowners were intent on extending their landholdings at the expense of their smallholding neighbors, not on making landownership easier. Even as the association began making progress in raising prices, tenant farmers briefly formed their own organization to demand better treatment from landowners; they were not sharing in the increased prosperity.[11]

Hillbillies

A large number of those who didn't join the association were small white farmers in the hillier, non-plantation areas. They were referred to by the derogatory term "hillbilly." Some who refused to join were black, although initially about the same percentages of Blacks as Whites joined.[12] Joining meant waiting for an indefinite period until the association was able to sell the tobacco at the higher price. It meant risking growing a smaller crop in hopes that everyone else would do the same. Poorer families therefore found it difficult to join and some well-off ones refused to. There were many editorials in the West County newspaper urging owners to make sure their tenants and sharecroppers joined. Many independent small farmers and dependent sharecroppers and tenants had to take out loans, often from bigger farmers and planters in the association, to tide them over until the association paid them. Those who couldn't get loans or who didn't want to go even deeper into debt than they already were, sold directly to American Tobacco Company.

American Tobacco played on and exacerbated these economic and class rifts among the farmers. Poorer families were far more vulnerable than others to the company's temptations, so the company paid hillbillies more for their crop than they paid to lowland farmers and planters who tried to sell directly to the company.[13] Farmers responded with violence among themselves and against the company. The state responded by sending in the military in defense of the company. The result was war in Kentucky.

Night Riders

The farmers' side of the violence was carried on by the Night Riders. This was a secret vigilante organization with perhaps as many as 10,000 members, which began organizing toward the end of 1905. It was led by an ex-Klansman and was organized similarly to the Klan. At least some of the members were also association members, although it is not clear whether the Night Riders had private approval from association leaders who denied any connection in public. Like the association itself, the Night Riders were led by large landlords and professional men, and operated in the interests of the large growers. At first the Night Riders "visited" farmers who refused to join, but reserved their violent activities for tobacco warehouses. They carried out commando-type raids, burning American Tobacco Company warehouses. They caused millions of dollars worth of damage, destroying warehouses, tobacco, telegraph lines—and homes in black communities surrounding the warehouses suffered severe collateral damage. Although the violence started in western Kentucky, and remained centered there, by 1907 it had reached central Kentucky.

But by mid-1906, company tactics began to pay off. Farmers began physically fighting each other rather than American Tobacco Company, providing the public relations justification for crushing their revolt: Kentuckians were hopeless savages in need of forcible civilizing. Media reports may have deplored the policies of American Tobacco Company, but they never took the next step. They didn't define children's malnourishment and long hours of work as violence on a par with that of the Night Riders, despite the fact that both left people dead and damaged in their wake.

The Night Riders performed Klan-like acts of terror against hillbillies; they killed several relatively well-to-do farmers who had refused to join the association and beat or whipped others. The Night Riders destroyed tobacco plant beds and burned the barns of people who hadn't joined the association; many were financially ruined. Night Rider strategy to reduce the size of the tobacco crop was shifting from an equal reduction for all to completely removing some of the farmers so that those who were left would get higher prices. Hillbillies whose crops had been ruined, as well as black and white tenants and sharecroppers, began a mass exodus of hundreds of families from tobacco-growing regions of Kentucky. They were soon joined by poorer association members who had obtained loans from richer members. When they couldn't pay, creditors began foreclosing and debtors lost their land to richer members.

Racial scapegoating

Black families bore more than their share of this violence. They were targeted because rich landowners sometimes broke the strike, and while they couldn't be driven out, their black sharecroppers could be. Big landowners could afford to go their own way, and they preferred to keep Blacks in their area under careful control as a powerless and cheap labor force, rather than have them driven out. In fact black sharecroppers may have been easier to control than white sharecroppers: complaining or challenging a landowner was safer for Whites than for Blacks, for whom it was rarely effective and sometimes suicidal. The Night Riders bit the race bait: despite a few attacks on wealthy planters, they turned their rage against Blacks. By early 1907 Blacks were becoming targets of night-riding violence even when they didn't oppose the association, and by 1908 they were the clear focus of night riding. The Night Riders terrorized black laborers and sharecroppers and warned landlords not to renew contracts with black tenants and sharecroppers. Once Blacks were defined as the enemy, violence escalated dramatically, from 15 recorded incidents in 1906 to 92 in 1907 and 158 in 1908.[14]

The Night Riders assumed that when Blacks lost farms, Whites would get them and tobacco prices would rise. But this was a flawed policy, even for the Whites who remained. It assumed that driving Blacks out would decrease the tobacco supply, and it was founded on the belief that supply and demand was the relevant issue. However, as Campbell points out, decreasing production could never lead to a better life for farmers so long as American Tobacco—or any other buying monopoly or oligopoly—had the power to set prices.[15] The weakness of this strategy was evident in the continuing poverty of those tobacco farmers who were left after the great exodus from western Kentucky tobacco-growing regions.

Because of the belief in whiteness, and because they were desperate, white association members were willing to watch people be driven out of farming to reduce the size of the crop, so long as it appeared that the majority of those driven out were black. So they stood by as Night Riders terrorized Blacks; they believed black competition was their problem. In South County between 1910 and 1925 the number of black farm owners dropped by about a third.[16]

Violence against Blacks was implicitly condoned in the West County newspaper. Night Rider violence against them was rarely mentioned, but alleged black crime was highlighted. At the same time the behavior that distinguished "good" Blacks was praised.[17] The West County editor and many others described such "good" Blacks as uninterested in bothering their heads with the difficult decisions of governing the country. In any case, the editors stated or implied, they were incompetent and needed white oversight for their own good. This interpretation upheld white supremacy, which supposedly provided protection against "bad" Blacks and the necessary oversight for "good" Blacks. With this background, Whites could accept almost any violence against Blacks as an understandable, or even praiseworthy, buttressing of white supremacy when the law was inadequate.

So enormous white farmer energy went into a strategy that couldn't work. In the process, many Whites as well as Blacks lost their farms to bigger landowners. Those Whites who got sharecropping, renting, and laboring positions found themselves economically in nearly the same boat that the Blacks they had driven out had been in. None of these farmers had benefited. Even the price rise they temporarily achieved often gave most help to richer farmers, who had bought up poorer farmers' crops or warehouse certificates and then sold them later at the higher price.[18] Landownership became whiter and more concentrated in the hands of the already well-to-do, while poorer white farmers lost their land or became even more indebted. Had they been able to see past their whiteness, perhaps they would not have supported, or stood by, while the Night Riders drove out Blacks. The lens of white supremacy had made it easier to define other farmers—black ones—as the cause of white farmers' problems. Jim Crow was functioning successfully, facilitating American Tobacco's policy of divide and rule and protecting the drainage system.

Nor did the tobacco associations, even at the beginning, grant leadership positions to black and white women or to black men, as the earlier Alliance had done, at least to a limited extent. Had women had a say in the matter, perhaps the family organization that supported the drainage system would have been questioned. Without such questioning, the associations assumed the continuation of the male head of household as the valve through which the labor of the entire family drained. The constraints of heightened patriarchy in turn supported white racial supremacy, constructing white women as white men's property and as racial property designed to provide the next generation of Whites. As racial property they were denied the right to love a black man and were said to require protection from black rapists.

Had Blacks had a say in the matter, it is far more likely that the association would have addressed the structures that created poverty for both races. Blacks in Alliance days and in the early 1900s in sharecropper and farmhand organizations raised these issues far more frequently than did Whites. They were less likely than were poor Whites to be subject to the belief that what was good for big landowners was good for them. By buying into these racial and sexual attitudes and strategies, the white farmers of the Tobacco Wars rejected the sources of strength that had led to the near-success of the Alliance.

Unlike the Populist revolt, the Tobacco Wars did *not* represent another fork in the road. The radical approach of the poorer Populists never got a hearing in the associations, which were fairly exclusivist from the beginning and became more so with the passage of time. Although it would have made a difference for landowners, there was never a chance that the associations would have improved life for most bony-fingered people struggling to live in an economy constructed around tobacco.

Restoring control

Meanwhile, the association was gaining strength. Its membership grew partly from conviction and partly from intimidation, and it had widespread local middle-class support. Its tactics were working. Less tobacco was being grown, partly as a result of members agreeing to grow less, and partly because so many farmers had been driven out of the region. American Tobacco's stockpile had been reduced by warehouse fires set by the Night Riders. Since so many remaining farmers were marketing through the association, American Tobacco Company was forced to more than double its prices, up to nine cents a pound. It now actually paid—although not very much, considering that the entire family put in a year's work—to raise tobacco.

American Tobacco fought back, using publicity from the state and national press to further its interests. The local press tended to be sympathetic to the association, supporting most of its economic aims, even while deploring the violence against Whites and against property, while barely mentioning violence against Blacks.[19] The state and national press, however, seemed to believe that the violence was evidence of the irrationality of Kentucky tobacco growers; these papers rarely addressed the system of underdevelopment, sharecropping, and debt peonage to explain the relationship between the company and the growers. Since feuding and other forms of violence in eastern Kentucky were being emphasized at the same time, the readers of these papers were likely to buy these warped interpretations. The stereotypes of Kentuckians as uncivilized savages that still afflict Kentuckians today became immensely powerful during this media campaign.[20]

Such reporting shaped the attitudes of some local non-growers and of many people outside the tobacco region across the nation, furnishing part of the excuse needed to subdue the farmers' revolt. Kentucky's new governor, elected in 1907, was Augustus Willson, a lawyer who had worked occasionally for American Tobacco, elected mainly by urban voters. With support mustered by newspaper reports biased toward American Tobacco, Willson sent state militia units to restore law and order in over twenty central and western Kentucky counties, where they "settled in as an occupying force."[21] He also said he would pardon any citizen who killed a Night Rider. White racism had once again backfired against Whites, since Willson used the violence against Blacks to justify sending in the troops to quell the revolt against American Tobacco Company. The state was providing a form of welfare—soldiers—to protect national capital in its struggle with local capital—the farmers who supplied the raw materials. In the face of such force, the association lost much of its strength and agreed to a compromise with the company in 1908.

Meanwhile, American Tobacco was declared in violation of the Sherman Anti-Trust Act and was divided up, forming an oligopoly from the former monopoly. The corporations in the oligopoly carefully avoided competition with each other, and prices quickly dropped back to the starvation levels of the pre-association days. There they remained until Roosevelt's New Deal, when tobacco growers got part of what they had originally fought for—a system for limiting production and some control over marketing.

THE WANNABE RESPONSE: NATIVIST VS. PRODUCER EGALITARIAN

It was the success of Jim Crow and the perception of an irresistible racial gulf between Blacks and Whites that distinguished the Tobacco Wars from earlier revolts, which had taken interracial organizing as a reasonable tactic, following class divides where they crossed racial lines. Organizers of the tobacco associations initially imitated the example of the Alliance, soliciting black membership. As pressure mounted, however, the example of the Reconstruction Klan gradually became the relevant organizing principle for many association members. Blacks were driven out and white landlords were warned, sometimes violently, not to take black sharecroppers and tenants.

This was not the first time tobacco growers had resorted to violence against other growers when a more inclusive movement had failed. There had been tobacco plant bed cutting riots in 1682, for instance, after the defeat of Bacon's Rebellion.[22] It is out of the bitterness of defeats of inclusive movements such as Bacon's Rebellion and the Alliance and People's Party that exclusivist tactics sometimes emerge. Given the lens of white supremacy, it was easy for white tobacco farmers to make this shift from inclusive to exclusive tactics. It was easy also because big guy/little guy analysis doesn't require a clear understanding of the role of race and gender in the U.S. class structure. This inadequacy provides the very elite they oppose with the tools to divide and rule them. Tom Watson, for instance, had been an important Alliance leader involved in interracial organizing, although his focus was on improving the position of white farmers. When the Alliance and interracial organizing failed, he simply tried another tactic. He joined the Klan after its rebirth in 1915, hoping to improve white lives through eliminating black competition.[23] Many in the Tobacco Association took the same approach. The compatibility of these farmers' views with racial exclusion is symbolized by the leadership of David Amoss, a member of the earlier Reconstruction Klan, who organized the Night Riders, and supported by the tendency of association members to be sympathetic with the Confederacy.[24]

I will use the terms "nativist" and "producer egalitarian" to distinguish between these exclusivist and inclusivist positions.[25] Both are "wannabes"–they want to become successful capitalist producers, owning their own means of production and controlling the conditions under which they live and work. Both are involved in big guy/little guy analysis. Beyond that, however, there is a real and important distinction between producer egalitarians and nativists. The Alliance and People's Party took a producer egalitarian approach. Producer egalitarians, while not free of racism and sexism, focus on the *equality* of those who produce, and on their moral superiority over people they think don't produce or who they think unfairly exploit others. Their approach is relatively inclusivist and class based; big landowners would be seen as reprehensible since they are not productive and instead are draining producers dry. Producer egalitarians are still around in North and South Counties. They do not particularly identify with capitalists who hire lots of people, since those are the people likely to do lots of exploiting. Nor do they approve of people getting educations and jobs that allow them to manage such businesses, orchestrating exploitation for the capitalist owning the business.

Nativists, on the other hand, like the white farmers in the Tobacco Wars, take an exclusivist approach, applying big guy/little guy analysis primarily to the rights of little guys who are both white and male. They believe that the big guys, the corporate elite, are using monopolistic tactics to deny them their natural right to local capital. The power of the corporate elite, they feel, makes it next to impossible to start businesses, buy farms, hire cheap labor, or even to control the labor of their own families. The nativist tactic in response is to eliminate those who are in competition with them for the scraps left by the big guys. Nativism, all over the world, claims that only those defined as "native" to a region have rights there; everyone else should leave or accept their inferior status, supplying labor to enrich the natives. Who gets to be called native is frequently a matter of intense cultural and political struggle. Nativists in North and South Counties today still take this approach. But they also believe that the government, in its role of servant to the big guys, is giving unfair advantages to white women and minorities. In their eyes these government policies encourage white women and minorities to leave their natural places under white male control, displacing white men as leaders and controllers of capital and denying them access to the labor supply they should naturally have.

The distinctions between producer egalitarian and nativist developed clearly in the Tobacco Wars, although their roots were visible earlier. In the space of a few years the farmers' revolt shifted away from defining Blacks and Whites, sharecroppers and landowners, as producers morally entitled to the fruits of their labor—or at least part of those fruits in the case of sharecroppers. Instead they began to define only Whites as appropriate producers, morally entitled to landownership. Both versions employed big guy/little guy analysis in their conspiratorial belief that big capitalists were out to get them—and it is hard to argue that they were wrong. Situations like American Tobacco's reestablishment of control led directly to the little guy understanding of the role of "big guys" in controlling and impoverishing "little guys." Whether the little guy perception of a conscious and coordinated conspiracy among big guys was correct is an issue for academics to argue about. Conspiracy or not, children were dying, parents were caught in a vicious cycle of lifelong toil, and owners' policies were unquestionably the culprit.

Both producer egalitarians and nativists accepted capitalism itself. They did not question the right of individuals to own and individually profit from their ownership of productive property. They had no problem with landownership or business ownership. They didn't try to force changes that would give rights to those non-owners who produce the wealth of others. They didn't define a decent price for tobacco or a decent wage for tobacco workers and sharecroppers as a human right rather than a privilege to be given by or forced from those higher in the drainage system. Instead they questioned only the right of monopoly ownership, which denied them the independence their own landownership was supposed to bring them or which made ownership more and more difficult to achieve or maintain.

The tobacco associations were guided by the interests of the bigger farmers and planters who had been their leaders from the beginning. Poorer Whites—sharecroppers, tenants, and indebted landowners alike— some of whom would have taken a more inclusivist route in Alliance days— allowed the leaders to get away with promoting exclusivist policies that didn't truly damage the grip American Tobacco Company had on their lives. They allowed this partially because their acceptance of white male supremacy blinded them. They assumed their leaders had the interests of all Whites at heart. Consequently their fight against financial oppression never addressed the class, gender, and racial relations that were basic to the new drainage system by which local elites drained black and white families and were themselves drained by Northern elites. The consequences of this inadequacy continued to enrich elites in their struggles with each other and kept us on the fork of the road that guarantees both bony fingers and corporate wealth.

9

NATIONAL CAPITAL
AND THE WANING OF INDEPENDENCE

So the elite worked to perfect Jim Crow and the racial state in an effort to guarantee that bony-fingered people would never again mount as powerful a threat as had been posed by the Alliance. At the same time, however, a potentially more dangerous threat was building momentum. It came with the flood of immigrants from Europe beginning in the late 1800s and combined with homegrown radicalism to challenge capitalism itself, directly questioning the rights of profiteering and exploitation that accompanied property ownership. Some even questioned the right of ownership itself. By the First World War, resistance of both the exclusionist and inclusionist varieties was intense and continuous. In the end, however, national capital tightened its grip on both local elites and poorer families.

CHALLENGING CAPITALISM

Despite the influence of Jim Crow, not everyone coming out of the ashes of the defeat of the Alliance followed the exclusivist strategy the tobacco farmers eventually chose. Instead, some took the Populist critique of monopoly capitalism to its logical conclusion. The problem, they said, lay not with other farmers or other workers, black or white, and not simply with *monopoly* capitalism. "I can see no way out," wrote Mother Jones in 1901,

> save in a complete overthrow of the capitalistic system, and to me the
> father who casts a vote for the continuance of that system is as much of

a murderer as if he took a pistol and shot his own children. But I see all around me signs of the dawning of the new day of socialism . . . [1]

In 1910 Eugene V. Debs wrote,

So long as the workers are divided, economically and politically, they will remain in subjection, exploited of what they produce and treated with contempt by the parasites who live out of their labor . . . The interests of the millions of wage workers are identical, regardless of nationality, creed, or sex . . . . [2]

About a decade later Debs received over a million votes as a socialist candidate for president, despite being in jail throughout the campaign.

The Industrial Workers of the World (I.W.W.), called the Wobblies, took the lead in class organizing, centering on the needs of so-called unskilled workers. At its inception in 1905, William D. Haywood declared that the Wobblies would not recognize "'race, creed, color, sex, or previous condition of servitude.' . . . We propose that this industrial movement shall provide, for every man and woman that works, a decent livelihood." [3] The Preamble to the I.W.W. constitution still says,

Instead of the conservative motto, "A fair day's wage for a fair day's work," we must inscribe upon our banner the revolutionary watchword "Abolition of the wage system." It is the historic mission of the working-class to do away with capitalism. [4]

These people believed that capitalism could not be reformed. Capitalists, they said, *inevitably* push wages and other costs as low as possible, turning to unfree or coerced labor when people refuse to work voluntarily under those conditions. They *inevitably* move toward monopoly to drive other capitalists out of business. With less competition, "trusts" like American Tobacco could sell their products at higher prices, buy their labor at cheaper prices, and amass more wealth. Economic power translates into political power. Capitalism therefore *naturally* leads to imperialism since owners, in their competition with each other, will be able to demand government help in getting access to the markets, labor, and resources of sections of the world that they don't yet control.

However, these critics said, reducing wages, coercing labor, and conducting imperialist wars fought with the bodies of the people who make their profits is a risky business. If enough people begin to object, or if those objecting are in a position of some strength, they may revolt, as they have done with great regularity. Capitalism therefore requires the "manufacture of consent," a massive effort to keep people believing that elite policies are beneficial for all.[5] This effort includes propaganda and the provision of some benefits to those in the middle who act as buffers and run the social control apparatus. It may also require buying off some of those who are threatening to revolt.[6] When people fail to consent, individually or jointly as they did in slave revolts, in Bacon's Rebellion, in the Great Strike, and in the Alliance and Tobacco Wars, the state's repressive apparatus comes to the fore.

INDUSTRIAL WAR:
THE REPRESSIVE APPARATUS VERSUS THE POWER OF NUMBERS

Those who came out of the Alliance questioning capitalism itself, rather than merely capitalism as practiced by monopolists who owned and controlled the "trusts," joined thousands of immigrants, mainly in Northern industries.[7] The immigrants' background in European class-consciousness led many to believe that capitalism couldn't be simply reformed to create a harmonious mode of existence in which employees and employers would benefit fairly. By the beginning of the 1900s these ideas were spreading rapidly, emphasizing the responsibility of government to the least powerful of its citizens. This responsibility included controlling the behavior of elites, limiting their property rights, and redistributing the wealth they had acquired by draining people dry. Socialists and Wobblies were gaining influence in the strategies followed in revolts. These new strategies were potentially far more dangerous to the elite than were strategies like those of the Night Riders in the Tobacco Wars.

These strategies (often described as "left" or "radical") worked on the assumption, first, that the means of production—tools, land, and factories—all actually belong to the people who use them. Secondly, they assumed that the oppression of one group of people is intimately tied to the oppression of everyone else. Strategies based on these assumptions tried to ignore the race, gender, occupational, and free versus unfree labor divisions that might give the elite the wedges they needed to divide and rule their workers. Nevertheless, Jim Crow and the long history of "race" in the United States continued to play themselves out even in the lives of people who tried to ignore them. Sometimes they were more successful than others. In 1892, for instance, free miners in Tennessee revolted by freeing at least 1800 convict miners. The convicts then joined with the waged miners in pitched battles with the militia that was brought in to force them all back to work at extremely low or no wages. Although the militia finally won, the miners came closer to winning than they probably would have done had they not organized across race and imprisonment lines.[8] In another such example, in 1910 black and white lumber workers in Louisiana ignored race—and the law—to meet jointly to organize.[9]

New tactics were introduced. In a sit-down strike workers quit producing but remained beside the tools and machines they used, making it extremely difficult to bring in replacement workers or to use military force against the strikers without destroying the factory in the process. General strikes, when all the unions in a city or in an industry strike together, became fairly common. General strikes required protesters to work together regardless of gender, race, or occupation. Organizing across these lines made it difficult to pit one group against another, denying owners their usual source of strength. Although there were many failures, such as that of the miners in Tennessee, strikers were getting better at crossing these divides during the two decades before the United States entered the First World War. At the same time, more and more people were working for wages, while there were gradually fewer but larger companies. This change brought bigger numbers of workers together in one place, making organizing easier.

Meanwhile, people's lives on the job were becoming even more difficult. As they consolidated, businesses took advantage of their power to cut costs. One example of this was the introduction of Taylorism. This system divided each operation into a series of repetitive motions that required little training, dramatically reducing the need for skilled employees. Employers could get rid of more expensive skilled workers and replace them with cheaper, less skilled ones.[10] With this "de-skilling," workers lost much of their leverage over employers, who could easily replace them, often with immigrants or children. Many children worked in textile mills, working ten-hour days, often losing fingers and hands in workplace injuries. Accidents, fires, and industrial illnesses escalated tremendously; for example, according to a 1912 report, one-third of mill workers in Lawrence, Massachusetts, died before age twenty-five.[11] The income gap between rich and poor wage earners widened.

Such conditions sparked rebellion. In 1904 alone there were 4,000 strikes involving thousands of workers, 10,000 in Lawrence alone. In 1903, in Kensington, Pennsylvania, 10,000 children struck with their elders, and some participated in a children's march on Washington. In Philadelphia, children working 60 hours a week struck, demanding the right to go to school. There were food riots in New York in 1917.[12] In 1919 one out of every five workers in the United States walked off the job.[13] And they began winning.

The corporations fought back with their usual tactics—race, control of the media, and violence. Black soldiers, for instance, were brought in to guard captured white miners in Montana. One of the white officers sent the miners' wives a letter suggesting that they "entertain" the soldiers, for which they would receive "due consideration."[14] Apparently this was a deliberate, although in this case unsuccessful, attempt to divert attention away from the wrongs committed by the mining corporation and onto race and gender. Businesses experimented with the use of Chinese laborers, and frightened native workers with the threat that employers would prefer supposedly docile, "effeminate" Chinese men.[15] Corporations hired private militias (Pinkertons, Baldwin-Felts detectives) who used machine guns to attack strikers and the tent cities where they camped with their families. A duly elected sheriff was removed in Colorado at the behest of mine owners and bankers.[16] The Bisbee Loyalty League packed 1200 striking copper miners into railroad cattle cars, left them without food and water in the desert for a day and a half, beat them up, then kept them in a federal stockade for three months. The strikers were never charged with a crime, but the press claimed they were "pro-German."[17] The National Guard was regularly sent to quell strikers who objected to working conditions that killed them or to minuscule wages that could not support themselves or their families. But occasionally even the National Guard rebelled, as did 82 of them in 1914, saying they "would not engage in the shooting of women and children."[18]

The owners of embattled corporations often demanded that reporters submit stories for approval to committees devoted to the interests of the company. This attempt at censorship was not always successful. In fact, censorship was often unnecessary since editors of major newspapers generally favored the interests of the big corporations, as did the editors of the Bisbee papers.[19] New South elites cooperated in this process since it was in their interest to bring in low-wage industry. They held wages down by busting unions and by providing incoming industry with a large labor surplus.[20]

Theodore Roosevelt and his administration, despite Roosevelt's progressive, trust-busting reputation, were guided by the needs of the trusts. National corporations were regulated only to preserve capitalism in the face of such massive unrest by making cosmetic reforms that would defuse people's anger.[21] Still, the Socialist Party continued to gain strength, particularly as government response made it clear that the power of the state was regularly and militantly used on the side of the elite to subdue protesters.

INDUSTRIAL WAR IN KENTUCKY

Contrary to the myths about industry bringing prosperity, industrial development brought poverty to most of the people living in Kentucky areas rich in industrial raw materials, as it has done in many similar parts of the world. Development in these cases meant *underdevelopment*—people's land and resources taken from them legally, by chicanery, or by force. The resulting profits are realized outside the area, are not reinvested locally, and do not contribute to local development. Local people, having lost their ability to feed themselves, become a low-wage work force.

Kentucky in 1900, before widespread development, was far from "backward." It had led the South in manufactures and among Southern states was second only to the far larger Texas in agricultural production.[22] By the Second World War this was no longer true. Most of Kentucky by then had become a source of wealth—raw materials and cheap labor—under the direct control of national capital. It had been "developed" and was close to the bottom on national rankings for most economic and social indicators. This had long been true of Kentucky's coal-mining regions, where by the early decades of the 1900s Northern coal mine owners and corporations like Ford owned most of the land. They bought out or kept out rival employers in order to keep wages low by preventing people from having a choice of employers.[23] National capital owned most mines; company stores drove out or marginalized local businesses. Many local people had to choose between leaving and working in the mines or timber industry. Some of those who still owned their own land practiced a way of life based on hunting, occasional wage labor, and nearly true subsistence farming.[24]

These conditions contributed to interracial union organizing and massive resistance by miners to alleviate the poverty, malnutrition, and sometimes starvation, as well as the life-threatening working conditions that came with the coal mines. Conflict between owners and miners was continuous, but at times flared into real warfare between the owners' private militia, state or National Guard, and armed coal miners. Many miners saw socialism as the only possible solution to the inevitable capitalist attempt to make themselves as rich as possible by making miners as poor as possible, or by letting them die in unsafe mines. Warfare flared in the western Kentucky coalfields in the early 1900s, at about the same time as the Tobacco Wars, in West Virginia in the 1920s, and in eastern Kentucky with "Bloody Harlan" in the 1930s.[25]

Most Kentuckians, however, worked in agriculture. There was still relatively little manufacturing in most of Kentucky; in 1849, 2.2 percent of the population of Kentucky was engaged in manufactures; by 1909 that percentage had increased only to 2.9.[26] However, Louisville itself was the second largest city in the South and a major industrial center at the turn of the century.[27] As elsewhere, smaller businesses were going under as capital became concentrated in the trusts. In 1893 there were approximately ten thousand unemployed in Louisville and many more whose wages were cut. Working conditions in Louisville were terrible, particularly for women, and especially for black women. Wages for most women working outside the home were below the minimal costs of keeping one person alive in the city. Women worked ten to fourteen hours a day, six or seven days a week; the least dangerous and physically exhausting jobs were reserved for white women. Nevertheless, because farming didn't pay or because the wages brought home by fathers and husbands were totally inadequate, women's wage work increased dramatically. At the beginning of the 1900s, 44,518 women and girls over the age of ten worked in Kentucky industries, mainly in Louisville. They worked in tobacco factories, where conditions were the worst and women's employment the highest, and in laundries, garment factories, and mills, as well as working as bookkeepers and clerks. By 1930 their numbers had approximately tripled. While some worked in factories, many rural women and some men did piecework under sweatshop conditions in their homes, often with the help of their children. They earned an average of $52 for a year's work in 1933, at a time when the minimum factory wage for comparable work was $12 per week.

As in Appalachia and among tobacco farmers, intolerable conditions led to resistance. There were at least 140 strikes in Louisville over wages between 1880 and 1900. There were also strikes by railroad workers—which women working in laundries supported by refusing to wash scabs' laundry—and by textile workers, mainly women. Some, particularly in northern Kentucky, expressed their discontent with votes for the Socialist Party. Even with most black votes eliminated by terrorism, in 1912 the socialist Eugene Debs got 11,677 votes, nearly 3,000 votes more than the Socialist Party had gotten a year earlier in a vote for governor. By the 1930s, communists and socialists in Louisville organized the Kentucky Workers' Alliance, opposed discrimination against Blacks, and staged a hunger march on Washington.[28]

Wage employment outside of Louisville and a few other smaller cities was primarily agricultural, except in eastern and western Kentucky where coal mining increased rapidly after 1900. But rural wage working conditions were even worse than in Louisville. Throughout the South, much rural industry was so dangerous, employment was so insecure, and wages so low that coercion was the only way employers could get people to work for them. Some of those forced to work were convicts. Most were not.[29] As landowners had done with their sharecroppers, mine owners frequently organized patriarchal control of mining families. Like landowners, they used debt peonage to force "consent" to conditions that regularly killed miners with unsafe conditions below ground and their children with malnutrition above ground. Surviving wives were left to cope with desperation when death or disablement of husbands or sons gave owners the excuse to evict them from company housing and withdraw all financial support.[30] By this time timbering by farmers in central Kentucky was going into decline as intensive lumbering used up the trees. However, timbering in the mountains continued under the control of large companies.[31]

So, although few Kentuckians in the early 1900s were engaged in industrial work, those who were suffered greatly. Many of those in agriculture weren't doing well either, particularly in counties like South County where many people depended on tobacco. Consequently many in the state had reason to distrust the trusts. Their personal experience with coal mine owners, with railroad owners, with tobacco companies, either as farmers or factory workers or as small business owners, had made it clear to them that Big Business was bad for "little guys." The editor of the West County newspaper railed regularly against the Trusts. Nor did people have much reason to trust their county governments, which regularly ruled in favor of the corporations.

RESISTING CAPITALIST WAR

Consequently, it is hardly surprising that there was considerable skepticism when the United States government decided to enter the First World War.[32] Many poorer people felt they were expected to put their lives on the line in Europe to make the world "safe for democracy," a war that they interpreted as making the world safe for the trusts. Others simply didn't see the point of taking men and their labor away from their already struggling families. Resistance in Kentucky and elsewhere, at least among poorer Whites, was widespread. Some of the strongest resistance was in the South, including that of the 800 to 1000 tenant farmers involved in the short-lived Green Corn Rebellion in Oklahoma.[33] Initially they expressed this resistance by failing to volunteer for the military; Congress resorted to force through conscription. Conscription, at least in some small white farming communities, was met by covert resistance. People avoided registering or failed to show up when called, or gave only a rather sullen "consent" when conscripted. Perhaps as a result of white resistance, proportionately more Blacks than Whites were sent overseas from Kentucky. Although Blacks made up 11.4 percent of the population, they made up over 16 percent of Kentuckians sent to Europe.[34] A massive campaign of "public information"–propaganda–was mounted, along with censorship of the news and sedition laws making it illegal to speak against the war. Socialists, Wobblies, and other people speaking their minds against the war were jailed as traitors or beaten by local mobs. Local committees of elites–frequently wives of prominent men living in towns–were appointed to orchestrate compliance with the war effort, to increase food production, and to institute more economical use of consumer goods.

The socialist vote in many parts of the country skyrocketed as a result of war resistance, with socialist candidates winning some local elections in 1917 and getting as much as a third of the vote in others. The socialist vote came mainly from working-class districts, regardless of whether or not the district had a large immigrant population. Thirty-two socialists were elected to state legislatures, and thousands of people came to hear socialists speak against the war at meetings around the country. Even in Kentucky, which was not a strong socialist state, some minor officials were elected.[35]

THE STRUGGLE CONTINUES AFTER THE WAR

The end of the war was accompanied by disillusionment in Kentucky.[36] Soldiers, having "made the world safe for democracy," many of them battered in mind or body, returned to find that the conditions of their own lives bore little relationship to the democracy they thought they had defended.[37] Black soldiers found themselves denied the manhood that soldiering was supposed to bring.

Fewer white men were able to claim the independence of landownership and of controlling family labor, adding to their disillusionment. Instead of owning farms, more and more Southern men were seeing a lifetime of wage labor stretching ahead. Northern industry was heading south to take advantage of their cheaper labor and of the South's greater success in the violent suppression of Wobblies, socialists, communists, and unions. Development under the direction of New South elites was designed to maintain the separate, cheaper, Southern labor market that had existed before World War I, but at the same time to harness it to Northern capital. Theoretically, this move would insulate businesses from demands that they pay workers enough to live on. It was backed up by the threat of moving the business to a more compliant area if workers did demand better pay, a policy Daniel describes as "New South business blackmail."[38] In practice, however, the abusive business policies that left workers dead, maimed, or utterly exhausted, and condemned many of their children to a repetition of the cycle, led to increased labor resistance in the South.

In an effort to construct "consent" to these conditions, more southern industries turned to the use of enslaved men. Most of them were black but some white; the "justice" system had processed them and classified them as convicts. Enslaved convicts were often used for the jobs with particularly high rates of sudden death, such as timbering in swamps in the Deep South. Jobs where death rates were a bit lower or more lingering were sometimes worked by convicts and sometimes by "free" workers controlled by debt peonage.[39] In either case, the problem for employers was that no one would voluntarily take such jobs, and coercion was required unless employers were willing to pay more, improve safety, and allow people to rest. Since this would diminish their profits, they chose coercion instead.

Frequently, however, this coercion was disguised if the work required skill and therefore a modicum of cooperation from employees. In this case, companies organized mill and mine towns where they "provided" housing, schools, churches, and that critical institution, the company store, which recycled wages back to the company. Company towns instituted patriarchal control of every aspect of the lives of their inhabitants.[40] Welfare workers hired by the company told women how to care for babies or cook nutritious meals. Ministers in company churches told them God wanted them to work hard and be grateful to the company and avoid consorting with atheistic agents of the Devil–socialists, communists, Wobblies, and union organizers. Schools repeated the message to children, and taught the gospel of development by outside capital. Those who didn't consent, the "troublemakers," were kicked out of their company homes. Debt peonage, organized through the company store, ensured constant debt and the legal excuse to force people to stay; indebted people who left were, if caught, brought back by the sheriff. Kentucky's vagrancy laws allowed men who didn't regularly work 36 hours per week to be arrested. At the same time, poverty was increasing.[41]

Jobs somewhat less disastrous to the well-being of employees could be filled without overt coercion. Nevertheless, as the 1920s wore on, even in these industries real wages dropped for unskilled labor and the "stretch-out" forced longer hours and harder work. Twenty-five thousand people were killed on the job each year in the 1920s, and another hundred thousand permanently disabled. The supposed prosperity of the 1920s proved to be only skin-deep and questions about capitalism itself became widespread.[42]

Among the already-bony-fingered, in contrast to those in the middle positions and in the local elite, the anger that resulted from these conditions often led to widespread left-leaning denial of the legitimacy of capitalism, rather than to nativist reactions. Lumberjacks in Louisiana, migrant wheat harvesters in the West, miners in Colorado, textile workers in Massachusetts and New Jersey all turned to the Wobblies in the 1910s and 1920s. A virtual state of war existed in many industries and in many areas. There was a significant socialist vote. In the 1930s Alabama sharecroppers and Kentucky miners, among others, became interested in communism.[43] The Southern Tenant Farmers' Union and other radical southern organizations continued the longtime cry of "land for the landless." In the 1930s they succeeded in making their voices heard—for a brief period the Farm Security Administration provided funds for thousands of sharecroppers and laborers to purchase land individually or as members of cooperatives.[44]

NATIONAL CAPITAL AND THE WANING OF INDEPENDENCE

Even for people who didn't directly question capitalism, national elite intervention in daily life was becoming a bigger issue. Local elites, who since frontier days had run Kentucky county government, began losing ground to national elites in the control of their counties. Since county government was extremely powerful in Kentucky—one scholar describes the counties as "little kingdoms"—this represented a major loss for the local elites.[45] For many non-elites, World War I was their first experience of direct contact with federal or even state government. Women were expected to register with their local committee for industrial work, recording the personal circumstances that affected their availability to contribute to the war effort. Men were told to switch to scientific commercial farm production, laying the groundwork for the mechanization that New Deal agricultural policies would later advocate. Mechanization created industrial expansion in fertilizers, petroleum products, and tractors, and would soon drive thousands of smaller commercial farmers and sharecroppers off the land and into wage labor. In Kentucky there was considerable resistance to using local taxes to support the Agricultural Extension organization, since it helped primarily larger farmers.[46]

On top of all this, more and more white men lost their expectation of eventual landownership and of controlling black labor and women's labor.[47] They had to deal with the "shame" of dependence on an employer and of taking directions indefinitely from another man, but in many cases continuing to be poor despite their hard work. The people they had been raised to expect to control were gaining greater independence. Women were getting the vote; cars and jobs gave some women physical and financial independence. Blacks were making serious organizational strides through the NAACP and other groups. Black nationalism and general black resistance to white supremacy were on the rise, and black veterans and other Blacks had begun to fight back against white aggression. White liberals seemed to be aiding and abetting black and feminist initiatives. Laws limited men's control of their families: divorce became easier for women, and children could be removed if a court judged it to be in the child's best interest. The patriarchal male head of household was losing ground: his control was less than absolute, his independence was compromised both by the greater likelihood of wage labor and by the intervention of elites in his rule of his dependents.

The First World War, like the Civil War and Reconstruction, had served as a wedge for a reorganization of the Southern drainage system. This time the reorganization was to accommodate wage labor under the control of national capital as the norm for white men and poorer white women. From the point of view of many Whites, the world they had known had been turned on its head. As usual when the drainage system was being reorganized, this time "developing" the South for wage labor to benefit national capital, the meaning of whiteness also had to be reconstructed. And as usual, it would take violence to do so.

10

THE REDEFINITION OF THE
PRODUCER EGALITARIAN ETHIC

As people increasingly came to depend on bought goods, and as cars and gasoline became necessities, their expenses rose, a trend many people in my area fight by continuing canning, sewing, and gardening. As expenses rose, people needed more more cash, and became ever more tightly tied to income-producing commercial farming or to wage labor, with less time for gardening and home manufactures. The resulting vicious circle tied people ever more tightly to capitalist organizations, both as laborers and as consumers. In the process more people became vulnerable to exploitation and found their lives more tightly constricted.[1] This shift was painful to an increasingly broad range of people in the working-class, but by the 1920s this pain had spread to the formerly more independent middle class as well: they had now joined the working-class as waged employees or were under the thumb of national corporations. As the previous two chapters have shown, unrest and resistance were widespread.

TRANSITIONAL DECADES AND THE BROKEN CONTRACT

The psychological wage, first of simple superiority and then buttressed by racial separation, was proving inadequate. Whiteness did carry with it a certain amount of protection from racial violence, but after all it was only Whites' own beliefs and actions that made racial violence dangerous to anyone. In reality whiteness didn't even carry complete protection from lynch mobs. Without the complicity and often active participation of poor

Whites, the planters and merchants, landowners, small business owners, lawyers and other members of the buffer class could never have achieved the reign of terror that controlled the South for decades and drained both Blacks and poor Whites. Most of the apparent advantages of whiteness were, for those Whites at the bottom of the drainage system, pure fiction. This fiction was avidly promoted by "racial agents," many of whom were the elite leaders of lynch mobs or who published, preached, or made political speeches buttressing the psychological wage.[2]

Buying off the opposition

During the 1910s, the effects of breaking the suffrage-instead-of-land contract reverberated through white communities. As farmers and industrial workers were increasingly squeezed by the trusts, whiteness and white privilege could no longer be counted on to control bony-fingered Whites. Many who could no longer vote in protest lost their sense of belonging to the system and felt they had little to lose in opposing it. Opposition was so intense that, in order to preserve their position at the top of a capitalist drainage system, the elite had to make some concessions to part of the working-class.

The First World War had brought huge profits to the major industrial capitalists. At the urging of the wartime committees, buying government bonds had been seen as a patriotic duty, which provided funds for the purchase from national corporations of industrial products used up by the war and therefore in constant need of replacement. As Du Bois points out, a small portion of this bonanza was eventually used to buy off part of the resisting working-class with higher wages.[3] Employers often gave these higher wages to those unions that were least threatening to capitalism. These were the unions that pursued nativist strategies of excluding white women, Blacks, or other minorities. Their leaders agreed to eliminate socialists, communists, and Wobblies and to grant capitalists their right to private property and private profit. These unions received a short-term benefit for their members—the right to a slightly larger share of industrial profits. The result was growing white inequality and the stratification of Whites into relatively permanent classes. Although employers began to discriminate in pay by race, changing the earlier policy of separate-but-equally-low-paid workplaces, only some Whites benefited. Others continued, with Blacks, to receive the low wages both had received before the 1920s, preserving a large low-wage, disenfranchised black and white component in the labor force to create the massive profits capitalists needed to compete with each other.[4] This was the compromise with the white "skilled" working-class coming out of the unrest of the 1920s and 1930s, although not fully stabilized until the 1940s.

At the same time this larger share of industrial profits became the material basis for a redefinition of whiteness and manhood. Higher wages would give material content to the whiteness of "real" Whites, a bonus beyond the psychological wage, distinguishing them from "white trash" and from European Catholic immigrants who didn't receive the higher wages. These redefinitions correspondingly revised the content of white male honor and racialized "white trash." "Real men" no longer had to be independent or in control of other people's productive labor; by that standard, too many would be defined as failures. Instead, they could bring home a paycheck big enough to "support" a family and could validate their ability to do so by being served by a non-producing wife. Even better, in much of Kentucky, was the ability to provide that wife with a black servant.[5] Money, hard work as a value in itself rather than as a step toward independence, and a wife's proper spending of a paycheck became the measure of manhood and morality; it was the proof of the real American. Those native Whites who failed to measure up on either count were deemed biologically defective and were categorized as "white trash."[6] Like Catholic immigrants, they belonged on the new, lower rungs of the racial labor hierarchy.

REDEFINING THE PRODUCER EGALITARIAN ETHIC

With this redefinition of whiteness and manhood came two major problems. First, the producer egalitarian ethic had to be redefined, so that "producing" for men no longer meant only independent production as farmers or craftsmen or small entrepreneurs.[7] Second, the failure of a great many Whites to meet the new standard had to be explained. It had never been true that all Whites were, or could reasonably expect to be, independent landowners or entrepreneurs. Previously, however, independence or a fairly good approximation of it had been common enough that Whites could use it as part of the white norm, a yardstick against which to judge themselves and others. But as wage labor became more and more common, and as serious exploitation spread to large numbers of native white men, using the yardstick of independence guaranteed that large numbers of them would be judged failures.

Wage labor itself was changing character. Previously, even when working for wages, skilled workers in factories had maintained the rights to use their minds as part of their craft, to make an entire finished product, and to work without supervision.[8] It was fairly easy to define such work as productive, even though the final product did not belong to the person who had made it. Monotonous work without decision-making rights had previously been deemed appropriate only for very young native white men, and then only as a temporary way to save money to purchase the land or equipment to become independent. Generally such jobs were reserved for some white women, but mostly for Blacks and not-quite-white immigrants. The new efficiency, however, as prescribed by Taylorism and Fordism, deskilled former skilled crafts and demanded work much like that reserved for Blacks, immigrants, and women. Dislike for the system was so intense that in 1913, for instance, Ford had to hire 963 people in order to increase his workforce by one hundred—people quit faster than he could get them hired, and he finally had to double wages in order to get them to stay.[9]

The number of skilled craftsmen in factories declined dramatically. Factory work for native white men in the new system was monotonous, repetitive, carefully supervised, and more likely to be permanent. This was work in which someone else held all decision-making rights, including even the right to prescribe exactly what motions to use while inserting a screw on an assembly line. And it was far harder work; breathers were impossible, changing position was impossible, and the struggle to keep up with the assembly line was continuous. If native white men engaged in the new factory work, and wanted to see themselves as producers and there-fore as moral "real men," robotic assembly line work would now have to be included within the producer egalitarian ethic—a difficult change.

Not only did permanent monotonous wage labor challenge the pro-ducer aspect of the producer egalitarian ethic, it also defied the egalitarian aspect. Industrialization brought with it a much more clearly defined class structure among Whites, one that was much harder to ignore.[10] Previously in small farm areas, but even to some extent in plantation areas, most white men were doing more or less the same thing as more or less independent operators. Although some white farming families were much better off than others, nevertheless each worked directly for its own interests; little farmers often weren't directly enriching big ones. All believed they were above the permanent labor class, which consisted primarily of Blacks. Under these circumstances it was fairly easy to pretend that all white landowners and local small business owners were equal. White tenants could be seen as soon-to-be landowners, equals in training, particularly when they were related to landowners. Since the power of planters and other local elites depended on the support of other Whites, it was to their advantage to encourage this conception of egalitarianism. But with permanent wage labor this was no longer true. Industrialization and development clearly meant that some who were formerly "equal" became far wealthier, while others became poverty-stricken; some determined how the screw should be inserted, while others inserted it.

This differentiation between classes was exacerbated by the centralization of formal decision-making power, substituting federal or state control for local control. This process got a temporary start during Reconstruction, but when home rule was returned to the former Confederate states local elites regained most of their former power. However, during the First World War the federal government began reaching deep into the structure of local communities. There was the attempt at thought control in the wartime propaganda campaign, dissent was criminalized, and government agents tried to change methods of farming and housekeeping. Local white men had less say over political decisions that affected their lives; it was still much easier for them to exert influence at the county level than at the state or national level. Decision making seemed to be sliding even further from the hands of "little guys" and from the hands of local elites.[11] Neither increased local class differentiation nor the centralization of political decision making provided conditions under which belief in white male equality could flourish.

Redefining the producer egalitarian ethic for white women also involved a revision of the meaning of productivity. A "good" woman now took responsibility for keeping her husband productive as a wage earner, providing him with a safe haven in which to recuperate each day from ten or twelve hours of exhausting and mind-numbing labor. She was responsible for the moral education of her children, particularly for making sure that they became hard-working and obedient employees or wives. She was to spend her husband's paycheck wisely and to engage in enough conspicuous consumption to make clear her husband's success as a breadwinner and her own success in producing a proper family. She was not to make as many of the household's necessities as before; she was to spend money instead, helping to fuel an economy based on consumerism.

As a result many white men found that their claim to manhood had become tenuous. They were being told how to run their lives and farms; increasingly the elite intervened in decisions and behavior that had formerly been under the control of local white men acting as patriarchal heads of families. New attitudes eroded a man's right to control his children's and wife's labor. Since production was no longer to be the basic function of a household, depriving a household of its labor force through divorce or the removal of children no longer mattered as much.[12] A household was particularly likely to be broken up if it wasn't performing its new wage-earning and spending functions adequately. Products such as shoes and "proper" clothing were now defined as morally necessary for raising children. Therefore children could be removed from households that weren't consuming properly.

This switch to consumerism did not happen automatically. National corporations worked hard to make it happen. They bombarded people with information—often deceitful—about the virtues of their products in order to "fabricate" customers.[13] Local merchants who might have sold other brands or local products were pushed into carrying the nationally advertised goods by this artificially produced "consumer demand" and by manufacturers who threatened not to sell their product to stores which didn't sell their brands exclusively. Customers might begin shopping at competing stores that did carry the particular brand they wanted, or they might turn to chain stores or catalog sales for their purchases. In Kentucky, as elsewhere in the nation, the worry that small businesses, both retail and manufacturing, would disappear under the influence of chain stores and catalog marketing companies like Sears was well founded. Fifteen percent of retail sales in Kentucky were made in chain stores by 1930 and in Louisville by the 1950s local owners of even the most successful industries and stores were being pushed out.[14]

Ignoring consumerism

Many North and South County white farming families maintained only a marginal connection with the consumption economy, living in a pattern that the elderly now describe from their own childhood and from stories their parents told them. These were landowning families that remained closer to subsistence farming and avoided heavy dependence on commercial farming, and therefore had little cash. Newspapers carried notices from stores specifying the farm produce they would accept in trade in lieu of cash well into the twentieth century. Most of the ads were for farming equipment, staple foods, medicine for "female troubles" and chronic exhaustion, shoes and overalls, cloth and sewing needs. This pattern in its essentials continued in my neighborhood well into the 1950s, although gradually more and more men spent part of their lives in nonagricultural wage labor.[15] In this pattern, families grew some tobacco for cash, but put much of their energy into providing most of their own food and clothing. Women born in the 1940s and earlier remember the dresses their mothers made for them from the flowered cotton sacks that flour came in. Along with coffee, overalls, and shoes, flour to supplement locally ground corn-meal was among the few necessities their families bought. Summers were spent preserving food for winter; women took pride in the shelves loaded with canning jars. Dried beans were the basic protein for much of the year, but men killed cows and hogs in the fall and whole families worked on butchering and curing the hams and bacon. Sides of beef hung in sheds during the winter. Foraging for wild food supplemented the diet. Huge cat-fish, the size of a six-year-old child, were shared at neighborhood or fami-ly get-togethers, since they couldn't be preserved. Pokeweed and other wild early spring greens provided welcome fresh food before gardens began their heavy summer production. After electricity came to my area in the 1950s, a huge chest freezer full of meat joined the canning jars as the backbone of the family economy. Since whole communities lived much the same way outside of the plantation areas, they could see themselves as equals, and, as many have commented, worked hard, but "ate real good and didn't know we were poor."

However, in former plantation areas there were more sharecroppers and tenants. They didn't have the luxury of opting to remain partially outside of the market economy. And the growing class of consumption-oriented experts on scientific farming and housekeeping defined anyone as "back-ward," landowner or not, if they dressed their little girls in flour-sack dress-es, no matter how cute those dresses looked. Thus, it was impossible for most sharecropping families, and for landowning but subsistence-oriented families, to become "proper" consumers.

WHITENESS AND THE NEW DEFINITION OF CONSUMPTION AND DOMESTICITY AS MORALITY

This is where the second problem with redefining the producer egalitarian ethic came in. The new pattern of productivity and consumption was a middle-class standard. Many middle-class families were able to afford a stay-at-home wife, particularly those in which the husband was a skilled professional, owned a business or was a landowner, or was part of the buffer social control class. Wives in bigger landowning families often had the help of women or children from their sharecropping families or had hired help. Many aimed for a lifestyle and pattern of consumption similar to that of the growing town middle class. Farm wives also "stayed home," but home continued to be their productive work site, although they didn't produce as many of the family's necessities as previously and were under pressure to advertise their family's successful farming by purchasing consumer goods. Most families who did meet the new criteria for productivity and morality were native Whites, but most towns also had a small middle-class black community whose members adhered to this standard. Some factory workers began to imitate the middle-class pattern, although with belts pulled extremely tight. This became possible as the conflict with the elite continued and unions gradually won more concessions for their members. Henry Ford's decision to double wages to five dollars a day, for instance, making a virtue of necessity, temporarily permitted fairly middle-class consumption patterns.[16]

Despite the apparent prosperity of the "roaring twenties," however, until the Second World War many white working men, like most black men, actually didn't earn enough to support the female domesticity that was the marker of a successful breadwinner. Such men didn't meet the moral requirements of the revised egalitarian ethic. With the racial discrimination in wages now prevalent, it was easier for native Whites than for Blacks or not-quite-white immigrants to meet the new standard, but even so, many didn't.

Many white wives did work outside the home, and not in the approved middle-class pattern: they were neither teachers nor social workers nor volunteer-club women doing good deeds. Instead, like black women before them, they worked under the control of some man other than their husband. Their sweat benefited capitalists far more than it had in diversified subsistence farming, and probably somewhat more than it did in commercial family farming. Farming had allowed families to maintain the fiction that women in the fields were just helping out, and that men were the real producers; factory work belied this fiction. Generally working in race- and gender-segregated occupations, white women maintained a toehold in white superiority and in white racial "purity." But the more ragged their children and husband, the less nutritious and appealing the meals they served, the less supervised their children and the more those children worked, the less she and the family met the new definition of morality. The bottom of the scale was employment that threatened their husbands' rights to claim white male patriarchy. Such challenges came when women worked outside of sex- and race-segregated occupations or worked as servants providing to another man the domestic services that they were supposed to provide only to their husbands.

So how was white poverty and lack of domesticity to be explained in the context of white supremacy? Whites presumably were biologically and culturally superior. They were given the "benefits" of Jim Crow segregation and discrimination. Capitalism and development were supposed to be beneficial to those able to take advantage of opportunities. How, then, could such superior and advantaged people include so many who were poverty-stricken? Why would some of those poverty-stricken native Whites continue to consort with Blacks and immigrants? What explanation could be given that wouldn't admit to the exploitation of Whites and upset the apple cart the elite had so carefully constructed in reorganizing the drainage system? And how could white men and women deal with the threat to manhood posed by their failure to meet the criteria, or by their precarious grip on those criteria? Whiteness had become partially behavioral; simply claiming European ancestry was no longer as effective as it had been.[17]

The contradiction posed by the failure of Whites to be equal, as prescribed by the producer egalitarian ethic, would eventually be explained away by making definitional distinctions among people formerly lumped together in a single category. They simply weren't all "really" white—they weren't "100 percent American." The conception of 100 percent American had been initially brought to the fore in the First World War propaganda campaign. It quickly became a centerpiece of the newly revived Ku Klux Klan's propaganda, differentiating "good" and "bad" Americans while continuing to define even bad white Americans as superior to Blacks.

Meanwhile, as working-class Whites were facing their problems with identity in the new system, the elite were having corresponding problems administering this reorganized drainage system. They needed a way to get a significant percentage of the population to believe that the continuous violence of labor repression was justified and beneficial to the nation. Second, there was the continuing need to manufacture consent to the new criteria of moral behavior despite the problems they posed. Finally, the elite needed an effective means of dividing and ruling the Northern working-class. In the North, more than in the South, new immigrants now made up a large percentage of the low-wage industrial workforce. They were demanding admission to whiteness and some were joining in spreading anti-capitalist ideas. The answer to both the white identity crisis and the elite control crisis came in the reinvention of the Ku Klux Klan and in the refurbishing of the old notion of "white trash."

The Klan and Redefinition

Although the Klan and its white sheets is now at the center of white American images of racial violence against Blacks, in reality that image provides a convenient smokescreen. It protects Whites from knowledge of the *pervasiveness* of white violence and of the *ordinary* quality of white individual and community complicity in it. The central place given to that white-sheeted image implies that real racism was and is practiced only by a marginalized and perhaps demented few. The image claims those demented few are poor white rednecks, denying the reality of middle and upper class leadership and complicity in the Klan. Central also to the smokescreen is the image of lynching as the basic Klan activity, obscuring from view all but a small—although critically important—portion of Klan violence.

The rebirth of the Klan in 1915 did not mark the rebirth of racial violence in the United States. Violence against Blacks had been continuous since slavery. After the Civil War they no longer had even the protection against destruction granted to property but not to black human life. It is true that, at least in plantation areas, lynching of Blacks was more frequent immediately after the Civil War than at any time since, and that the Reconstruction Klan carried out part of this violence. However, there were at least one hundred lynchings a year from 1882 to1901; lynching remained in the double digits until 1932 and in the single digits until 1951. White Kentuckians lynched as large a percentage of their state's black population as did Whites in the Deep South.[18] During much of this time there was no Klan. The Reconstruction Klan had been forced out of existence in 1871 and the second Klan, organized in 1915, didn't become a major force until about 1920. Even during Reconstruction, not all violence was performed under the auspices of the Klan. Between the demise of the first Klan and the birth of the second, groups of "regulators," "whitecappers," "night riders," and local mobs continued lynching.

However, lynching was only the most visible and most reported form of violence. Whippings, beatings, rapes, castration, harassment, threats of violence, or hearing about violence were daily occurrences. Even those Blacks or those black communities without direct experience of the more violent expressions of white supremacy would be well aware of the possible consequences of violating it. Nor could Whites be totally ignorant of the acceptability in most white communities of enforcing taken-for-granted white privilege with violence if necessary. Even if they themselves claimed to abhor violence, most took white supremacy and the racialized state as normal and accepted the violence as an unfortunate but necessary means of maintaining order. They believed that Blacks accused of rape or murder had actually committed those crimes and deserved punishment, and that the "justice" system couldn't be trusted to execute them. The lens of white supremacy made newspaper reports of what appears now to be extremely dubious evidence appear to provide credible proof of guilt. This remained true as the "justice" system pushed out lynch mobs and took over the killing of Blacks, performing "legal lynching."[19] Thus most Whites, consciously or not, were implicated in the violence by their silence.

The second Klan, in other words, despite its violence against Blacks, was not *needed* to perform that function—systems of violence were already in place, part of the taken-for-granted white culture. Instead, it acted as a tool of national American elites who used the nativist response for their own ends, choosing to institute fascist processes to enhance their own power in their quest for international control. The redefinition of the nativist crusade helped to manufacture middle-class consent to its own loss of privilege as the repercussions of the takeover by national capital reverberated through their lives. Simultaneously, it permitted capitalists to ratchet up the level of exploitation of their workers. It split the white working-class, controlled the black, and eliminated political and activist dissenters: communists, Wobblies, socialists, and radical unionists. Increased exploitation allowed them to extract the extra value national capital needed to push out local capital and then to compete with each other in the race to dominate as international capitalists.

11

THE KLAN AND THE MANUFACTURE
OF MIDDLE-CLASS CONSENT:
SPLITTING THE WHITE WORKING-CLASS,
TERRORIZING THE BLACK

The success of the second Klan, reborn in 1915, long after the death of the Reconstruction Klan, and rising into prominence in the 1920s, reflected yet another reorganization of the drainage system, this time around permanent wage labor under the ascendancy of national capital. It flared briefly into national prominence and power during the transition between systems in a vicious response to middle class and local elite loss of power. It continued the tradition of violence against Blacks and brought a return of violence against people of European ancestry. It scapegoated communists, socialists, inclusive unions, Catholics, immigrants, and Jews. In the process of manufacturing consent to the new system the Klan played myriad and sometimes contradictory roles ranging from resistance to accommodation of the new system, but ultimately it was used by the national elites to gain control of local labor and resources. Once national elites had wrested control away from the local elite, the Klan was outlawed and prosecuted, but never fully eliminated; it continued to act as a marginalized terrorist organization, kept on ice to be allowed out when needed again for labor control.

THE SECOND KLAN

Millions of mainstream white Protestant Americans joined the Klan in the 1920s, and many more were fellow travelers, sympathizing with and furthering the ideals of the Klan without actually joining. In Kentucky the

Klan was strong all through the 1920s, with estimates of membership ranging from 50,000 to 200,000 members. The overwhelming control of politics that the Klan achieved in places like Indiana never completely materi-
alized in Kentucky. Nevertheless, its influence in state government was
very real, as it was in local government. Half of Shelbyville's city council
were Klan members in 1925, for instance, and the Klan maintained an
active presence in many small communities.[1]

It is unlikely that these members joined *simply* because they were racist.
In a racialized state racism is endemic, and their racial attitudes probably
were not significantly different from those of many who didn't join.[2]
Instead, apparently most joined because they felt threatened by the world
around them. They were generally middle class, neither "unskilled" labor
nor national elites. Those who joined were not the middle-class local professionals who represented national capital as lawyers, bankers, and
administrators. Instead, joiners were of the middle class associated with
local small capital—landowning farmers, merchants, or skilled craftsmen
running a small business. Others were allied with local capitalists as doctors, lawyers, teachers, and Protestant ministers. Others held mid-level
skilled white-collar positions in national corporations, for example, as railroad conductors, clerks, supervisors, or bookkeepers.[3] Many in the middle
class felt they were working hard and getting nowhere. Nevertheless, they
still precariously maintained more control over their own labor than did
the mill-working and sharecropping Whites around them. The comment
of a small business owner near here, watching a wagon carrying a hard-
working sharecropper to his burial in the 1930s, revealed awareness of the
contrast with his own position. The sharecropper, he said, "will be out of
luck if he misses Heaven, because he surely never had any pleasure *here*."[4]

Those who joined the Klan felt their position was being eroded both
from above them in the drainage system and from below. Local elites in
North County, for instance, were gradually losing control of their banks as
a result of mergers and acquisition by national capital, and chain groceries
were beginning to make their presence felt.[5] From below, Klanspeople worried about erosion of their position as recent immigrants and northward-
migrating Blacks competed with them for a better rung on the labor hierarchy. Small entrepreneurs and landowning farmers had been the economic base of local communities, but there were now far fewer such people. In the new economy most middle-class people would have to work for
large corporations rather than expect to eventually become their own
boss.[6] Skilled craftsmen in the working-class were disappearing as assembly lines took over and roboticized most production. Consequently skilled

craftsmen often felt threatened, just as did the disappearing old independent landowning and entrepreneurial middle class. But most working-class men's lives were already organized around wage labor with little realistic hope of becoming their own boss. For them the shift from local to national control of capital made less difference than it did for the middle class.

Klan propaganda

The Klan had an enormous centrally controlled hierarchy that adapted to local situations. Klan organizers picked issues that were currently hot in individual communities, always intending to separate white Protestants from everybody else. They were backed up by the national Klan's Propagation Department, which supplied direction, literature, and ideas for speeches. The Propagation Department's message thus found its voice in thousands of Sunday sermons, speeches at fairs, letters to newspapers, and editorials, as well as Klan meetings. It was even more widely disseminated through organized "whispering campaigns" conducted by women in the Klan. Such campaigns supported boycotts of Jewish and Catholic businesses, passed along stories of prostitution rings run by Catholic convents kidnapping Protestant girls, of Jewish greed, and of poor white and immigrant immorality. All the while, the organization's militaristic structure kept it tightly tied to central authority.[7]

This propaganda was aimed at the Klan's middle-class audience. If the middle class objected to the way capitalism was operating, their consent had to be won, not overtly forced. They voted and had a modicum of power at the local level and therefore couldn't be shot by militias or lynched if they got "out of line," as white and black people at the bottom of the drainage system often were. Equally important, they needed to be enlisted in the fight to control those below them.

In fact, many middle-class white people were deeply angered by the power of big business. Because they felt that money in large quantities, in the hands of national elites, controlled government policy, they saw little point in placing hope in government for the relief of their problems.[8] Some gave in to apathy; some joined the Klan. Klanspeople advocated direct action against Jews, who they thought controlled the country's finances, and against Catholics, whose Pope they believed orchestrated foreign dominion over the United States. Both groups were accused of supporting socialism, and socialism, according to the Klan, would eliminate the sanctity of property and profit. Capitalism would die out, and with it the entrepreneurial route to individual freedom, independence, success, and power over others. Socialism would allegedly take the power of individual self-determination away from native white men—supposed descendants of the initial "founders" of the nation. It would destroy the nation by undermining the racial heritage that they believed was their due.

CLASS, THE KLAN, AND EXCLUSIVIST EGALITARIANISM

Klan dues and regalia were expensive, excluding poorer industrial and agricultural workers. Many of them weren't interested in joining anyway, especially those involved in the interracial or inter-ethnic unions of the 1910s and 1920s. Since extremely wealthy local elites and those associated with bringing in national capital were also unlikely to join the Klan, Whites within the Klan could see themselves as equals, ignoring income differentials. They saw themselves as the hard-working, patriotic, moral, family-oriented, white Anglo-Saxon Protestant descendants of the individualistic and enterprising stock of the Founding Fathers. They felt they lived up to the revised producer egalitarian ethic and should be rewarded for their "virtue" with upward mobility and a chance of independence.

A large proportion of businessmen and professionals in the Klan had not inherited their positions; they saw themselves, like small landowners, as hard-working entrepreneurs who, through their individual effort, had achieved success. Others, although employees, had likewise come from poorer origins.[9] As potential or actual entrepreneurs Klanspeople advocated the sanctity of private property and private profit—they believed that white Anglo-Saxon men should be in a position to benefit from both. And they believed that white Anglo-Saxon potential was held in check by lack of capital. Access to startup capital actually was limited for non-elite men; even local elites had trouble getting loans or locating investors for business ventures or expansion. National financial and manufacturing elites now controlled most investment capital. Unless local elites worked through them, orchestrating "development" to enhance national elites' profits, they were unlikely to get the capital they needed to compete. Klan propaganda helped insulate national elites from the anger their control of capital provoked, focusing it instead on supposed Jewish control of capital and Jewish immigrants' supposed radicalism and communism, all part of the alleged Jewish plot to control the world.

Although most in the Klan didn't hire labor, many hoped to. Defining themselves as potential employers, Klanspeople opposed organized *group* efforts to raise wages, claiming that wages should reflect *individual* merit and achievement, not collective political or union strength.[10] The Klan denied the reality of conflicting interests and inequality between employer and employee, claiming a harmonious community of interest among those who sweated and those who benefited from that sweat. It advocated what it called a "closer relationship between capital and labor."[11] In practice, the Klan interpreted any resistance on the part of labor as anti-American. Consequently, the Klan engaged in verbal and physical union bashing, ranging from cross burning to murder of labor leaders. Not coincidentally, union activity and membership dropped in the early 1920s as Klan activity and influence reached its peak.[12]

Klan anti-unionism, however, was shaped by conceptions of who *should* provide the labor to enrich employers. In the South they admitted no right of poor Whites and Blacks to organize; in the North immigrants were added to this mix. But the Klan paid little attention to craft unions composed mainly of white Anglo-Saxon Protestant men who practiced exclusionary tactics to defend the native white right to the few remaining skilled jobs. A de facto collaboration between Klan, exclusionary unions, and corporate owners contributed to constructing a new hierarchy of labor, buying off native Anglo-Saxon Protestants by placing them on a higher rung with higher wages than immigrants, Catholics, Blacks, and other people of color.[13]

New Rungs on the Labor Hierarchy

In the North many of the people on the new lower rungs of the white labor hierarchy were Catholic immigrants, but in the South, many were native Whites. So "white trash," "Catholic," and immigrant came to have a not-quite-white race-like character shaped by "bad blood."[14] Their supposed inadequacy was described as the result of generations of alleged incest, poor nutrition, and improper training. But bad white blood didn't lead to inferiority quite so irretrievably as did membership in the "lesser races." As a Kentucky Klan organizer explained, "the very foundations of the country are in danger through . . . the mighty host [of 'aliens'] streaming in . . . " As a result, the "melting pot has changed to a garbage can . . . fouled by the mass of foreign, unassimilated stock," and, with some exceptions, only the native-born should vote.[15] Superior productivity and intelligence, and even a good individual work ethic, were claimed to be biological attributes of native Whites but not of white trash, southern and eastern European immigrants, or Blacks. The Klan publicized the work of scientists who claimed that such cultural differences had a genetic basis.

Catholics and the alleged Jewish conspiracy

Part of the bargain struck by the national elite with the Klan and other nativists in return for their support was the establishment of severe immigration restrictions in the early 1920s. This limitation on new recruits for low-paid jobs meant a labor supply problem. Part of the cure lay in the northward migration of several million poor Whites and Blacks, bringing the Southern labor reserve north.[16] Mexican labor was brought in as another piece of the answer, and vagrancy laws were enforced to keep people working.[17] Another part lay in moving industries south, cooperating with New South elites in using Southern labor there. But an additional part of the solution lay in denying upward mobility to the not-quite-white eastern and southern European Catholics and Jews who already made up a large percentage of the low-paid workforce. Then they, like Blacks, could serve indefinitely as a source of cheap labor. Religion could act as a permanent identifying mark setting them off from "true Americans" and justifying discrimination. Anger at the national elites would be redirected and neutralized as the Klan set Protestants and Catholics at each other's throats, and both turned against Jews, splitting the working-class.

Before Klan propaganda gained ascendancy apparently anti-Catholic and anti-Semitic attitudes among Protestants did exist but were not particularly pronounced. There had been Jewish mayors in Kentucky, and Catholics and Protestants bought from each other's stores and lived peacefully as neighbors.[18] It took Klan and elite encouragement to fan those existing sparks into flames. Local Protestants boycotted and often drove out Jewish and Catholic businesses. However, in so doing they often unwittingly cleared the way for national corporations, rather than for themselves. Thus, despite its intentions, Klan strategy decreased native white male access to capital. As usual, exclusivist tactics had backfired, damaging those who used them as well as those they targeted.

"White trash"

In promoting 100 percent Americanism, Klan attitudes helped justify the idea that not even all native Whites were equally deserving. Over one-sixth of native Whites were "not the type that furnished in earlier years the brain, muscle and moral fiber of the land," constituting "a might army of defectives and social delinquents."[19] The fact that some white Anglo-Saxon Protestants experienced low pay, dependency, and confinement to unskilled work totally controlled by others was explained as the result of their biological or cultural inferiority—they were white trash, not "100 percent American." Biology, not the drainage system, explained continued poverty in the land of opportunity, so 100 percent Americans could deny the importance of class inequalities. In popularizing such racialized beliefs about poverty, the Klan aided and abetted corporate interests.

Klan attitudes and influences outside the Klan were mutually reinforcing. Talk about, and government investigations of, "shiftless" white sharecroppers, laborers, and mill workers became common, and in fact all these groups actually did move frequently in search of better conditions.[20] Describing them as white trash made the problem appear to be within the worker rather than within the job. Once again, employers complained about the difficulty of finding decent help. Stereotypes of Kentuckians received nationwide attention, epitomized by famed historian Arnold Toynbee's 1934 description of Appalachian mountaineers as "barbarians."[21] Others saw them as genetic diamonds in the rough, representing the "original Anglo-Saxon stock," a resource to use in resuscitating the white race and highly preferable to eastern Europeans as well as to Blacks.[22] Other stereotypes characterized textile mill hands as "lintheads," a derogatory term implying they were so inferior that the low wages, child labor, and the total control of their lives in company towns was actually a form of benevolence. Employment in mills and schooling could "rescue" some white trash. It would teach them part of the new morality: how to labor.[23]

THE KLAN AND THE HOUSEHOLD DRAINAGE VALVE: REDEFINING GENDER

Ideas of 100 percent Americanism and white trash depended heavily on reshaping gender around paychecks and consumption. The flow of value through the head-of-household valve had been mostly one-way in commercial family farming. The entire family produced salable commodities, and the husband/father fed all of the value they produced into the drainage system.

But in families dependent on wage labor the nature of the flow of value through the valve changed. A woman no longer produced salable commodities or as many products for home use. Instead, her job was to keep the wage earners in the family going back to work and preparing children to be hard workers as adults. The value she produced, in the form of cooked meals, clean socks, perhaps canned garden produce, and cared-for children, went to subsidize the wage received by the husband and perhaps other wage-earning children or relatives. In other words the employer got two employees for the price of one. One of these employees worked at the employer's workplace and the other performed support services in the home. Some employers in company towns recognized this, and, as slave-holders had done earlier, provided a garden plot and canning and preserving instructions. Others provided social workers to teach women how to "scientifically" care for their families on the tight budgets necessitated by the low wages their husbands were paid.[24] Women were encouraged to find fulfillment in service, not in household production, for, in fact, many white women now spent full-time servicing their own households. They now produced most of the value flowing out of the wage-dependent family through the head-of-household valve, since men in these families no longer produced goods or crops at home. But the value the wife produced—a husband who continued to work—couldn't be sold, leaving her entirely dependent on her husband in a way that farming women generally were not.

The role of head of household also changed. Men's wages now flowed through the valve into the family; he received status and responsibility within the family as the "breadwinner." Men were to place most of those wages at the disposal of their families and provide broad guidelines for expenditures, hopefully under the wife's scientific household management. Families measured themselves and others by their consumption patterns; keeping up with the Joneses became a moral issue.[25] White men whose paychecks weren't big enough to keep up and white women who failed to organize consumption properly risked exposing themselves as "white trash." "Real men" redefined the work ethic; hard work was good for its own sake, not because it allowed you to eventually gain independence or get ahead of others. Proof of a good work ethic came in the paycheck, not in goods produced or acres plowed. So the paycheck became the measure of manhood. Clean clothes and well-disciplined children became the measure of the moral woman.

The Klan came into this redefinition of gender and whiteness by enforcing men's obligation to produce, if not as entrepreneurs, then as employees, thereby ultimately enriching the elite who employed them. The Klan threatened and sometimes whipped "shiftless," vagrant, or immoral Anglo-Saxon Protestant men; the implication was that they should become "God-fearing . . . industrious toilers," who supported families.[26] White women were believed to have the right to be "supported" and protected—and controlled—by men who acted as properly patriarchal benevolent despots within their families. While few were actually whipped, those few whippings underlined the Klan rhetoric that publicized and moralized about "family values" and the new criteria for white manhood.

This emphasis on supporting families also justified looking down on men who didn't. Since the definition of a properly supported family was a wife in the home serving her family, any man who couldn't earn enough was morally suspect. He must be too stupid or too lazy or so interested in sex that his numerous children forced him into poverty. Alcohol became both a symptom and a cause of inferiority. Catholics, so the claim went, drank; men who drank didn't support their families. Good hard-working 100 percent American Anglo-Saxons didn't drink. Succumbing to drink could turn 100 percent Americans into white trash. Hence the Klan insistence on prohibition; in some parts of Kentucky this became the primary overt Klan issue.[27] They inveighed against alcohol, which led women to sin and divorce and men to neglect their families, against dating in cars where girls were out from under their fathers' control, and against any erosion of the family and the father's authority within it.[28] Controlling wives and daughters was critically important because, they felt, "[a] nation can rise no higher than the spirit and virtue of its womanhood," whose duty it was to instill virtues and urge men to live up to them.[29] Thus if the nation–or a native white man–went under, the fault would lie with women who weren't 100 percent American and proved to be trash.

Thus was white stratification both justified and explained. Whiteness could still work for 100 percent Americans because only the inferior and immoral failed. Stratification, poverty, and low wages were biological, natural results of the fact that white trash and immigrants simply didn't have what it took to rise in the world.

AN APPARENT CONTRADICTION:
NATIONAL CAPITAL SUPPORTING NATIVISM

Although national elites benefited from the presence of the second Klan, they didn't control it. In fact, despite the Klan's hatred for them, national elites made no effort to control it until the new drainage system was well established. In a comparable situation, planter elites had made no effort to control the earlier Reconstruction Klan until Blacks and poor Whites had given up their hope of better things and sharecropping was established. Once sharecropping was the norm, however, and the Reconstruction Klan still continued driving out black sharecroppers and tenants, big landowners in Kentucky reversed direction, withdrew their support from the Klan, and allowed Blacks to testify against Whites in night-riding cases. As marginalized terrorists, however, Klansmen and other whitecappers continued to serve elite purposes. Too small to succeed in driving Blacks out and replacing them with white tenants, Klan offshoots were still adequate to endanger Blacks who didn't have white patrons. Eventually white terrorism helped tie Blacks to sharecropping by making the "protection" offered by their big planter patrons a necessity.[30]

Had the second Klan, like the Reconstruction Klan, not served the interests of the controlling elite, it would never have gained the respectability it did, despite its large membership. After all, large membership hadn't brought respectability to the Alliance or to unions. There was no concerted effort to control Klan violence until the middle of the 1920s, when its credibility was undermined, and various states followed Kentucky's lead in passing anti-lynching laws.[31] Despite the law, however, mob members were rarely punished for murder of a black person, even when, as frequently happened, the murder was a public event.

Although national elites didn't join the second Klan, some nevertheless aided and abetted it. A syndicated series ran in about twenty newspapers in 1921 castigating the Klan but failing to point out its usefulness to the elite. Thousands of insecure Whites who had never heard of the Klan liked what they read and membership soared. Congressional hearings followed, but were called off without making recommendations even against those Klan activities that were clearly illegal. Legislators certainly seemed to be giving the Klan a green light.[32] Other elites, like President Harding, were supporters of nativist groups that cooperated with the Klan.[33] The film *Birth of a Nation*, produced by Kentuckian D. W. Griffith, was the most technologically advanced film of its time. It lauded the Reconstruction Klan in its role as the savior of pure white womanhood and was shown all over the country. Woodrow Wilson enthusiastically praised the film as "like writing history with lightning . . . terribly true" at its White House showing.[34] Some Northern capitalists, Pierre DuPont and Alfred Sloan of General Motors, for instance, provided funding in the 1930s for Southern politicians promoting white supremacy. Henry Ford published an anti-Semitic newspaper. Such activities generally supported the Klan conception of Jewish conspiracy and a biological racial hierarchy.[35]

National elites initially had good reason to let the Klan grow, despite its opposition to national capital. Feelings of powerlessness against big business may have led many middle-class people to join the Klan, but a more radical response was also quite possible, given the salience that socialism, communism, and the Wobblies had gained since the turn of the century. And potentially this challenge could be violent, since large numbers of those most exploited had been denied the vote and with it even the hope of working within the political system for redress of what they saw as injustice. Bony-fingered people could have mounted a serious challenge to the elite if they had reached across race and gender lines. Various radical groups, including inclusivist unions, radical Christians, and communists, were trying to get people to do just, sometimes successfully.[36] From the point of view of the elite, anything that could split this potential alliance among people being drained was beneficial, even if it meant putting up with rhetoric denouncing them as blood-sucking capitalists.

And that is exactly what the Klan did. It siphoned off many white Protestants and set them against the rest of the potential members of such an alliance of drained people. Anti-immigrant, anti-Catholic, and anti-Semitic fervor could all join with anti-labor attitudes under Klan auspices. Together these attitudes could derail the radical unionism that gained its greatest support from immigrants, both Catholic and Jewish, and at times from Blacks and native Whites at the very bottom of the drainage system. It refocused protest energy into a protest that, compared to communism, was far less dangerous to the elite. It used its huge propaganda machine to tell precariously middle-class Whites that the root of their problems with national capital actually lay with Jews, Catholics, Blacks, and immigrants, and immoral women. It encouraged worried white Protestants to define themselves as the moral backbone of the nation, as people who defied nonproducers, be they business moguls, white trash, or ignorant immigrants. On the surface the Klan actively opposed national capital, supporting local capital in the fight against a "development" that damaged local businesses. However, the Ku Klux Klan actually aided the very national corporations it despised.

New South Elites and the Marginalization of the Klan

Klan propaganda gave a new twist to old explanations of supposed black inferiority; it inveighed against the New Negro.[37] The New Negro was supposedly even more dangerous than the old. The new version compounded the old alleged uncontrollable desire to rape white women with a desire born of military service during the First World War to upset the status quo with radical notions of male equality. Black radicals, particularly those who were also union leaders, were in continuous danger from the Klan. Violence against radical Blacks, unlike violence against white men who failed to support their families, was frequent and often ended in death. At the same time, more conservative black leaders like Booker T. Washington, who advocated self-help for Blacks within the racial hierarchy, were given prominence by white liberals and New South advocates of national capital. As a result of de facto collaboration between the Klan, liberals, and New South elite, many black radical activists and union leaders were silenced by terror or death. By the middle of the 1920s, most Wobblies and other radical labor activists had been killed, jailed, driven into exile, or had gone underground. At this point New South elites began complaining about the Klan and its violence. Many employers now said immigrants and poor Whites could be "Americanized" and that Blacks, given the kind of industrial training Booker T. Washington had advocated, could likewise become good workers.[38]

This New South "business liberal" or "progressive" position on race and ethnicity, including the support of conservative black leaders, amounted to a compromise with the Klan and other whitecappers.[39] Race riots, such as those that had broken out all over the country in 1919, were not conducive to profits or to a stable, disciplined workforce. National business elites' apparently more accepting attitude compared to that of local elites reflected their desire to obtain the cheapest labor possible. Whether that labor came from Blacks, Chinese, Hungarians, or white trash made no difference to them. Regardless of ancestry, terrorized labor is frequently cheaper labor; the Klan was good at terrorizing, and therefore had played a useful function. However, most in the Klan didn't *intend* to make black and immigrant labor cheap for national elites. Instead they intended to drive out black and immigrant labor so that elites would have to hire Whites at higher wages, or so that they could take black or immigrant farms and houses for themselves. Therefore, if the Klan was too successful it would damage elite interests.[40] Thus, just as earlier planter elites had eventually pulled the rug out from under the first Klan, New South elites eventually did the same thing to the 1920s Klan in the second half of the decade. Once black radicals and the inclusive unions had been suppressed and Whites had accepted white stratification, the Klan was more of a liability than an asset.

It was at this point that an all-out effort was instituted at the state and national level to discredit the Klan and even occasionally to prosecute—although not to execute—for violations of the anti-lynching laws. National elites took the right of informal mob enforcement of whiteness, and the control of cheap labor, away from local elites.[41] They replaced it with formal enforcement controlled by the new buffer social control class that mediated between national capital and local people. At about the same time that the anti-lynching law was passed, reflecting the declining power of the local elites who led the Klan, the Kentucky state legislature made Federal Hill a "state shrine." What it enshrined, and mourned, was the passing of the old South and its old local planter elite. After the vote was cast, the entire legislature rose to sing "My Old Kentucky Home."[42]

The Klan was reduced to a marginalized terrorist organization; its whippings and lynchings were now carried out in secret, rather than as public rituals. When needed, the lid could be lifted; the media could "advertise" a renewed tolerance for the Klan by carrying reports of unpunished violence against whoever was causing serious trouble for the drainage system. Rationales for middle-class audiences could explain the dangers to business—and therefore allegedly to the country—posed by these threats to the drainage system. Such rationales could help to organize middle-class tolerance for violence by the Klan and, if necessary, by the National Guard in defense of American business. Thus in the 1930s when the Congress of Industrial Organizations (CIO) began inclusionist union organizing, rather than the well-tamed exclusionist American Federation of Labor (AFL) version, the Klan was allowed to revive temporarily. The CIO was accused of communism, and the Imperial Wizard declared that the Klan would not "allow the CIO to destroy our social order."[43] The Klan contributed its own violence, but probably more importantly it helped to spread anti-communist and anti-socialist propaganda. Communists actually did participate in the union organizing and other activism of the 1930s, and the communists actually included black and white leaders and members.[44] Thus the Klan's combination of anti-Black and anti–white trash racism and anti-communism was particularly relevant. Its propaganda matched with attitudes of many who were not necessarily in sympathy with the Klan. Ministers claimed that CIO stood for "Christ is out," or "communist insanity organized."[45]

This propaganda was used to explain why black, immigrant, and native white miners and miners' wives in Kentucky and West Virginia needed to be killed for demanding an end to debt peonage and lethal working conditions. It could explain why sixty protesting unemployed autoworkers needed to be shot by Ford employees and police. It could explain why women textile mill hands should be beaten and sometimes killed when they resisted inhuman work speed-ups and demanded wages high enough to support a family, perhaps to let their children complete school instead of working in the mills beside them, breathing lint-laden air.[46] The Klan and its exclusivist nativism had served its purpose.

12

BROWN SHIRTS/ WHITE SHEETS: FASCISM AND MIDDLE-CLASS DEMOTION

In Kentucky and in the United States generally, the relationship between the Klan, the middle class, and the elite was strikingly similar to the relationship between the early Nazis, the middle class, and the elite in Germany. Fascism, however, was not institutionalized in the United States as it was in Germany. National capital–big business, as it was often called–was putting extreme pressure on local capitalists in both countries. Nativists–both white-sheeted Klansmen and brown-shirted early Nazis–supported "little guy" capitalists and wannabes in their efforts to control property and labor in a racialized society.[1] Generally speaking it was not lower-class laboring people, but the same more-or-less middle class mix of local business and professional people, white-collar employees, and local landholders who formed the backbone of both groups. In each country they saw themselves as faced with two enemies. From above they feared social demotion at the hands of big business, but they also feared that people they considered inferior to themselves might challenge them from below. In the end, in both countries, national capital first used exclusionary nativism to disrupt what they saw as a much more threatening radical attack on the whole structure of the drainage system. But once that was done, the national elites of both countries de-fanged the nativist "little guy" attack on monopoly capital. The Klan was put on hold by U.S. big business after the mid-1920s; the Nazis were simply taken over by German big business. Early nativist Nazis who stubbornly continued attacking the "big business" enemy were purged from the party or killed, leaving the party now threatening only supposedly inferior people.[2] Nazi economic policy eventually came directly from German big business: I. G. Farben essentially ran the German economy.[3] During the Second World War the United States also tightened the connection between the state and major corporations. The heads of the biggest industrial corporations, which received enormous government war contracts, took leaves from their corporations. They worked as heads of departments concerned with war production and economic affairs. They continued to receive their corporate salaries, and worked for the government for a dollar a year.[4] Their powers weren't as direct or as extensive as those of the German officials: in the United States the corporate heads worked, at least technically, as government employees rather than as heads of their corporations.

That fascism was not institutionalized in the United States as it was in Germany may be related to the fact that German big business was somewhat hamstrung by that country's mildly socialist Weimar government. Resistance to tightening the drainage system was more institutionalized there: German unions were some of the strongest in the world, and the social safety net was one of the best.[5] United States businesses, on the other hand, had always been able to count on help when they needed it. Businessmen and Chamber of Commerce members led anti-union mobs that tore the clothing from strikers' wives, whipped strikers, and hung the leaders.[6] Others oversaw more organized violence, in which police or security guards did the real work. They shot and jailed protesters. In 1920, for instance, Attorney General Palmer initiated a roundup of immigrants and radicals in which 6000 people were arrested and about 550 people were deported. Demonstrators were shot at Ford, there was open war in the coal mines, and Rockefeller's private militia killed men, women, and children in their strike camp. Historian James Weinstein maintains that the resulting reign of terror against those fighting the corporations in the United States during the First World War and its aftermath was worse than anything going on in Europe at the time, including Germany.[7]

In both countries, local and national elites cooperated initially in constructing lower rungs on the labor ladder through discrimination or terrorism or legislation; both wanted cheaper labor. But national elites had an advantage over local elites in actually using those lowest rungs. National corporations in both places were more Taylorized. They had greater access to the credit needed to install the latest technology that made deskilling labor efficient.[8] If in addition only big employers had access to people confined to the lowest rung, they would have another competitive advantage over smaller employers. This was certainly true in Nazi Germany where for the most part only the large national corporations were able to get free concentration camp slave labor. In the United States it was mainly bigger employers—mining companies, for instance—that got convict slave labor. Thus by helping to construct new low rungs the Klan and the nativist Nazis contributed, unintentionally or not, to the downfall of local elite control of business and labor.

Legal construction of a racialized labor hierarchy

German national elites, in choosing to increase their exploitation of the German working-class, supported the Nazis because Nazi nativism was useful. The Nazi propaganda machine helped discredit the existing government, which from the elite point of view was much too friendly to labor. After the Nazis gained power and the national elites took over, nativist rhetoric justified the official creation of a racialized state, as it did in the United States when Jim Crow was institutionalized. The Nazi state, however, legislated the details of its ranking system more formally than did the United States. Good Aryans were legally at the top and given Aryan privilege—good wages, the reservation of jobs with better working conditions, and minimal middle class welfare. Aryan privilege, like U.S. white privilege, helped to buy off a big section of the working-class. It designated those supposedly hard-working, productive men who deserved the service of a biologically fit wife who would stay at home and raise the next generation of pure Aryans according to state social worker instructions. Couples that weren't "biologically pure" didn't have the legal right to this kind of life. Such couples had only limited rights to children, and the wives were required to have jobs. Below pure Aryans was the rest of the population, placed in steps carefully graded by biological fitness and marked legally by decreasing access to wages, rations, and welfare. These lower categories included women whose behavior marked them as biologically undesirable as mothers—women who didn't clean house properly, who disobeyed male authority, had mentally disturbed relatives, or were not "pure Aryans." Other low rungs included unionists, "voluntary" foreign labor, and prisoners of war. With them at the very bottom were "community aliens." Among them were Jews, Gypsies, communists, homosexuals, and others, such as the "work-shy," tramps, and prostitutes, whose values supposedly marked them as biologically impure.[9]

Once war production began, Aryan males at the top of this hierarchy were forced to work up to their physical capacity.[10] There were official discussions of just how much work they could stand, and their families were provisioned just well enough that they could raise many healthy children.

Abortion and birth control for this group were forbidden. Further down the ladder, women could be sterilized or forced to abort; they were unsuitable for raising good Aryans. Instead, they were to work at very low-paid, physically demanding labor.[11] Those at the very bottom, German and foreign conquered "community aliens," were murdered in gas chambers if they were judged unsuited for hard labor. If judged suitable, they were worked in Taylorized concentration camps with almost no food until they could work no more, were murdered, and replaced. The owners and managers of I. G. Farben and other national corporations clearly concluded that the efficient use of human resources made certain people disposable, like paper plates.

Meanwhile, Nazi propaganda used slogans such as "self-realization through work," "the gospel of work," and "beauty of work," and over the gate into the Auschwitz concentration camp are engraved the words "Arbeit Macht Frei"—"Labor Liberates."[12] National elites grew wealthy, local elites went out of business, and workers suffered in carefully graded amounts. Given the unlimited power that came from actually running the government, big German corporations chose to push exploitation to the limit as national policy.

WAR BENEFITS FOR AMERICAN ELITES

American national elites were not as desperate as German elites before the war. Leftist and anti-capitalist sentiment hadn't gained as much power in the United States, despite severe unrest. Since the U.S. government was already dominated by business interests, the U.S. elite had a much bigger welfare program for itself than did the German elite. Legislators, governors, and presidents were all willing to use tax-payers' money to protect big business interests, with legislation and enforcement through the "justice" system where possible. If necessary they were willing to stage mock trials or to bring out the guns of the military, the National Guard, state militias, and the police.[13]

With the advent of the Second World War, U.S. national elites rapidly became the capitalist world's most powerful. Fifty-six companies got 75 percent of all U.S. war contracts, an incredible bonanza. As a result small businesses and small farmers went under, and the concentration of capital in the hands of the national elites intensified.[14] But the formerly widespread criticism of big business, of greedy trusts, and of monopoly became muted during the war. That such criticism still existed, however, is revealed by a South County newspaper editor's reference to capitalism as "unpopular" in an editorial equating capitalism with freedom, and in the frequency with which the paper delivered diatribes against socialism.[15] The glorification of American big business capacity to out-produce the enemy became a common component of patriotism; it was becoming un-American to criticize the corporate elite.

During the war, the editor of the South County newspaper lauded the role of capitalists in the war effort. "Private enterprise," he said, in a typical issue of the paper, "working in its full production and service sphere, in full cooperation with our armed services, can match its strength against any dictatorship yet devised." An accompanying article pointed out that "[p]roduction hinges on the drive of independent citizens. Industry is run by independent citizens. The problem in the future will be to see that it stays that way." Nevertheless, remnants of the nativist objection to "big guy" power are visible in another issue, in which the editor says that the "cornerstone of every community is the business man—the man who invests his money in local property, who employs labor, pays taxes, and helps in every way to build a better town" but can't succeed "in a community where the local money is being spent a thousand miles away."[16]

New lower rungs on the labor ladder

In fact, American elites did work people to death and they did use slave labor in prison labor camps. Agricultural elites forced labor from prisoners of war and arranged for almost-free labor from contracted Jamaican, Bahamian, and Mexican workers, and used race and race-like designations to determine who would receive a living wage.[17] Some mining and landowning employers could pay in scrip, a legal fake wage. Employers didn't formally have the right German employers had to starve, eventually kill a captive labor force, and then replace it. Nevertheless their policies sometimes produced similar results on a smaller scale.

However, American employers did all this without a state-sanctioned and regulated hierarchy of labor. This was a de facto system, much less carefully organized and less powerful than that in Nazi Germany, and more informally enforced. In the United States, at least outside of prisons, the compulsion to remain in dangerous jobs that didn't pay a living wage came mainly from economic necessity and lack of alternatives. That compulsion was often orchestrated through debt peonage or through terrorism or discrimination, but it was not a direct result of legal regulations, as it was in Nazi Germany.

Not only were the elites of both countries pursuing similar policies in relation to both labor and nativism, but there were also strong direct connections between German and American corporate elites. For instance, during the war the Rockefellers' Standard Oil Company maintained its cartel with I. G. Farben, the corporation that ran the Nazi economy, organized the Nazi four-year plan, received 72 percent of German four-year-plan investments, and ran the Auschwitz slave labor program.[18] Henry Ford had fascist connections in Germany. General Motors produced trucks in Germany for the Nazis throughout the war, and even received reparations after the war for damage inflicted on their German plant by Allied bombing.[19] That relationship continued after the war when many Nazi scientists were brought to the United States.

NATIVISM AND THE MANUFACTURE OF CONSENT

Like German elites, American employers depended partially on nativist attitudes and organizations to support the continuous violence that was required to keep the drainage flowing freely in the 1920s and 1930s. In America the Klan helped distinguish white trash from other Whites in order to explain why whiteness and America weren't working for some Whites. In Germany the Nazis separated out community aliens—like U.S. white trash—to explain why some apparent Aryans deserved to suffer poverty and exploitation. These apparent Aryans actually lacked the "racial essence" of true Nordics, though some who didn't look Nordic—like Hitler himself—nevertheless could possess the "racial essence." Their behavior marked them as members of the "Volk" community, the mystical folk community Hitler invoked as the essence of the German fatherland. Thus, like the redefined whiteness, Aryan-ness was partially behavioral.[20] In nativist eyes only the influence of Jews, Gypsies, leftists, and the genetically impure stood in the way of the all the benefits that should come to the Nation and its pure members.

Both Klan and Nazi tactics helped to make nativist attitudes respectable even among those who were not members or even real sympathizers, making the suppression of dissent appear reasonable. These same tactics contributed to the repression of the bony-fingered people at the bottom of the drainage system, those among whom consent was much harder to manufacture by persuasion. This repression required more than the passive consent of not knowing or not caring about what was happening, or of simply accepting newspaper accounts describing massacres and mock trials all as if they were natural events. Active consent was also required. At least some people would have to be willing to participate in legal and illegal violence. They would need to elect politicians who believed that the state should operate for the benefit of big business and would send tax dollars to a massive welfare program provided by the National Guard, police, and "justice" system. They would have to be willing to look the other way when lynch mobs took action. White-sheeted Klansmen and brown-shirted Nazis similarly discredited or terrorized politicians who talked about real equality or about the real causes of bony fingers.

Equally important, nativist rhetoric focused attention on "values," away from elite policies that caused so much misery and made it so hard for many people to live up to the new standards of morality. Powerful Klan rhetoric, beatings, and murders focused on scapegoats for white problems: immigrants, Blacks, Catholics, Jews, unions, Wobblies, socialists, and communists. Nazi rhetoric and violence, in making the same points, defined certain people as sub-human and therefore expendable in the name of race and profit. Nativist Nazi consent to elite Nazi policies eventually brought upon the nativists themselves inhuman working and living conditions. They themselves became expendable as soldiers or workers in the name of profits for the few. Only force—Allied guns—brought an end to this system. Once again exclusionary tactics had backfired.

Similarly, American corporate elites used nativism in their orchestration of the de facto system of labor control. Like the German formal system, the U.S. system led to the deaths of some of those who were treated as disposable labor. Many of these deaths would be defined as accidental—the result of mining disasters, of bad luck, as the "natural" result of poverty or illness—or as the inevitable result of confrontations with the National Guard who "naturally" had to defend corporate private property. Like the German elites, U.S. big business owners showed no signs of voluntarily relinquishing this system and the riches it brought them. Instead, American elites between the two world wars conducted a running battle with protesting workers. They managed to maintain their edge largely because of nativist initiatives that had been naturalized with the help of Klan propaganda. These included the heightened racism directed against Blacks and immigrants of color; the division of Whites into 100 percent Americans, white trash, and Catholics; and the redbaiting that made the destruction of inclusive unions and union leaders and the suppression of dissent appear patriotic.

The crisis was put on hold with the patriotism and jobs of the Second World War, but by the end of the war, big business was firmly in control of local elites and markets. During this time national industrial elites used their influence in government to consolidate their power. The long struggle between local and national capital ended, and the new controlling elite backed off from fascist processes. The association of patriotism with production had smoothed this transition. Many now believed that "What is good for GM is good for the nation," a rather ironic attitude considering GM's production of Nazi trucks.[21]

In the aftermath of the war what U.S. national elites needed was uninterrupted production to take advantage of the new markets around the world opened up by the war, so they backed off a bit from policies that pushed workers into revolt. Higher wages, a real forty-hour week with benefits, and a welfare safety net combined to buy off a large and vocal proportion of U.S. wage earners. The middle class finally gave up its expectation of entrepreneurial independence, and the people who held factory production jobs adjusted themselves to robotic work. Both finally accepted the definition of their wage labor in the reorganized drainage system under the control of national capitalists as productive, manly, and appropriate for white men.

CAPITALIST CRISIS, THE WITHDRAWAL OF PRIVILEGE, AND FASCIST PROCESSES

Nativist attitudes tend to become far more prevalent and broadly accepted among "little guys" and the use of fascist processes becomes far more prevalent among "big guys" under a specific condition–and that condition can occur again.[22] Fascist processes are likely to be chosen when a new elite, representing a different level of capital, is fighting to wrest power from the elite that currently holds controlling power over the economy and social structure. To gain this power the new elite chooses to *break* the contract that had been previously "negotiated" between the old controlling elite and the groups below it in the middle of the drainage system. These middle groups have some degree of power, making it difficult to use direct force on them to reorganize the drainage system. The old contract with the old elite had granted privilege to people in the middle in return for their consent to elite rule, but that privilege is withdrawn as the new elite takes over and reorganizes the drainage system to suit its own needs. The new elite is placing itself in a new, higher position on the drainage system above the already existing top positions of the old elite. The old elite is forced into an intermediate position and the old middle is correspondingly demoted. The new controlling elite in the newly created top position can then drain the lower-level elites below them, and through them, those still lower in the drainage system.

According to this interpretation, fascism is the process of adding lower rungs and demoting the previously privileged. It is only the elite, with their control of capital, who have the power to *institute* fascist processes. But they gain consent to their policies by manipulating and encouraging already existing middle-class and working-class nativism. Fascist processes do require some form of state support for enforcement, but a totalitarian fascist state like that in Nazi Germany isn't necessarily needed to provide that support. Regardless of whether a totalitarian state is involved or not, carrying out fascist processes successfully requires more than just enforcement. Ideological justification and legitimation are needed before it is possible to withdraw previously negotiated privilege in order to increase the exploitation of large numbers of people. The Klan, like the early Nazi Brown Shirts, performed exactly this function. Ultimately, then, the power of the Klan derived from its complicity with fascist processes in the United States. Denying the existence of fascism in the United States or describing the Klan either as an organization of marginalized extremists or as ordinary respectable citizens helps to provide a smokescreen for the fascist processes that actually are invoked from time to time.[23]

Another fork in the road

In order to keep draining people at the new rate, both U.S. and German elites chose to support the nativist route; it was less threatening than the left-leaning route. The alternatives presented by those who opposed capitalism itself were real. Although there was never a communist under every bed, as was later claimed, communism and socialism were widespread and the belief that the United States could move toward a European-style socialist government was not far-fetched. Had this happened, U.S. elites would have had their hands tied in the way German elites had before the rise of the Nazis. Their right to exploit people's labor and the country's natural resources and keep the profits for themselves would have been severely limited. Instead of permitting this to happen, they chose to protect their wealth. They encouraged the racial hatred that had contributed to the defeat of earlier efforts by bony-fingered people to control elite behavior and limit drainage. They polished the lens of white supremacy, which they had helped to perfect with Jim Crow segregation, through which many people now viewed the world. Local elites became Klan leaders. National and New South local elites covertly provided support through publications and racially discriminatory hiring and wage policies. Overtly they frightened the white racist working-class with the specter of black and immigrant competition for "white" jobs. The two elites kept race in the forefront of many angry white people's minds, distracting their attention from capitalism itself as the source of their problems.

Many of those who managed not to be distracted joined communist, socialist, or Wobbly interracial organizing to limit the capitalists' right of exploitation. Corporations and landowners met them with illegal violence; the state met them with legal violence through the military and "justice" system. This violence eliminated radical leaders and cleared the way for a kind of reform that accommodated segments of the working-class while maintaining a large reserve of bony-fingered people who desperately longed for low-wage jobs. This kind of reform now appeared more practical to most Americans than demoting capitalists to equality with everyone else so that all would share equally in the benefits coming from land, resources, and labor. As historian Robin Kelley points out, people who took the route of challenging capitalism itself, rather than merely reforming it, faced "the possibility of imprisonment, beatings, kidnapping, and even death."[24] The critical role played by violence that Lerone Bennett emphasized in creating and maintaining the power of the elite in the social structure of the 1700s applies equally in the twentieth century as former white privileges were withdrawn.[25]

13

NATIONAL CAPITAL, THE RETREAT
FROM FASCIST PROCESSES,
AND THE SUGAR-COATED CONTRACT

American Whites after the Second World War finally settled down and accepted a self-definition many had contested off and on since the turn of the century. It included white stratification and submission to a very small, extremely wealthy white elite that now dictated foreign and domestic policy and governed life both at work and at home. Their intent in so governing was presumed to be benign; their right to do so was taken as natural. The new definition withdrew formerly granted white privileges such as a reasonable hope of personal, political, and economic autonomy. It substituted a sugar-coated contract with wages large enough to support a family and to provide a white picket fence around the home. Whites could still dream the American Dream of unlimited opportunities for those who try, but in reality whiteness, at its bottom line, would now mean only an adequate wage, independence would mean merely the ability to pay bills, and not all Whites would qualify—white privilege, 100 percent whiteness, would now belong only to those people identified by European descent who also behaved correctly. White trash and radicals, like Germany's community aliens, would not qualify.

The postwar contract included concessions from national capitalists in return for working-class cooperation. Labor unions (purged of communists) were legitimized.[1] Corporations could no longer use convict slave labor. Taxes provided welfare funds and a variety of programs to prevent revolt among those who suffered most from economic decisions made by the elite; poverty declined dramatically.[2] The tax burden that provided these funds for individuals, families, and communities, as well as the much larger funds used for elite welfare, rested more heavily on the rich and on corporations than before. More jobs carried good wages and benefits, so more people could afford the goods and services produced by corporations using their labor; to some extent that purchasing power made up for the hours of grinding labor and degradation that many experienced on the job.[3] But at the same time any hope of a poor people's revolution also disappeared.[4] The sugar coating on the contract had co-opted too many people, and those who were bought off frequently turned against those to whom the contract had never been offered. Divide and rule continued alive and well, but for twenty or thirty years, the 1950s into the 1970s, before the effects of the intensifying struggle between capitalists for international dominance became widespread, there were somewhat fewer bony fingers.

National Capitalists as the Undisputed Controlling Elite

A combination of factors had tipped the scales definitively in favor of national elites by the end of the war. The association of patriotism and "efficient" mass production had been established during the Second World War, partially with the help of wartime films portraying national corporations as America's saviors, not as greedy trusts destroying America. Union demands for decent wages and safe working conditions appeared selfish, even though industrial deaths exceeded those of soldiers.[5]

Massive profits and dominance over the economy during the war had followed on the heels of New Deal policies that favored big businesses over small, big landowners over small, and owners over sharecroppers and tenants.[6] And industry boomed as the United States gained hegemony over the capitalist world after the Second World War. This boom, creating many new lower-wage jobs, offset the down-sizing that occurred when manufacturers adopted new technologies. Even more important, U.S. hegemony meant vastly increased markets around the world for American corporations and therefore temporarily decreased competition between national elites. Employers wanted industrial peace so that, instead of battling their workers, they could focus on producing goods to sell in the new worldwide market. And a vast internal market for consumer goods sprang up, partly due to increased wages. Sometimes, though, internal markets were forced into existence. General Motors, for instance, sometimes working with Standard Oil and Firestone, had already bought up and destroyed streetcar companies to make sure that people would have to use the buses and cars, and gasoline and rubber, that became necessary as streetcars disappeared.[7] While local elites never completely disappeared, they no longer held complete sway over conditions in their own areas.

The struggle between national and local elites and capital started and ended at different times in different places, even within a single state like Kentucky. But looking at the nation as a whole, by the 1910s national industrial capitalists had gained control of factory production in the United States. By the 1920s many people in a wide range of class positions were feeling the effects of their control, and many in the middle class had responded by joining the Klan. However, it wasn't until the Second World War that national capitalists consolidated their control over the social and political structure of the United States and then backed away from fascist processes.[8]

CONTROLLING DEMANDS FOR EQUALITY

The national elite struck a bargain with the working-class in order to gain industrial peace and to focus on production to take advantage of the new worldwide markets. This bargain involved instituting a new system for controlling demands for equality. If wages for Whites rose as part of the sugarcoated contract, then the industrial labor force needed to be expanded to provide another source of cheaper labor and to limit the extent of the rise. This meant an end to job segregation and pay discrimination; national corporations wanted to be free to hire both Blacks and Whites. But if segregation and the Jim Crow system of labor control ended, how would it be possible to limit black demands for equality in order to maintain a low-wage Southern black and white segment of the labor force?[9] Equally important, how could apartheid end without letting Blacks and Whites become equal again, thereby risking empowering the very people most likely to object to capitalism itself? Anti-capitalist sentiment couldn't be permitted to regain legitimacy. Finally, what would focus the entire working class on the apparent benefits of allowing national elites to set national and foreign policy in their own interests? And producing weapons—the biggest single source of corporate profits—at a wartime rate during peace had to appear necessary.[10] How could all this be done without disillusioning the growing numbers of white middle-class liberals who thought that U.S. postwar prosperity should apply at least marginally to all citizens?

The answer was found in emphasizing the threat posed to the United States by communism.[11] Fear of the USSR soon provided a substitute for the labor control functions and middle-class propaganda functions that had been earlier played by the Klan. Consent could now be manufactured by fear of an external enemy, the military-industrial complex could be defined as a benign protector against communism, dissent could be defined as unpatriotic or communist, and the American Dream of ever-increasing consumption could be held up as the proof of American superiority over communism. But until this persuasion process was well under way, it would continue to be unsafe to back off from expensive fascist processes.

Squashing dissent: McCarthyism

American film, starting with *Birth of a Nation,* and then television, became powerful propaganda tools under the control of national corporations that monitored their content.[12] Day after day television portrayed the USSR as an imminent threat to the American Dream, providing the backdrop for anticommunism. McCarthyism mopped up of much of the remaining opposition to capitalism. It scared into silence academic and other liberals in the white middle class who hadn't been in labor unions and thus had escaped earlier purges. Even the appearance of opposition to capitalism became frightening to middle-class people worried that they, like many of those confronted by McCarthy, might lose their jobs or their reputations.[13]

Oppositional newspaper voices disappeared; except during the thought control of the two world wars, such papers had at least made alternative viewpoints available. But most of them were unable to survive the combined onslaught of the Second World War censorship, McCarthyism, and the marketing power of newspapers backed by national capital. Even mainstream newspapers that were locally owned became more compliant with the needs of national capital. Pointing to particular policies an editor thought were misguided, or publishing opinions about which particular representative of the national elite would do the best job in leading the nation became the limit of editorial dissent. The West County newspaper before the First World War had regularly published articles about the efforts of the greedy trusts to control local people and local business. By the 1950s, however, it no longer discussed the machinations of Big Business or assumed there was a conspiracy of "big guys" out to get "little guys."

More and more local newspapers folded. Even as early as the 1920s corporate ownership of newspapers had meant that many people genuinely had no idea about the extent of poverty during a supposedly prosperous era.[14] After the Second World War such facts and viewpoints became even more inaccessible. People became addicted to television as newspapers grew increasingly boring, presenting essentially the same information in essentially the same way. The formerly widespread leftist and nativist critiques of either capitalism itself or of national capital were marginalized by stereotypes about "commies" and "pinkos" or about "white trash" and "rednecks." Both North and South County newspapers maintained a steady stream of anti-socialist and anticommunist editorials. Mainstream religion equated economic redistribution with communism and socialism, and both with godlessness; religious institutions thus acted as defenders of capitalism and property rights.[15]

Limiting the civil rights protest

Many Whites were frightened into silence by violence or McCarthyism, or bought off with good wages. Some were simply part of a generation that had no memory of earlier examples of interracial cooperation.[16] So it was now "safe" for the federal government, with national elite and New South local elite backing, to take the lid off the black struggle for justice. The Supreme Court abandoned its support of Jim Crow, and the balance began to shift. Southern white supremacists, elite and non-elite alike, gradually caved in to the pressure exerted, at the risk of their lives, limbs, and freedom, by thousands of Blacks and a few Whites during the 1950s and 1960s. Many of the tactics used in the 1950s and 1960s were not new—for instance, there had been earlier bus and streetcar boycotts. What had changed was the degree of force local elites were willing to use, and national elites to countenance, to stop them.

Elite and white opposition to the civil rights movement was comparatively muted for a number of reasons. "Muted" may seem an inaccurate description, considering the lynchings, beatings, and harassment that were arrayed against the movement. But this degree of violence would have seemed half-hearted indeed even one generation earlier. By the1950s, elite needs had changed. Mechanization meant that landowners were not as dependent as before on controlling sharecropping labor.[17] With the postwar industrial boom working-class Whites may have felt less threatened by Blacks gaining limited access to factory jobs.[18]

Equally important, however, was the fact that now Blacks pushing for *real* equality and *real* justice could be, and were, defined as communists, as could Whites who might be tempted to join or defend them. The government had conducted a "successful campaign to equate the advocacy of socialist ideas with high treason.[19] Blacks who demanded individual civil rights, such as the right to vote or to sit in the front of the bus, received white liberal support. Other Blacks, however, pointed out that capitalism around the world inevitably depended on a large pool of cheap labor at the bottom of a labor hierarchy, and that the pool at the bottom was frequently defined by race. In their view the "race problem" in the United States was not a result of individual white prejudice or of ignorant Southern politicians and landowners, but was instead the result of the normal operations of capitalism. Leaders who brought out this point of view were blacklisted, like Paul Robeson, jailed like Eldridge Cleaver and Angela Davis, driven into exile like W. E. B. Du Bois and Cleaver, or killed, like Fred Hampton and even Martin Luther King when he began talking about class as well as race.

The Ku Klux Klan of the 1950s and 1960s, although small, played its part by terrorizing and killing Blacks and a few of the Whites who supported them, making it easier to limit black demands to civil rights only. It continued to function locally as a terrorist organization serving the labor control needs of local Southern elites who depended on belief in white supremacy to get poorer white votes and to keep black labor "in line." Some working-class Whites continued to support the Klan because they depended on white supremacy to reduce competition for jobs.

An equally important role was played by the White Citizens Councils, made up mainly of local business leaders, members of such organizations as the "Farm Bureau, Rotary, Kiwanis, and Lions Clubs."[20] Their undercover encouragement for violence, their pressure against political and racial moderates as well as radicals, and their continued resistance to desegregation contributed to the preservation of a segmented Southern labor force organized by de facto segregation.

RETURNING THE VOTE TO POOR WHITES AND BLACKS WITHOUT RISK TO ELITES

Poorer people were more likely than richer people to vote for economically and racially liberal politicians, whose policies would generally have been somewhat helpful to poorer people.[21] This had been true earlier, when elites had used Jim Crow to take away poor Whites' and Blacks' vote to stop them from overturning the drainage system, and it was still true. To prevent a class-based alliance of poor Whites and Blacks when the vote was given back to them as a result of the civil rights movement, national and local elites used misinformation. National industrial elites claimed to be Blacks' natural allies in the fight against discrimination. Since they wanted access to all labor, not just white labor, the myth claiming that the upper classes were less racist than poor Whites appeared to be true. Correspondingly, they also promoted the myth that poor Whites were naturally racist. This claim was supported by spurious research, by a media cover-up of upper-class racist activities, and by middle- and upper-class "genteel" aversion to the Klan of the 1950s and 1960s. In fact the white middle and upper classes may well have been more actively racist than the white working-class."[22]

Both myths were needed to drive a wedge between Blacks and poorer Whites because, instead of being natural enemies, they actually tended to act together on the basis of class unless race-baiting diverted their attention away from class and economic issues. Such wedges were critical if the elite were to maintain their position, since 70 percent of the newly reenfranchised voters in the South in the 1960s were poorer Whites, and elites worried that they would vote by class rather than race.[23] These wedges helped in making it politically possible to end segregation, and still to restrict high wages and a secure living to only a segment of those whose sweat trickled up to the elite.

THE LOW-WAGE WORKFORCE AND THE SUGAR-COATED CONTRACT

Despite the death of formal segregation and despite the sugar-coated contract for one segment of the workforce, desperately poor people continued to be available to work their fingers to the bone. Their work contributed to employers' ability to pay other workers higher wages; their presence contributed to elite willingness to back off from fascist processes. The contract itself—and those employees who benefited from it—thus depended on the continued poverty of those below them.

Blacks and poor Whites, freed from sharecropping debt peonage as a result of the combined effects of mechanization and the civil rights movement, continued their massive Northern migrations. But as they moved north industry was leaving Northern cities, so most found themselves dealing with poverty due to low wages in manual and service work, lack of benefits, lack of full-time jobs, and, for those without jobs, the inadequacy of welfare or the dangers of providing services defined as illegal.

Among those who remained in the South, poverty was widespread. Farm laborers, black or white, continued to work for a pittance, as did many of those who had jobs in towns and cities. Local elites and already existing industries made sure that new industries continued the policy of low wages, since Southern communities would lose their attraction for investors if wages rose. Industrialists and local elites alike worked to keep out unions, at times even going to the extent of allowing a corporation to select and pay the town's police force.[24] To a large extent the workforce remained segregated, with the better factory jobs reserved for Whites. Industries sometimes refused to locate in areas where the population was more than 30 percent black.[25] Such policies contributed to maintaining an even lower-paid segment of an already low-paid Southern workforce. In practice, therefore, the lowest positions on the labor hierarchy, North and South, industrial and agricultural, were still disproportionately filled by Blacks.

But the new policies were changing the U.S. workforce; overall it was less exploitable than previously. With the whitening of European immigrants, the shifting of a significant number of Blacks and poor Whites into industry, the provision of welfare for women and children without an able-bodied man in the home, and the removal of prison labor from private manufacturing and agriculture, there weren't enough people to fill all the positions at the very bottom of the labor hierarchy.[26] But tightening the screws on Americans could upset the fragile industrial peace. Instead, employers turned to non-Americans to get a nearly enslaved workforce.

The Bracero program during the 1940s and 1950s brought in temporary migrant workers from Mexico. They were controlled by labor contractors, paid minuscule wages, and forced to return to Mexico when no longer needed. As in the case of prison labor, labor unions objected, and with increased mechanization agricultural employers, at least, no longer needed as much stoop labor. So the Bracero program was canceled and agricultural employers turned instead to illegal immigrants supplemented by extremely poor legal immigrants and native-born Blacks and Whites. Even among migrant workers, the very poorest of the American poor, Whites benefited from white privilege. They were more likely to avoid control by labor contractors because many had cars and because they couldn't be threatened with deportation, as were both legal and illegal immigrants who didn't "look" white or whose mother tongue was Spanish or Creole.[27]

THE RETREAT FROM FASCIST PROCESSES

Since fascist processes demote some and increase the exploitation of many, they frequently provoke resistance. In that sense fascist processes are "expensive," and once their dominance is stabilized the new controlling elites tend to back away from the fascist processes they used to establish control. That point had been reached by the mid-1950s. Opposition to capitalism was well muted; the dominant ideology ensured that most people would "police" themselves and their neighbors should they begin to wonder about the new world in which they found themselves. High industrial wages for those at the top of the labor hierarchy, good benefits, the feeling that government was on their side in enforcing minimum wage laws, the forty-hour week, improved safety conditions, social security, unemployment pay, strong unions to protect their interests, and a generally skyrocketing standard of living with a long secure retirement at the end of a hard-working but not bony-fingered life—all these went a long way toward making the new definition of whiteness acceptable. Television lauded the new arrangements and assuaged nostalgia for the "good old days" with mistily sentimental small-town stories about "real" Americans punctuated by ads extolling the benefits coming to consumers from the new system.

At the same time the dismantling of apartheid gave legitimacy in the eyes of the world to U.S. opposition to communism. Without Jim Crow the USSR could no longer make international hay by accusing the United States of hypocrisy in advocating freedom outside its borders but keeping Blacks terrorized and in subjugation within its borders.[28] High wages and good benefits for many defused USSR accusations of wage slavery in the United States, and the social safety net of welfare, unemployment insurance, retirement, school lunches, and free health care for the indigent defused USSR accusations of capitalist exploitation.

For the only time in U.S. history, much of the elite paid lip service to the idea that humans living in what is often called "the wealthiest nation on earth" had the inalienable right to a minimal level of food, health care, and housing.[29] Factory workers with secure income and benefits, and with some middle-class welfare such as the GI Bill and low-interest home mortgages, acquired middle-class trappings. Their children often went to college; they took vacations; they retired in comfort; they had good health care. The new labor hierarchy was securely in place, with Whites focused on the importance of gaining a home surrounded by a white picket fence, and willing to accept the fence and all it signified as a substitute for personal autonomy, willing to accept their demotion from the expectation, and often the reality, of entrepreneurial independence, so long as they could support their families and could believe that anyone who tried could do the same.

RACE AND GENDER IN THE NEW DRAINAGE SYSTEM

Despite the persistence of poverty, for the majority of Whites the end of the Second World War marked the beginning of approximately three decades of increasing material security.[30] This security underwrote a widened definition of whiteness–the not-quite-white European immigrants, including Jews, were now white and qualified for white privilege.[31] Conquered Mexicans of the Southwest and most Latin American immigrants, however, did not. Nor did African Americans, although with greater access to jobs and education, the black middle class did grow. Large numbers of Blacks, like Whites, experienced significant financial improvement, although often without the security that Whites had, nor in as large numbers, nor, on average, for equal educational attainment did their wages approach those of Whites.[32] Many found union jobs, and as formal discrimination in the armed forces and civil service ended, others found service sector jobs that paid a living wage.

Black commitment to education had always been intense and as educational and job segregation became less intense, some children in relatively secure black working-class families began getting a better education than some of the children from poor white families.[33] Their qualification for service sector jobs was therefore higher than that of many poorer white children, particularly among boys. As a result, very occasionally Whites found themselves working under black supervision. More frequently, however, Whites found themselves working side by side with Blacks.

For many this constituted a loss of the psychological wage and was a bitter pill to swallow. But for others the sugar coating of decent wages and security diminished feelings of imminent threat. Desperation was no longer rampant among Whites, and many did finally swallow the pill; Blacks could share in a few of the benefits that had previously been reserved almost exclusively for Whites. White trash, despite being white, would not share many of the benefits of whiteness. But they still had the psychological wage, they still had the remnants of the white male right to riot–their violence against wives and against minorities was rarely punished severely–and should they or their children try to "pass" as 100 percent Americans, their physical characteristics were not likely to give them away.

The fact that the attainment of the "American Dream" was severely limited–by race, gender, and engrained ideas of what it meant to be 100 percent American–could be ignored by most white Americans and by many non-whites who watched television and listened to news produced by media companies owned by massive national corporations. Many people believed that the United States was somehow "different"—here anyone could succeed in climbing the ladder of the labor hierarchy. What *Whites* received as wages was interpreted as what *Americans* received; immigrants of color, conquered Mexicans in the Southwest, Native Americans, Blacks, and people of Asian ancestry, many of whose families had been part of the United States far longer than the families of many white Americans, were all considered aberrations. Real Americans were white; in white American eyes what happened to everyone else—including white trash—was simply irrelevant to understanding America. Likewise, real Americans were men; what was happening to women was also irrelevant, even in the eyes of the many white women whose husbands earned the new higher industrial or managerial wages. That women's wages remained low, rarely affected by the benefits of the sugar-coated contract, was considered natural. The influence of class was denied; the advantages of silver spoons were ignored. The shape of a capitalist economy is a pyramid, with limited positions at the top or even near the top. Nevertheless, the perception was one of unlimited opportunity for positions at or near the top for those who would just try. So the fact that poverty was widespread during the 1950s and 1960s was ignored by most Whites or explained away as a result of people's stupidity in not taking advantage of their opportunity to achieve the American Dream.

Blaming the victim

The "discovery" with the 1962 publication of Michael Harrington's *The Other America* that, in fact, many people in the United States didn't have adequate food, health care, or housing provoked widespread dismay. But, given the power of the dominant ideology, this discovery led, not to a serious white examination of the drainage system, but to numerous forms of victim blaming. "Culture of poverty" theories blamed poverty on the culture of the poor, a revision of the inferiority of white trash to include other races. Poor Whites in Kentucky were frequently cited as examples of the culture of poverty. Urban Blacks were frequent targets, with an added twist that blamed black women for their lack of submission to men, causing men's failure to hold jobs that paid a living wage. Since no one had ever accused poor white women in Kentucky of dominating their husbands, they were blamed instead for their failure to rise above their ne'er-do-well husbands and convince their children of the value of an education that would free them from their defeatist culture.[34]

The success of the civil rights movement in getting the vote returned to Blacks and poor Whites and ending Jim Crow segregation ironically contributed to the ease with which Whites turned to victim blaming to explain the failures of the American Dream.[35] From a common white perspective, Blacks no longer had any excuse for poverty or for claiming that the United States "playing field" wasn't level. According to this perspective, the American Dream was real and attainable for anyone who tried. And some Blacks, particularly in the middle class, agreed. The logic of finally guaranteeing voting rights to Blacks and poor Whites was remarkably similar to the logic employed when poor Kentucky Whites in the 1790s were given the vote instead of land. If revolt is in the air, giving people an apparent say in their government and a stake in the political system goes a long way toward defusing a threat to power holders. With the idea of the American Dream thoroughly in place and the belief that voting matters—even when none of the candidates truly represent people at the bottom of the drainage system—poor people, unable to find a living in the new system, could be told to use the vote, try harder, and stop complaining.

14

LOCAL ELITE CHOICES AND
THE REORGANIZED DRAINAGE SYSTEM:
"OLD SOUTH" AND "NEW SOUTH"

The sugar-coated contract had been offered by national, not local, elites. Local elites had to cope with the pressures coming from national capitalists as the areas they used to control became more and more tightly tied to the national economy. Compared to Louisville and the coal-mining regions of Kentucky, North and South County were less directly shaped by national capital until the Second World War. As the sugar-coated contract took hold in the North, elites in the South responded to national corporations' quest for cheaper Southern labor. North and South County elites made predictably different choices in their own interests, corresponding to the differing economies of the two counties. Those choices still influence lives here.

Elite choices took place against the backdrop of agricultural mechanization. In many areas of the South mechanical harvesters replaced people and mules. The result was a labor surplus and a massive exodus of displaced tenants and sharecroppers heading for cities in search of jobs. Some of those families were better off as a result.[1] But local business and professional men saw their profits dwindling as consumers disappeared, and often responded by working to bring in national capital to provide jobs. Factories with their payrolls would help keep people from leaving and would give them wages to spend on the goods and services of local merchants, doctors, and lawyers. This "boosterism" gradually spread to a wider and wider range of Southern communities.

Life in North and South County

In South County in the mid-1970s when my husband and I first arrived, there was almost no national capital visible. The only chains were a grocery and a Dollar Store. Banks were local operations. Nearly all of the few businesses were locally owned. Even McDonald's didn't make it here until the early 1990s. Because national capital wasn't visible doesn't mean it had no effect on South County, however, for South County did produce a valuable raw material–tobacco. North County, on the other hand, had many businesses and some industry, and national capital was readily visible. Both counties were being drained, but drainage here was organized differently from the coal mining areas, and South County was drained differently from North County. The difference between South and North County is similar to the distinction Numan Bartley draws between the agriculturally oriented "Old South" and the industrially oriented "New South."[2]

SOUTH COUNTY: "THE OLD SOUTH" AND AGRICULTURE

Local elites in South County had, to use the old plumbing analogy, remained tanks as national capital took over. They were collection points for much of the sweat of the county. They had, however, been forced to add small pipes out their far side, connecting them to the national drainage system. Particularly in the southern part of the county, the former plantation area, commercial tobacco farming remained dominant in the economy. Slightly over one-third of the white men in the county in 1970 were still self-employed, most as farmers. Like the plumbers my husband and I worked with, others were independent contractors, setting their own prices, choosing the jobs they took, and determining their own time schedule. They worked hard, but took time out as they saw fit. Most hired one or two helpers, often on a rather sporadic basis, and some of the helpers eventually went into business for themselves. Others remained dependent on the contractor and consequently remained "boys" all their lives. However, 60 percent of white men in the county had been independent 20 years earlier; many more were now answering to bosses.[3]

Big landowners and lawyers dominated the South County social structure, presiding over the drainage system.[4] Local elites owned the tobacco warehouses, managing the flow of tobacco for the national cigarette-manufacturing corporations. They controlled the sharecropping, tenant farming, and hired labor force; they ran the judicial system and county government, or were connected to those who did. And finally, they controlled credit either through personal loans, furnishing sharecroppers, or through their control of the banks. This system effectively provided the steady, large, and low-cost supply of the raw material national industrialists needed for the manufacture of cigarettes.

A scarcity of waged jobs in the county other than in the low-paid sewing industry, retail, and services helped to maintain the system by limiting options outside of agriculture. In the mid-1960s a Louisville company had opened a new branch, provided additional jobs, mainly for women as sewing machine operators. Other people found employment in schools and county government. One town had a small company making camper tops. The huge tobacco warehouses in the southern part of the county provided seasonal employment, as did farmers who hired help during tobacco harvesting in the late summer. Locally owned stores, restaurants, banks, feed mills, sawmills, and stockyards, mostly in the county seat and other small towns in the southern part of the county, hired a few more people. But many people made most of their money in agriculture and received most of that in November or December when they sold their tobacco at warehouse auctions. They lived much of the year on credit and on their gardens, canned and preserved garden produce, and homegrown meat. There was a countywide paying off of debts as people made the rounds of stores and feed mills after cashing their tobacco check. What was left frequently went to make a good Christmas. As a community with very little cash to spend, South County wasn't a particularly attractive target for national capital retailing until country roads were paved in the late 1960s and early 1970s. These roads began making long-distance commuting to jobs feasible and more people had paychecks to spend and needed to buy products they had formerly grown or made.

NORTH COUNTY: THE "NEW SOUTH," INDUSTRY, AND WAGE LABOR

When we arrived in the 1970s the North County seat, like South County, still had a functioning, although diminishing, locally owned downtown. White women I know who grew up in North County in the early 1960s fondly remember dressing up—with white gloves—for Saturday shopping, driving to the county seat, walking around the downtown stores, and eating lunch at a soda fountain. None of that would be possible now. It was still possible, barely, in the 1970s, although the white gloves had disappeared by then. For the most part the downtown stores are gone now. The big old brick buildings that used to house them are empty or are used by representatives of national capital: the insurance companies, banks, and corporate lawyers. A few fairly high-priced lunch spots have sprung up, catering to people working in those offices. Families now have to drive to the edges of town for an affordable family lunch, where the malls, car lots, groceries, and fast-food places congregate.

But even in the 1970s there were enormous differences between North and South County; North County was already significantly directly organized by national capital. Many North County elites, instead of remaining tanks in their own right, had become pipes, as representatives of national capital.[5] There were chain stores and shopping centers on the outskirts of the county seat in North County, there was some non-textile manufacturing, business leaders had recently succeeded in establishing a community college, and the town was growing rapidly. However, wages compared to the rest of the state remained fairly low, even by 1980, although higher than in South County. Family income was much higher in North County, but more residents bought everything they used than in South County. Fewer people heated with wood, which even in 1990 was still the single most common fuel in South County. Fewer town dwellers had gardens, there were fewer outhouses, and more homes were connected to the public water system. Many women in and around the county seat worked for wages, in a pattern very different from that followed by many women in the more subsistence-oriented families in North and South County, although in both counties about one third of women are listed as being in the workforce. All in all, more people in North County lived lives shaped by the demands of a job. They arranged child care, leisure activities, care of elderly relatives, when they got up and went to bed, and even when and where they ate, all around work schedules in which they had no say.[6]

Farm families in North County didn't share in the higher income of the county seat, having a median income only about two-thirds that of the town dwellers. Compared to South County, however, North County farmers were doing well. Farm family income in South County was only about three-quarters that of farm families in North County. South County farmers' lower income may reflect fewer supplemental jobs and a greater percentage of sharecroppers and tenants resulting in a greater gap between rich and poor, a gap that is still evident in the 1990s, and wider in Kentucky than in all but eight states.[7] But Bartley also points out that in Kentucky, Tennessee, and Virginia the scattered pockets of farm families growing a wide variety of cash crops—like North County farmers—have generally done much better than those caught in dependence on a single crop, like many South County farmers.[8]

A history of divergence

The divergence between the two counties appears to have begun before the Civil War and become more marked with the introduction of burley tobacco. North County appears to have kept aspects of its diversified subsistence economy alive longer than did former plantation areas like southern South County. It never put heavy dependence on tobacco; the farm economy appears to have centered on corn and wheat at the turn of the century. Farms produced a wider range of crops, and household manufacturing, at least as long as the U.S. Agricultural Census charted it, was much greater than in South County. It was one of the state's bigger producers of fruit and mules.[9]

North County's "poverty" had been quite noticeable in the 1880s. Pigs slept in the courthouse, and the roads were so bad that few people used buggies. The town looked neglected and 40 Blacks lived in a deserted tannery. Nevertheless, the town's dozen saloons did a good business, especially on court days, when as many as 500 men—and presumably some women—rode into town.[10] Apparently, because North County produced little in the way of resources needed by industrial capitalists, not much tobacco and no coal, there was no particular reason to underdevelop it at this time.[11] The resulting low cash income didn't necessarily mean poverty in the sense of lack of necessities for Whites in northern South County or in North County; real poverty was probably more prevalent in southern South County where sharecropping was more common.

Population in South County remained static or shrank slightly. By contrast, by the 1920s the North County seat was beginning to grow slowly and to change.[12] So long as roads were bad and cars few, people did most of their shopping in the many tiny towns that were then thriving little centers of business. Small towns in the more diversified subsistence areas centered on the business brought in by farm families coming to get corn and flour ground at the local mill. According to a local historian, when tobacco finally came in to the area where I live after the First World War and people quit growing wheat his town began going downhill.[13] Crossroad towns that now have little more than a gas station, video store, florist shop, funeral parlor and church—maybe even less—once had doctors, lawyers, dentists, banks, millinery shops, grocery stores, movie theaters, schools, and railroad stations. With cars, things changed. Business in the bigger towns like the county seats increased, and the little towns began to die.[14] Financial control—and banks—concentrated more and more in the bigger towns in the 1920s. It gradually became harder and harder for people in outlying areas to avoid trips to the North County seat.

Businessmen, with a few professionals such as doctors, controlled town government. Fewer of them appear to have defined themselves primarily as landowners, as did those who controlled South County.[15] In North County, as in many other New South communities, "far-sighted citizens . . . induce[d] manufacturers to locate [in the county seat] . . . "[16] But the county seat in the 1940s and 1950s, judging by the ads for goods and services in the paper, remained oriented toward retailing to the farming community. The paper rarely bragged about the importance of farming itself, as did the South County paper, which was more agriculturally oriented.

The beginnings of a major shift toward wage labor in North County occurred in the 1940s with the enormous wartime growth of its military installation. The military gradually became a large employer of civilian labor, and large numbers of soldiers began spending small amounts of money locally.[17] By 1958, according to a North County editorial, the local farming population had declined significantly, and many country dwellers were now industrial workers. Nevertheless, ads about farm auctions frequently mention both a "nice home" and a "tenant house," indicating that farmers still thought tenants were important. As one ad put it, "the Government and the tenant will pay for this farm."[18]

Despite the shift toward wage labor, about 42 percent of white men in 1950 were self-employed. This was far more independence than later, after development policies began to take their effect. By 1970 only 13 percent of white men were self-employed, and about half of them were farmers; and in 1990 only 7 percent of the entire workforce were their own bosses. Many Whites in North County in the 1950s were still farming, and most of them were to some extent diversified subsistence farmers. Unlike South County, there were few black farmers, and few black men were self-employed. Most black men in North County in 1950 were in low-wage laborer and service positions.[19]

ALTERNATIVE ROUTES AND LOCAL ELITE CHOICES

When national and local elites fight for the power to shape local economies in their own interests, some people in the community benefit. But this is rarely true for those at the bottom of the drainage system, and often not true even for those a bit above the bottom. In Kentucky, unlike much of the rest of the country, counties are a significant unit, still run by local elites in the 1970s as "little kingdoms."[20] In looking at North and South Counties it is clear that local elites have had an enormous impact on how lives were lived after the Second World War, as they have had all along, and as they have now. It is also clear that local elites have had to operate within the constraints imposed on them by the needs of national capital and now international capital. The policies that resulted depended very little on whether individual local elites were personally good people, believing that what is good for them is good for all, or were greedy cynics out to squeeze the last drop of sweat from those below them. They were caught in a process; they could have fought increasing inequality and dependence, but those who had done so earlier had frequently paid with their lives or their careers. They would have lost the respect of their peers, and they would have had to work toward the destruction of their own positions of power. And, of course, they had been carefully taught that economic equality was godless socialism.

To boost or not to boost

New South "boosterism" reached some Kentucky communities in the 1920s and 1930s. Elites in smaller Kentucky communities jumped on the "boosterism" bandwagon in the 1950s, becoming part of Kentucky's "strong tradition of state-directed economic development."[21] Local chambers of commerce worked with local governments to put together attractive bids for national corporations. They competed in offering enormous tax cuts and used taxpayers' money to subsidize the companies, financing bonds, providing nearly free buildings and low-interest loans. They controlled or busted unions in order to lure corporations with promises of low-wage, non-union workers to replace Northern unionized manufacturing labor. Local business leaders advertised the virtues of their workers, touting particularly their work ethic and their willingness to work for little because they grew their own food.

Since the industries that went south were mainly older ones that technology had bypassed, cutting labor costs with low pay and poor safety measures was their primary means of competing with each other.[22] People took jobs with these corporations only because of lack of alternatives. "Development" benefited mainly local merchants and professionals and was associated with a drop in Southern income between 1960 and 1980 relative to the rest of the country. Kentucky's income dropped even relative to most of the rest of the South, while ownership of its industry became increasingly concentrated in the North.[23]

South County elites chose not to become serious boosters. Although the Chamber of Commerce did take some steps in that direction in the late

1950s, until the early 1980s a group of farm and business owners actively opposed bringing in industry, and support apparently was minimal, judging by how rarely the newspaper advocated industrialization compared to North County newspapers.[24] South County's labor force in the 1950s was still more or less absorbed by tobacco. Burley tobacco production has yet to be thoroughly mechanized. It is one of the most labor intensive of all crops—about 300 hours of often back-breaking work per acre.[25] Newspaper ads in the late 1940s suggest this lower level of mechanization in South County, with fewer ads for tractors; references to mules and horses last considerably longer. In the early 1970s a number of farmers in our area still used mules for plowing out tobacco, although they used tractors for other work. In southern South County big landowners apparently hung on to their black labor force. Black men in South County worked almost exclusively in agriculture, as hired hands, tenants, or as farm owners. Blacks in North County, however, either left or were driven out of farming shortly after the Civil War.

South County's elite, at least until the 1980s, had little reason to encourage national capital to come in. They needed tenants and hired hands; customers for their stores were not leaving since mechanization had relatively little effect on burley and small farm owners continued buying what they needed locally. The low-wage industry and retail that did exist hired mostly white women.[26] Most of the black women and a few of the white women who had jobs in North and South County in 1950 worked as domestics, as did many even in 1970. Women's paid jobs didn't conflict with elite needs for an agricultural labor force. They did farm work, but many of them did it in addition to their day at the sewing factory or at someone else's house, or used vacation time to cut tobacco. This pattern left men free to work their own or their landlord's farm. Women's wage labor supplemented farm income and made it possible for farmers and tenants to continue producing tobacco at extremely low prices, subsidizing the tobacco companies. Bringing in jobs for men would have been contrary to the local elite's need for a large, cheap labor force in tobacco.

North County elites' position in the 1950s would have been quite different.[27] They had reason to want to attract industry, and industry would have had reason to be attracted to North County. Business owners were worried about people leaving the area; tractors were taking over, and since North County grew little burley farming labor needs would have dropped significantly.[28] North County's elites had no particularly lucrative use for this labor surplus. Nor, without tobacco, did they have a good means of draining people still engaged in diversified subsistence farming.

They had more to gain and less to lose by bringing in national capital than did South County elites when the opportunity arose in the 1950s. Unlike South County elites, they took the New South booster approach, soliciting national capital and raising their own incomes by allying themselves with national capital.[29]

North County's booster history

In 1949 a talk was given about Kentucky's industrial development opportunities to an industrial committee district meeting in the North County seat. In 1951 the high school band paraded Louisville industrialists into town from the railroad station for a meeting with the local Chamber of Commerce. Programs about development often emphasized its inevitability, as did the 1955 "Date with Industrial Destiny."[30] Newspapers didn't discuss the fact that such development depended on low wages. Nor did they talk about the way local elite boosters across the South generally attracted industry with tax subsidies and subsidies from farming families who fed themselves.

Like other New South leaders, North County boosters advocated improving schools enough to attract business and industry. Typically, however, New South leaders opposed raising taxes enough to provide a quality education for all local children.[31] Business leaders in many counties soon began agitation for establishing community colleges to provide low-cost education. One result has been a surplus of trained workers in a number of fields, keeping wages relatively low and part-time. At the urging of boosters the town was beautified, a community center and an airport for private planes were built, and many businesses and homes began flying American flags.[32]

Many incoming industries in the 1950s and 1960s hired an almost exclusively female workforce, expecting to keep wages lower than they would have been for men. As a result, North County employment for women began to include a much broader range than did South County, and it was no longer primarily unmarried women who worked in manufacturing, as had been the case earlier.[33] Many more women found employment in the growing number of service sector jobs, particularly at the new hospital where my daughters were later born. Serious industrial growth, however, didn't come until the early 1960s, following a decade of intense and continuing development efforts by the local elite.[34] By this time, much of the industry coming into North County hired men. The county seat began growing exponentially as it became a magnet for people looking for jobs. Including the suburbs, in the 36 years following 1940 its population increased by 400 percent.[35]

Since coal miners and others had already unionized and fought for higher wages, these new industrial workers had better working conditions and higher wages than employees in non-industrial jobs in the area, although their wages were significantly lower than Northern wages. While union membership was fairly low, those unions that did exist kept the pressure up for higher wages.[36] Nevertheless, the sugar coating on the contract in Kentucky, and in the rest of the South, was thinner than in the rest of the country. Wages were proportionately lower, benefits fewer, and working conditions more dangerous.[37]

Advocating consumption: making boosterism pay off for local elites

With development should come greater consumption and greater profits for manufacturers and for the local businessmen who had worked to bring in an industrial payroll. However, farming families' avoidance of consumerism and reluctance to spend enthusiastically could thwart this strategy. Efforts to persuade them to buy more extensively, to become good consumers, are evident in the postwar South County newspaper. An editorial entitled "The Right to Choose," for example, equated the right to decide which consumer goods to buy with freedom and the American Way.[38] Ads, editorials, and news items touted the virtues of electricity and of electrical gadgets. Local homemakers' clubs appear to have been urged to compete in buying consumer goods. Unusually high numbers of washing machines, televisions, electric blankets, stoves, refrigerators, mixers, hot plates, and power mowers purchased by the members of a particular club or county was considered newsworthy.[39]

The North County editor apparently felt less pressure to shame North Countians into becoming good consumers. Judging by the far wider variety of ads in the paper, and the greater number of people working for wages, consumerism was probably already well established. As public transportation declined and traveling to jobs became more common, owning a car—and buying gasoline—switched from being a status symbol to being a necessity. Ads relating to cars, clothing, and groceries dominate the North County newspaper after the war. Store-bought clothes became a necessity as more women worked outside the home and didn't have the time, and eventually the skill, to make their family's clothing. Eventually homemade clothing became a mark of inferiority, just like cornbread and beans have become, although in neighborhoods like my own, with more recent diversified subsistence roots, they are still preferred cultural markers among the older generation. In the early 1980s, for instance, one of my neighbors complained about her daughter-in-law's inability to can and garden well. In the mid-1990s one of my daughters was told she would "make some man a good wife" because she can sew and cook.

THE RENEGOTIATED CONTRACT

Life in the two counties was thus shaped by the way in which the contract with Whites was renegotiated. In those sections of North County and South County that remained closer to diversified subsistence farming, people like my neighbors resisted consumerism and wage labor well into the 1980s. They continued to believe household autonomy and productivity was the ideal. Religious opposition to television made hanging on to this ideal easier—in my area homes with televisions were rare until the mid-70s, although my neighbor believes even the remnants of that attitude will disappear when the older generation is gone. In much of South County it was not obvious that the contract had been renegotiated. North County, however, was different. Consumerism was rapidly becoming a common pattern, and with it the white picket fence and a comfortable retirement for well-behaved, hard-working Whites who agreed that the paycheck and the proper spending of it were basic to morality. But what would happen when international capital began taking over from national capital in the late 1970s and reneged on the contract, again pulling the rug out from under the middle class and creating lower rungs at the bottom of the labor hierarchy?

15

HOOKING IN THE REST OF THE WORLD: THE REORGANIZATION OF DRAINAGE IN THE NEW WORLD ORDER

These days, people in North and South County who were once relatively secure struggle with the loss of the sugar-coated contract. They deal with overwork, layoffs, and the threat of poverty. They struggle to run a household with two parents working full-time, or with the even greater difficulties of single parenthood. Employers are trying to increase profit margins in an internationalized economy by cutting back on safety, on wages, on benefits, on full-time work, and on jobs themselves. At the same time, the United States now sports 170 billionaires, one of whom alone is wealthier than the combined gross domestic product of all of Central America.[1] Wealth has been concentrated recently into far fewer hands in yet another reorganization, as international capital took control from national capital. The seven wealthiest people in the world could entirely eliminate world poverty if they shared their riches.[2] Their wealth is the flip side of the poverty of people like my friends, neighbors, and students in Kentucky—and in much of the world. International capital no longer needs the sweat, or the purchasing power, of workers in any particular country. Lives in North and South County are being reorganized for the internationalized drainage system of the New World Order.

THE GROWING DOMINANCE OF INTERNATIONAL CAPITAL: INITIAL PHASES

National capitalists solidified their control of the United States during the Second World War and finalized the sugar-coated contract with the Taft-

Hartley Act in 1947. The act paid lip service to unionized industrial democracy, but actually made it possible for employers to use and control unions in order to ignore those rights.[3] Many workers gave up the struggle; some union leaders gave up on efforts toward social justice and simply worked for good contracts for their members. Some colluded with management to produce a docile workforce.

This process was simplified by the postwar economy. Industry boomed because of the enormous worldwide market for military and consumer goods. Median income rose steadily until the early 1970s, fueling spending for consumer goods in the United States.[4] Young white men expected their wages to rise to meet expenses as they aged and their children grew. Income inequality decreased somewhat, and even the poor were a little better off than their parents had been. Minimum-wage jobs and welfare payments placed people about at the poverty line. While race and gender, and whether one lived in the North or the South, continued to influence income significantly, living standards rose at least slightly for most Whites and some people of color in the United States.

With a now more cooperative working class, national capitalists set to work to take advantage of the world markets opened up by American military might. Some of the richest and most powerful men in the United States played major roles in foreign and domestic Cold War policy, keeping profits flowing to themselves in a "rejuvenated" capitalist system. Charles E. Wilson was president of General Motors Corp., which sold enormous amounts of goods to the military; later he became secretary of defense under Eisenhower. He articulated the policy that was eventually followed: "a continuing alliance between business and the military for 'a permanent war economy.' "[5]

THE GROWING POWER OF A LIMITED GROUP OF NATIONAL CAPITALISTS

The result was a welfare system for the corporate elite that dwarfed welfare for the needy.[6] It also dwarfed previous elite welfare. Billions were spent on defense products between 1945 and 1977; this spending escalated later to 1 trillion dollars during Ronald Reagan's first administration. Part of this money went to buy weapons systems that even military analysts thought were unnecessary. Defense contractors produced defective equipment, charged excessive prices, and were occasionally slapped on the wrist when caught in a wide range of illegal but profitable practices. Likewise in their private sector operations, corporate giants engaged in illegal practices to keep prices high, and were rarely seriously punished. All of this justified Eisenhower's warning as he left office in 1961 of the need to "guard against the acquisition of unwarranted influence . . . by the military-industrial complex. . . . We must never let the weight of this combination endanger our liberties or democratic processes."[7]

The propaganda strategy

Capitalists during the early postwar years focused on producing goods in the United States to be sold on worldwide markets as well as to people in the United States. For cheap labor they moved industries south or brought in contracted Third World labor. When they felt that their right to cheap labor was under threat during the 1960s, the country's largest employers sponsored secret committees consisting of lawyers representing, among others, General Motors, Chrysler, General Electric, and B. F. Goodrich. Funding came from the Chamber of Commerce and the National Association of Manufacturers. The Labor Law Reform Group acted as a steering committee for the much larger Blue Ribbon Committee, which included more than one hundred lawyers representing large corporations and employers' organizations, which met in secret, to protect their interests.[8] It fought the Kennedy and Johnson administrations' mild attempts to control employer behavior, and paid particular attention to preventing unionization of the South, a critical source of cheap labor within the United States.

The Labor Law Reform Group hired a public relations firm to manipulate public opinion. Scripts were given to companies owned by group members to be used in school textbooks, TV comedies, comic strips, and newspaper articles. The anti-union messages they conveyed often operated subliminally through derision or by portraying labor leaders as power-hungry and coercive. More serious discussions of the supposedly disastrous effects of unions were placed in magazines read by people in influential positions. This policy built on already existing perceptions among some that unions were exploitative. It gradually succeeded in turning public opinion against unions, building support for further changes in labor policy to benefit employers.

With surveys of public opinion rating labor leaders on a level with used-car salesmen, early in the 1970s the group merged with other employer organizations to form the Business Roundtable. The roundtable did not attempt to maintain secrecy and expanded its agenda beyond union-busting, mounting a general attack on anything they felt impeded their ability to compete in a global market. Targets included government regulation of safety and pollution, consumer protection, welfare, pensions, and the movement toward national health insurance. It influenced public opinion, for instance, through ads that looked like articles in *Reader's Digest* in the mid-1970s about the value of business and the free enterprise system.

INTERNATIONAL CAPITAL AND THE INCREASED INCORPORATION OF THE THIRD WORLD

By the end of the 1970s, however, this initial phase was ending, and international capital gained more and more dominance, paralleling national capital's overwhelming of local capital in the 1920s.[9] This process had actually started centuries earlier in specific businesses; the slave trade, for instance, had been international, as were the early sugar and tobacco industries. And throughout the 1950s major banks were buying smaller ones. Eventually major bank stockholders or their associates held positions in government, and this minuscule percentage of American men gained policy and lawmaking oversight over the internationalization of their own corporations.[10] At the same time financiers in other wealthy nations were doing much the same, so that the world economy came to be more and more tightly controlled by a few extraordinarily powerful men connected with corporations whose wealth exceeded that of most nations.

Laws were rewritten by the early 1980s to favor international capitalists. It was now easier to move their investments to places where they could make greater profits. It was also easier to form transnational corporations. By the mid-1980s corporations were receiving massive aid from the U.S. government to move to the Caribbean, rather than simply moving South as they had done earlier.[11] At the same time transnational corporations with main offices in other countries rapidly increased their investments in the United States. By the 1970s half of all such foreign investment each year was in the South, where labor was cheap and state governments cooperative.[12] By 1993 there was more foreign investment in the United States than in any other country.[13] International capital, headquartered in the United States, the countries of Western Europe, and Japan, created a financial network spreading across much of the globe, so that national boundaries carried less and less meaning. This network used labor and resources wherever and however they were most profitable. First and Third World workers were essentially part of the same labor market.

Investment in new manufacturing jobs during the 1980s was primarily outside of the United States. Within the United States well over half of new jobs, replacing those lost, paid wages that left families below the poverty line. By 1989 one in seven full-time jobs paid $2000 less than the poverty level for a family of four.[14] Since U.S. workers were unlikely to agree to lose good jobs, a combination of force and propaganda was needed to manufacture consent.

MANUFACTURING CONSENT

Employer groups such as the Business Roundtable in the 1970s and 1980s got labor law and policy changed so that the force of law was now squarely behind management decisions to shift to a cheaper workforce, or to places where they could pollute with impunity, or obtain cheaper resources without worrying about safety standards.[15] Repressive client governments that cooperated with American-owned corporations, such as Somoza's in Nicaragua, Pinochet's in Chile, Noriega's in Panama, Marcos's in the Philippines, or Saddam Hussein's in Iraq, received U.S. aid. During military actions to discipline misbehaving clients like Panama and Iraq, news programs were tightly controlled and appeared to demonstrate the continued need for U.S. weapons production and a technologically efficient military—that could drop bombs and kill only the right people, for instance.[16] Still, after the dismemberment of the USSR, there was no sufficiently exciting and threatening enemy to rally large numbers of Americans around transnationals in whose interests American soldiers were supposed to give their own lives or take others, and in whose interests American workers were supposed to tolerate bony fingers, ill-health, or death. Propaganda was needed extolling the benefits of business and presenting corporate decisions that damaged people as if they were inevitable results of natural forces such as business cycles or free enterprise or the "natural rate of unemployment," rather than made by humans deliberately pursuing profits.

Such theories said that plant closures in the United States were natural results of union insistence on wages that were "too high." American industry was unable to compete in a global economy and capitalists were "forced" to move elsewhere. In fact, American wages had risen along with productivity until the 1970s, when productivity continued rising but real wages (wages in relation to buying power) began dropping.[17] Somehow CEOs' incomes, which became astronomical in the 1980s, were never "too high."

Other theories claimed that the decisions of the corporate elite were not only natural, but also beneficial in the long run. The trickle-down theory of economics said that making it easier for the rich to get richer and for corporations to make bigger profits would, in the end, benefit everyone. In fact, this didn't happen. Instead, much of the additional profit went to buy other corporations, a process that usually decreased rather than increased the number of jobs available and concentrated wealth in fewer and fewer hands.

Finally the icing was added to the propaganda cake. Allowing the corporate elite to make greater profits was supposed to improve the lives not only of Americans, but also of people in Third World countries, through "development." In fact, it hasn't. Study after study has described the disastrous consequences of continued colonial-style extraction of cheap labor and resources from Third World settings.[18] Local elites still benefit from orchestrating the expropriation of land and organizing a low-wage workforce; they likewise organize the violent repression it takes to control people who object to starvation or near-starvation. But Americans are told that these people are starving because they "don't know how to feed themselves" and need development, not because they have been deprived of land and resources and are paid starvation wages. Such people also are now tightly connected to the international drainage system. Should they successfully defy the violence directed against them and force corporations to pay wages that are "too high," factories can and do move elsewhere.

INTERNATIONALIZING THE ECONOMY OF NORTH AND SOUTH COUNTY

People in North and South County came to be positioned differently in the internationalized labor hierarchy. South County remains primarily a source of raw material for the tobacco industry and of low-wage employees for employers outside the county.[19] It is now tightly tied to the wage economy, but as a peripheral "labor reserve" area. As in labor reserves around the world, people living here continue to produce some of their own food. They generally work for low wages and provide their mostly distant employers with a flexible supply of labor, moving in and out of the labor force as needed. Their flexibility depends on the ability of kin, of farms, of the informal sector, and of government transfer payments and welfare to provide a minimal subsistence for those times when they are without adequate wages.[20] North County's role is quite different. It is definitely part of the periphery, a low-wage area in relation to the rest of the country, and even in relation to the rest of Kentucky. However, it has increasingly become an organizational center for international capital controlling drainage out of its own and surrounding labor reserve areas like South County.

SOUTH COUNTY'S TRANSITION TO A WAGE ECONOMY

Development ended most sharecropping and some tenant farming in South County, but it did so at least partially by getting rid of people rather than by reorganizing so that people could support themselves locally. South County particularly lost young people. We "hippies" were made to feel welcome, though odd, in the early 1970s because we were young and thought that South County was a place to move into, not out of, and were interested in learning "old time" skills rejected by many younger South Countians. While the process of development has clearly provided many people in South County with more cash than their parents ever had, they also need to spend more. Dependence on the vagaries of the international tobacco market has been partially replaced by dependence on the vagaries of internationally controlled wage labor.

When it became possible to get to jobs by driving long distances on new roads, South County slowly began changing. In the 1960s and 1970s a few of our neighbors, for instance, made a daily 150-mile round-trip commute into Louisville. Earlier if people had jobs in Louisville they had to move there, as the grandparents of a friend of mine did in the 1920s, and as other neighbors did in the 1950s. Commuting men could work on the farm in addition to their wage labor, and their wives and children did much of the farm work. The combination of wages and the income from raising tobacco and beef cattle supported such families in a pattern Ann Kingsolver describes as a "strategy of multiple livelihoods."[21] This pattern has become more common as more jobs have become available in North County and other surrounding counties, requiring only a 60 to 100 mile round-trip commute. There are many for whom no jobs exist in South County, although earlier they might have been sharecroppers or hired agricultural labor. Those who can't commute, or who can't find jobs under conditions that make the commute worthwhile, subsist on a combination of welfare, occasional jobs, under-the-counter wages, social security, disability payments, and extended kinship networks.[22] Altogether this means a bit more money to spend locally, and people are gradually becoming more enmeshed in the consumer economy.

At the same time some changes occurred in burley tobacco. Insecticides, herbicides, "sucker dope"—which stops the development of unwanted extra shoots—and later baling rather than tying cured tobacco leaves contributed to a small decrease in the labor needs of tobacco growers. Meanwhile, the profitability of tobacco dropped. The new chemicals were expensive, but more importantly tobacco companies no longer depended on Kentucky for their burley. They began buying leaf grown outside the United States, particularly in Brazil. This move gave them cheaper tobacco grown without the costs of pesticide regulation or tobacco price supports by underpaid farm families under contract to transnational corporations.[23] It was justified by citing the agitation against smoking in the United States and by the inaccurate claim that tobacco price supports come out of taxpayers' pockets. In reality farmers pay a percentage of their tobacco receipts to provide the entire funding for price supports.[24] By the 2001 crop year, tobacco companies were instituting contract tobacco farming in Kentucky, a system that gave them direct control over growers.[25]

But at the same time that tobacco companies are turning to the Third World for labor, bigger farmers here are doing the same. They bring to their farms, often illegally, Mexican and Central American workers for the tobacco harvest and sometimes for tobacco stripping. It is no longer unusual to see people of apparently Hispanic ancestry in South County, most frequently riding in the backs of pickups or on wagon loads of cut tobacco on the way to the barn. Some farmers house them in old chicken sheds, in barns, and frequently in rundown and crowded old mobile homes. Without transportation they are totally dependent on the grower, often in very isolated settings.[26] Other growers are turning to recently established Amish communities for tobacco workers. Both groups work for wages far too low for most Americans to live on, the Amish because they have religiously avoided consumer culture and the Mexicans because the process of "development" in Mexico has produced massive poverty there.

As tobacco profits declined, so did the power of the old local elites whose lives had been built around a tobacco economy. And as the population dropped, so would customers at their stores. As the old elite died, boosterism began to flourish, making sense for some South County elites.[27] Many local businesses became subsidiaries of larger companies, as did our local hardware store, grocery store, and fertilizer plant. Selling land, increasing local payrolls to improve retailing, and positioning themselves or their children for managerial jobs all made attracting industry a sensible strategy. Some local elites and entrepreneurs and some newcomers became involved in organizing national and international capital investment.

However, successfully attracting national and international capital takes decades of planning and a great deal of money, and even now South County's booster efforts run on a shoestring compared to North County. So although a few fairly small manufacturing plants arrived in the 1950s and 1960s, supplementing those that were locally owned, for the most part South County remains a labor reserve. Local elites have less clout than formerly, but carry on as real estate owners or contractors or as landlords who use more machinery, some tenant labor, and temporary Mexican and Amish labor. Others have maintained their position as part of the social control stratum as lawyers and judges. McDonald's came to South County in the early 1990s and small restaurants disappeared. People spend their money near where they work and no longer flock into the county seat on Saturdays. Many of the small retailers around the courthouse square have disappeared, making it harder and harder to shop locally, snowballing to make local businesses even more precarious. During the 1990s boosterism began to succeed, bringing in a few relatively small Japanese and American transnational corporations, and most prospective businesses visiting South County are Japanese.[28] Most new industrial employment comes from two new plants and an expansion at the old sewing factory; now slightly under half the jobs in the county are industrial. Tourism and a professional theater have increased the incomes of a few local business owners and provided a few low-wage service industry jobs.[29]

As farming becomes less profitable and as South County becomes a labor reserve in the national and now international economy, and as more jobs require a high school education, more and more boys remain (at least technically) in high school until graduation. Those who want jobs during their teenage years are now usually unused to heavy agricultural work, and can earn more at minimum-wage jobs than by working in tobacco. School officials no longer look kindly on students who are truant because of cutting, housing, or stripping tobacco. So, as older people here point out, a major source of the short-term help tobacco farmers need has dried up. The hue and cry again went up: "we can't get decent help; they don't know how to work any more." The man I most recently heard making this complaint was sitting on his tail. He was resting, worn out from a brief stint of tossing hay bales into our barn, while his hired hand, probably paid less than minimum wage, kept working and surely overheard this comment.[30]

North County as a node for national and international capital organization

When we first moved here, North County's biggest manufacturing plants were national plants established mainly during the 1960s and 1970s.[31] A few local industries were established throughout the 1980s. Then in the late 1980s foreign capital began arriving. By 1998 the three largest foreign-owned factories employed over 39 percent of the manufacturing work-force. The largest national corporation employed an additional 9 percent.[32] This means that four companies control nearly half of the best-paying jobs in North County, aside from white-collar jobs.

The arrival of foreign capital in North County was the result of a sustained effort on the part of Kentucky as a state and of North County's Chamber of Commerce and Industrial Foundation. Kentucky's governor, Martha Layne Collins, had made numerous trips in the mid-1980s to Asia, principally Japan, to tout Kentucky's workforce. Laws in Kentucky were rewritten to provide "Free Land, Free Buildings, and Free Money," as one county ad puts it, to corporations relocating in Kentucky or coming in from foreign countries. Corporations taking advantage of these programs say they save tens of millions of dollars as a result—dollars that would otherwise be paid into the state and county treasuries as taxes. Information to attract industry put out by the North County seat's Industrial Foundation and by the state emphasizes the importance to prospective businesses of the generally low-wage, hard-working, highly motivated, loyal, and team-oriented Kentucky workforce.[33]

North County, and the area around the county seat in particular, became a regional centralizing point for the drainage of sweat out of surrounding labor reserves like South County. This meant many managerial and other high-paying positions in the county seat. Some of these jobs are held by local people, but many are not. The Chamber of Commerce and the Industrial Foundation worked hard to convince potential industries that upper-level employees would want to move here, producing a video in the 1980s portraying the town as a lovely environment with a choice of big old homes or newer ones, a small town atmosphere with rural beauty, modern amenities, and all the cultural opportunities of a big city either in the town itself or in "nearby" Louisville. Shots portraying all this were carefully chosen, indeed!

The presence of these newcomers certainly raised per capita income, and the increased number of people living or working in the county seat certainly enhanced the profits of local branches of retail chains.[34] However, it is less clear how much *native* North Countians, other than local elites, benefited from all this.[35] Their per capita income can't have risen as much as the relatively high per capita and median family incomes seem to indicate, since a significant percentage of the highest wages went to newcomers. Furthermore, most new jobs are not industrial. They are close to minimum wage, often part-time or temporary. Average wages are relatively low, while the cost of living is only slightly lower than the national average, not low enough to offset low wages.[36] Nevertheless median family income is significantly higher in North County than in South County and in the other counties drained by North County industry.

This would appear to mean that the route chosen by North County elites has been successful not just for the elites themselves but for their fellow North Countians. Maybe. But there is another way of looking at this. Many of the higher-paid North County manufacturing jobs are in unionized plants.[37] It could easily be argued that North County's higher wages are a result, not of booster policy, but of the long union struggle to force industry to pay decent wages. Given elite efforts to keep unions out it could even be argued that those high wages represent a failure, not a success, of local elite strategy.[38] At least some incoming corporations have refused to hire anyone with even past employment in a unionized company. One such corporation was recently charged with unfair labor practices for its tactics in preventing the formation of a union.

North County provides much of the region's buffer social control class. They control and direct those below them in the region's drainage system, for the benefit of those above them, through the justice system, social services, and educational establishments, as well as through managerial positions in business and industry. Thus North County's relative prosperity is built significantly on organizing the drainage out of the surrounding region. Equally important, many of those higher-wage industrial jobs depend on materials produced by the lower-paid work of people in surrounding labor reserves, in Third World countries, and in North County itself.

From this perspective, what the local elite strategy accomplished was merely to put significant numbers of North Countians a notch higher than most South Countians in the drainage system; they became overseers. This has meant continued poverty for South Countians, and despite higher wages for some in North County, it has meant continued poverty for many others in North County. Because local boosters chose to organize the North County workforce as a relatively low-wage servant of national and then international capital, North County workers have been vulnerable since the sugar-coated contract has come to an end. They are now in direct competition for jobs with desperate people all over the world within the global economy of the New World Order.

TRANSNATIONAL ORGANIZATION: THE NEW WORLD ORDER

By the 1990s the power of international finance capital overwhelmed that of nearly all governments in the entire world.[39] In the face of such power, even the U.S. government stands little chance of winning a direct confrontation. Indeed, according to then Speaker of the House of Representatives Newt Gingrich, "the purpose of the American government is to strengthen American companies in the world market."[40]

Reflecting the needs of the newly dominant international finance capital, new transnational organizations have been created by the world's most powerful capitalists. These include the International Monetary Fund (IMF), the World Bank, and the Trilateral Commission, all acting to coordinate international finance capital. The IMF and the World Bank directly control conditions in its member countries or in Third World countries by withholding or granting loans with strings attached to force "austerity measures" that enhance profitability.[41] The Trilateral Commission was founded in the early 1970s to analyze the needs of its American, Japanese, and European members and issue policy recommendations.[42] Its members were chairmen of the boards of the biggest international corporations, heads of the biggest foundations, think tanks, elite universities, TV networks, the biggest newspaper and magazine editors, and a few other people in major leadership positions. Many of its members move back and forth between government and business or other private positions and can influence policy. In 1975, for instance, the commission issued a "crisis" warning about the dangers to "governability" of a "highly educated, mobilized, and participant society," an internal threat they claimed was greater than any external threat. They recommended that educational institutions should "lower job expectations" and that a college education should become job training.[43] Perhaps it is merely coincidence that the media began talking about the necessity of getting business involved in education shortly thereafter.

President George Bush Sr., in declaring his New World Order, was making a double statement. First, he was acknowledging that the world was being realigned by the power of international finance capital expressed through transnational corporations. By the 1980s competition among international capitalists had become intense. The USSR fell apart, and the whole world, no longer excluding the communist bloc, was opened to capitalist penetration, setting off a scramble among corporations for access to former communist markets, labor, and resources.[44] China turned toward capitalism and threw its enormous weight into the competition, and Japanese and other Asian elites joined European and American elites in the fight for control of U.S. markets, labor, and resources. The result in the United States was concern that the United States was losing its "competitive edge." This concern, well publicized by magazines, newspapers, and television, became the justification for reneging on the sugar-coated contract.

Second, Bush was implying that transnational corporations in their positions of world hegemony were actually instruments of U.S. world hegemony. As a former member of the Trilateral Commission, however, he was surely aware of the commission's report, which stated that people who thought this way lived in "a mental universe which no longer exists—a world of separate nations."[45] In the New World Order it is relatively meaningless to talk about American or any other nationally identified hegemony.[46] Instead, international capitalists, who happen to reside in one part of the globe or another, roam the world looking for those conditions that will profit them most. Their decisions are influenced by the degree to which people in one part of the globe or another have managed to forge protection for themselves against the depredations of roving national and international capital.

The New World Order that Bush heralded represents yet another reorganization of the United States drainage system to include far more people who are not living in the United States, mostly bringing them in at the bottom. Their work replaces that of people in the United States who, due to the previous reorganization of the drainage system under the sugar-coated contract, couldn't be forced as easily into work so ill-paid or so unsafe that people died of it. Most people now treated as "disposable labor,"[47] to be used up and thrown away when they are no longer productive, are no longer U.S. citizens. Just as those employees receiving higher wages were dependent on the low wages of those below them in the drainage system within the United States, they are now also dependent, as are their employers, on the dying wages of people outside the United States. The old contract has fallen apart, and unfree labor has revived. The result of reorganization has not been the kinder, gentler America that Bush predicted would emerge along with the establishment of the New World Order.

16

THE RESUMPTION
OF FASCIST PROCESSES

"**S**ixty hours? That's nothing! They're working eighty hours at Xcorp!"

"At Wcorp they never paid me for staying after they closed to clean up my area . . . they didn't pay anybody, we all had to do it."

"If they keep this [welfare reform] up, there's going to be a revolution!"

"It ain't right, [university basketball coach] making millions when there's kids out there hungry—and the rest of us are working, too, not just him."

"I'm selling drugs, yeah, but am I more immoral than the people living in those big new houses? Well, I'm not getting rich off other people's sweat like they are . . . !"

"They disabled the safety mechanism so we could work faster . . . "

"Nursing care is going down the tubes . . ."

"Where I am everybody is like that, a full-time job and something on the side . . . you can't make it otherwise."

"When you look up from the bottom of a very deep hole you can't see the light even though you know it's a hole. When you look up you don't see hope, you see darkness. Until government gets a grip, or until we on the bottom make them get a grip, [this desperation] will continue. With welfare reform the hole is just getting deeper."

"They treat people like that, and then complain about how they can't get decent help!"

"We don't even see each other enough to fight."

"I have to drop this class to work—my father lost his job . . . "

The sugar-coated contract is definitely falling apart as far as these central Kentucky white people are concerned.[1] The contract had said that white men who worked hard and followed the rules would be able to support families and pay their bills. Instead, these families cope with low-wage or part-time jobs, or with better-paid jobs that require so much overtime that they eliminate family life.[2] Either way, they are working their fingers to the bone and getting only bony fingers. Myths about lazy, uneducated, boozing, barefooted, violent, pregnancy-prone rednecks "naturally" receiving low wages notwithstanding, workaholics are common among people in North and South County. Kentucky workers rank among the most productive in the country.[3]

The anger reflected in these comments comes in reaction to the resumption of fascist processes as the effects of the reorganized New World Order trickle down to more and more Americans, including those previously protected by the sugar-coated contract.[4] Intensified competition for control of the world's economy has led to new, lower rungs on the U.S. labor hierarchy. There has been a return to unfree and semi-free labor, and to dying wages, recently spreading to a wider range of employees. To control the inevitable discontent the elite have chosen increased repression, a renewed emphasis on racialized tactics of divide and rule, and, as usual, a redefinition of whiteness.

THE NEW WORLD ORDER AND INCREASED EXPLOITATION

As competition between international capitalists heated up, headlines in the early 1990s blazoned the prediction that corporations would have to be more "efficient" and "leaner" to survive. The implication was that workers who survived downsizing would have to work harder or international capitalists would turn instead to labor outside the United States. They have done exactly that—when they can. Fruit of the Loom, for instance, recently fired its Kentucky employees and headed for Guatemala, where they can pay workers a bit over a dollar an hour.[5] But not all can do that. McDonald's needs burgers flipped here, not in Mexico—although conceivably they could be made in Mexico and shipped here to be heated. Wal-Mart needs cashiers here, not in Calcutta, if it is to sell goods here. If Toyota makes cars in Kentucky it gets tax advantages, cuts shipping costs, and gets comparatively cheap labor.

When Fruit of the Loom and other workers lose jobs the number of people in the reserve labor force increases. With more people desperate for a job, corporations have greater freedom to exploit their employees. If, for instance, a North County company chooses to speed up production by disabling safety mechanisms, and people lose fingers and arms as a result, most employees are afraid to complain.[6] As they well know, whistle blowers often get fired regardless of what the law says, and there are plenty of other people out there waiting for that job. The employment office in a nearby county, for instance, had 6,000 applications for a new plant that eventually hired about 250.[7]

CEO pay in Kentucky doubled during the 1990s; CEOs in some industries make 143 to 812 times the median income of employees; the highest paid make more in a single year than low-paid workers could make in three to six lifetimes.[8] With a larger labor reserve it is easier for North County corporations to institute policies that bring these benefits to decision makers but hurt people and communities. They can fail to raise wages as fast as inflation. They can cut benefits, for instance, by making workers pay a larger percentage of insurance costs. They can downsize, making the people left work harder and faster, often with vast amounts of overtime. They have plenty of "volunteers" for part-time or "temporary" contract work that sometimes lasts years at a time, and that most people find less than satisfactory. They can replace mid-management, engineering, clerical, and production positions with computers, robots, and other high-tech solutions, or substitute lower-paid women for men. Eventually, around the country even corporate vice-presidents began feeling the pinch.

Reneging on the sugar-coated contract

None of this accords with the sugar-coated contract.[9] The expanded middle-class that contract created is now a liability in the eyes of corporate owners and managers. Those living wages, benefits, and relatively safe workplaces now look more like lost profits than the price of industrial peace. With a worldwide market, sales lost in the United States through the declining buying power of lowered wages can be replaced by sales elsewhere. As Peter Jennings eagerly pointed out on *ABC News* during the visit of China's president to the United States, China has one billion potential customers and needs nuclear power plants.[10] This promises an enormous bonanza for American-based transnationals if the U.S. government orchestrates power relations with China in the interests of business.

The "renewed efficiency" achieved through improved technologies and downsizing led to a "jobless recovery" in 1992 from the recession of the late 1980s and early 1990s, followed by what is described as a full

economic recovery. But in many respects this recovery has been mythical. While employment statistics and corporate profits look healthy and
the stock market skyrockets, and while upper-level management income
and wealth reach unimaginable heights, poverty, lack of health care,
hours of work, part-time work, and chronic exhaustion have all
increased. While such conditions have historically plagued those toward
the bottom of the drainage system, they now affect many who formerly
had middle class security.[11] Things are even worse for the many who
haven't been able to avoid the looming threat of poverty. Some probably
answered a 1995 North County ad placed by a temporary agency for
"laborers . . . capable of heavy lifting, working twelve-hour shifts seven
days per week."[12]

LIFE ON THE POVERTY LINE

Let us be clear: life at the poverty line, or even somewhat above it, is a life
lacking what all Americans agree are basic necessities. It marks an inability to participate in the customary life of our society.[13] This isn't the poverty which combines little cash with a decent roof and plenty of food grown
on your own farm, as experienced by many Whites earlier in North and
South County's history. This is the poverty of people dependent on cash
in a consumer economy.

Life at or below the poverty line—in 2000, $17,463 annual pre-tax
income for a family of four—is very often a life one paycheck away from
homelessness.[14] A minor car repair becomes a major financial strain; an illness can mean financial catastrophe. So can jury duty, since it often translates into lost wages—some stay off voter lists to avoid the risk of being
called. In counties with a small population and a low percentage of regis-
tered voters, like South County, the risk is quite real—I have been called
four times. Poverty-line homeowners have to let leaking roofs continue
leaking; for renters a leaking roof often means a drawn-out, ulcer-produc-
ing fight with the landlord. Cavities remain unfilled. Children gaze long-
ingly at toys or clothes and parents have to decide between the child's
desire to be like other kids, the child's need for nourishing—not just filling—
food, and the child's need for heat in the winter and electricity year-round.

Even for those who succeed in filling all these needs, the process is
incredibly time-consuming. Shopping at yard sales is cheap but slow.
Paying bills without a checking account necessitates trips to the post office
for money orders, or to utility companies to pay in cash. Since checking

accounts require as much as a $1,000 minimum balance, many find them an unaffordable luxury. Even shopping with food stamps requires fortitude: people "look at you funny" or "make comments." For the working poor, people whose jobs pay so little that they qualify for food stamps, such reactions are doubly offensive. After all, they work as hard, or harder than, those making the comments. Adding insult to injury, those commentators are perfectly happy to buy products made by people who are paid wages so low that they need food stamps, as one ex–food stamp recipient bitterly pointed out. Working long hours or several part-time jobs adds to the strain; so does working at night. Mental and physical exhaustion becomes the normal state of affairs and adds to the difficulties of coping with an already difficult life.

Members of poor extended families depend on each other for a social safety net, for instance, in caring for children while a parent works or providing transportation to a hospital for tests, or for a place to live when someone can't pay the rent. Because of this interdependence, problems in one part of the family have repercussions for everyone else. Money, time, energy, and emotions are all involved. The continuing necessity to be involved through a combination of duty, love, and dependency with an abusive and abused set of extended family members can be devastating.

REVIVING THE FREE-TO-UNFREE LABOR CONTINUUM

Because of poverty and the threat of poverty, and because of the belief that *white* men support families through their own work, it has been possible to force Whites into accepting the kind of work that formerly was reserved for the not-white, the not-quite-white, and white trash. Referring to his upbringing in the 1960s, one North County man explained, "Back then, it was 'Niggers are on welfare. . . .' Being a [drug] dealer was okay, but not being a nigger. . . . Men work, pay their own way—that idea was literally beat into me."

Similarly, some white women turn to minimum-wage factory work, knowingly risking brown-lung and disabilities, because, as one woman put it, their families would "rather see them dead than on welfare." She had become pregnant and married at fourteen to escape intolerable conditions at home, only to find herself struggling with a part-time job, child care, and farm work. She slept only four or five hours a night in a vain attempt to keep the house clean enough and meals pleasing enough to avoid being beaten by her husband. She decided she had to leave when he began beating their son—who when I last talked to her was showing signs of abusing his girlfriend. An aunt got her a job at the local sewing factory, where she earned enough with overtime to allow her to leave her husband. Leaving without a job was not an option: she had been taught that being white meant self-sufficiency. Her family would have disowned her had she turned to welfare, even to avoid serious abuse. But turning to the sewing factory, she says, amounted to trading one form of slavery for another. Since then, however, in a clear rejection of her nativist upbringing as she pursued a college education, she has moved from rejecting welfare and the people on it to a critique of the elite role in creating both the conditions that lead to the need for welfare and the policies that make it difficult to leave it. Her explanation for her problems now, like that of many other producer egalitarians in North and South County, focuses primarily on class. She is convinced that the "big guys" conspired to profit from her difficulties, benefiting from her cheap labor and waiting to take advantage of any "misstep," such as her early pregnancy, which might make her vulnerable to exploitation.

So pride and definitions of whiteness, not just the threat of poverty, kept all these people working, providing much of the low-wage workforce on which Kentucky employers depended. But when Kentucky employers no longer want them many of these same white people are forced onto welfare, or into other less secure employment, or back to school for training. They, or the people they have displaced in their downward move in the labor market, are desperate enough and proud enough to accept jobs that bear no resemblance to the jobs of the sugar-coated contract. Bumper stickers saying "I'm po' but proud" became one common response. The result has been a revival of the racialized free-to-unfree labor continuum.

REVISING THE SEGMENTATION OF THE FREE LABOR FORCE

It was never true that all Whites could realistically expect the sugar-coated contract to provide men with permanent full-time jobs with benefits and wages high enough to support a family on about forty hours a week. Nevertheless, that did happen often enough to make the expectation *appear* reasonable. It no longer appears reasonable. Older people here laugh or get angry when I mention that many jobs used to pay enough for one man to support a family—they remember those days. But younger people often just look puzzled. This is not the reality they have encountered.

Their reality has been that full-time permanent jobs are scarce; temporary employment companies are now the country's largest employers.[15] This is why, when Fruit of the Loom shut down in a nearby county and 3,500 people lost their jobs in an area already hard hit by layoffs, 4,000 people applied immediately for 500 lower-paying jobs with a new Amazon.com warehouse—in Fruit of the Loom's old buildings. These jobs are projected to average (presumably for those who can get full-time jobs) a bit over the poverty line for a family of four.[16] And it is why people continue taking jobs at ZCorp in North County despite stories of the remarkably high rate of missing fingers among its employees—people who work there are sometimes greeted by a raised hand with a finger bent out of sight. And it explains why they work there for a time despite the frequent involuntary eighty-hour work weeks; the pay, for central Kentucky, is good, but most can't stand the job for long; the enormous annual turnover is mentioned regularly when Zcorp is discussed.

The role of welfare for the poor: providing welfare for the elite

One of the most basic myths of the United States is that having a job will end an employee's poverty. In fact, many jobs don't. In North County, 73 percent of the net increase in jobs between 1980 and 1993 came in the low-paying service and retail sectors, whereas between 1968 and 1980 that figure was only 48 percent.[17] Some people work at jobs that pay less than minimum wage, usually illegally under the counter. Others, paid minimum wage, are eligible for welfare in the form of food stamps. In the heyday of the sugar-coated contract one full-time minimum-wage job put a family of four close to the poverty line; now it takes nearly two.[18]

Welfare, in other words, is subsidizing employers who refuse to pay a living wage. Once again, the elite are on welfare. The sweat shop, the motel paying illegally under the counter for room cleaning, the farmer who legally pays less than minimum wage, the retail chains and fast-food joints hiring part-time labor—they all pay only part of the employee's wage. The taxpayer pays the rest, and the employer makes bigger profits from cheaper labor provided at taxpayer expense. However, given global competition in the New World Order, such welfare for employers is apparently no longer deemed adequate. Not only does the welfare reform of the 1990s create a bigger and more desperate workforce, allowing employers to push everyone's wages down, but special new rungs are being added at the bottom of the workforce, providing additional forms of subsidized labor for employers.[19]

Indenture? The return of semi-free labor

While conditions in the free part of the labor hierarchy have worsened, people who were already toward the bottom have become increasingly miserable. Some are losing their freedom. The Personal Responsibility and Work Reconciliation Act, passed by Congress in 1996, is the cornerstone for the legal structure by which semi-free labor is being re-created in the United States.

To justify the act the myth that jobs automatically end poverty is supplemented by the myth that there are enough jobs to go around, so people too lazy to get them must be forced into jobs for their own good.[20] These myths persist despite the fact that most poor people *have* jobs—in Kentucky over 80 percent of poor families with children, for instance. Nor are there enough jobs—in 1998 there were job openings for only one-third of the people expected to leave welfare in Kentucky.[21] Nevertheless U.S. policy persists in equating poverty with evil and with defective personalities. Historically some allowance has been made for the "deserving" poor, usually white widows. The refurbishing of white trash in the 1920s tightened this—not all white women were considered deserving. The Personal Responsibility Act carries it a step farther, for it is mostly women who may be pushed into semi-free labor by the "welfare reform" it mandates.

Limiting welfare eligibility provides more people "willing" to take jobs at the bottom of the free labor hierarchy. These are jobs that people normally avoid because of their low pay, lack of benefits, or danger. Those who can't find jobs may be required, if they are to continue to eat, to do "volunteer service," which in Kentucky sometimes means working for a business without wages.[22] In return, they will continue to receive minimal support from the government—food stamps, medical care for themselves and their children, subsidized housing if they are lucky, and a pittance for all the other expenses of life. Their "pay" will leave them far below the poverty line, and their work can replace that of some employees previously better paid. They will work for food and shelter and the right to medical care, seeing very little actual money. Are these women being forced into a new form of indenture, this time to the state? Like sharecroppers, people in these positions are not slaves, but neither are they totally free, and like slaves and sharecroppers, their relationship to their employer is not based on wages.

There are other hints of a revival of indenture. Job Corps, for instance, in some cases contracts with corporations that work young people for several three- or four-month periods without pay. During these "training" periods the worker receives pocket money, food and shelter, and, upon graduating, a lump sum of up to $1,000.[23] The company may eventually hire the trainee at minimum wage for an indefinite period; later pay is supposed to be at least $6.50, undoubtedly substantially lower than prevailing wages in many cases. Apparently accepting low wages is supposed to "pay back" for the "training," much as earlier indentured servants were expected to pay back their employer for the costs of their passage by ship. In fact, *Job Corps in Action,* holding up an innovative Oregon program as a model, referred to the program's graduates as "fully 'indentured' " to the corporation that had provided the training.[24]

Another hint of indenture comes from Pennsylvania, where a study analyzed the results of a 1982 precursor of welfare reform that barred most cash welfare payments to thousands of "employable" people. The study found that two years later nearly half of those cut were being taken care of by relatives, which in many cases must have increased the burden on already struggling households. But one-third—approximately 22,600 people—were keeping body and soul together by a return to "indentured relationships." They were working, but received no pay. Their employer provided room and board and nothing more.[25] Less dramatically, America Works, a private welfare placement corporation, "keeps a significant portion of the salary its clients earn during their first four months on the job."[26] And some Kentucky programs propose that the state subsidize the hiring company, not the employee.[27]

Other forms of semi-free labor

Probation, parole, and work-release provide another source of semi-free labor for employers. Those outside the prison but under the control of the criminal "justice system" are generally required to work; if not, they can be returned to prison. This means that they cannot resist unfair or even illegal treatment. Nor can they hold out for decent wages and benefits, or even for a forty-hour workweek. They are completely at the mercy of their employer, and often must return a large portion of their wages to the state to pay the costs of their supervision by parole officers.[28]

According to one activist it is now possible for employers in Kentucky to impose a form of semi-free labor on highly trained immigrants in normally well-paid jobs. The law lets immigrants work for only two employers during their first six years in the U.S. Some employers downsize immigrant employees and arrange for a new job at a different company. Since the employees are now on their second job, they cannot leave. The new employer returns the favor to the first company. The employee is only semi-free.[29]

Some Latino immigrants and other migrant workers come to Kentucky illegally and are held almost captive by their employers, who threaten to turn them over to the justice system if they complain about low pay or abysmal conditions. Many work in agriculture, others in industries in near-by counties. Others are legal immigrants and some are citizens, but all operate under the suspicion of illegality. Even those whose Latino and Native ancestors became U.S. citizens by virtue of U.S. conquest of the Southwest, whose ancestors had been there long before the arrival of their conquerors' ancestors, feel the bite of discrimination. And of course there have been scandals about the use of unfree sweatshop labor around the country as employers take advantage of illegal immigrants, sometimes even importing them specifically for that purpose.[30]

The revival of slavery

At the very bottom of the labor continuum, as in Nazi Germany, we find slave labor in prisons, dedicated to the increase of corporate profits. The brief period when free workers, backed by the sugar-coated contract, were able to force employers to forgo unfree labor ended during the Reagan years. States that now require employers to pay wages to prisoners they employ—usually far less than the prevailing rate for such work—also require prisoners to return most of their wages to the prison to pay for their "room and board." In other states they work directly for the state, generally for pennies per hour, saving the cost of hiring free workers. During the 1990s prisoners were, for instance, answering telephones for Best Western, making computer chips, building prisons, fighting forest fires, cleaning hospital waste off beaches, making furniture and blue jeans, and wrapping products for Microsoft. The companies hiring them find them highly prof-itable—cheap, productive, and reliable workers.[31]

Prison labor is a corporate bonanza, partly because it lowers labor costs for employers who use it, but more importantly because it lowers labor costs for all employers. Like welfare reform, it provides employers with a large and desperate labor reserve that can be used to push everyone from mid-level managers to janitors into accepting lower wages. In West County prisoners in a discussion group said they were used to displace state workers on the local road crew. They worked late into the night clearing snow, while former paid employees were fired. Several Kentucky state parks couldn't operate without prison labor, since the state doesn't hire enough people, according to a Frankfort union activist. In Kentucky and elsewhere corporations have used prisoners to bust unions, bringing them in to replace strikers.

The U.S. rate of incarceration is skyrocketing. As in earlier periods of our history, the available slave labor force is highly racialized. Young black and Latino men in particular are targets for incarceration. "Street sweeps" are conducted principally in their neighborhoods, and their drugs—crack, for instance—are defined as more dangerous than the alcohol or cocaine used by the more affluent and the more white. But some Whites, mostly from among the ranks of the poor, do become unfree prison labor. Whiteness no longer grants the total immunity from slavery that it did before the Civil War, nor even the near immunity Whites had from enslaved convict labor under Jim Crow.

THE DEMOTION OF THE MIDDLE CLASS: REVISING GENDER, REVISING WHITENESS

The New World Order added a new layer of capital at the top of the drainage system—international finance capital—and, in re-creating the free-to-unfree labor continuum, it pushed down many who were relatively privileged in the old system. Middle-class Americans, both the blue-collar and white-collar variety, began experiencing a demotion similar to what happened earlier this century in the United States and Germany when national capital took over from local capital and the small entrepreneurial, craft, and landowning middle class lost its independence. Instead of losing independence, this time they are losing security and their access to the American Dream.

Even white men who play by the rules can no longer expect the elite to live up to their side of the contract: they can't count on being able to pay the bills associated with a reasonably comfortable life, nor on retiring in comfort. The picket fence has become obsolete as home ownership becomes less and less likely. This process has been devastating to men's sense of honor and identity.[32]

The sugar-coated contract had defined successful manhood as the ability to support a family, marked by the service of a full-time wife who managed the consumerism that advertised their success. Raising children and getting her husband back to work each morning in a reasonably productive frame of mind was defined as a woman's duty and as the fulfillment of her womanhood.

While many white women during the sugar-coated contract did work for wages, people often claimed they were working just for "pin money," or just until they could pay for some particularly desirable and expensive consumer item. Or they claimed a woman just wanted something to do during the day while the kids were in school. Correspondingly, the claim that women really didn't need to work justified the low wages they received even when doing jobs identical to those of better-paid men. These lower wages allowed men to keep a modified sense of head-of-household honor, even in families where it was blatantly clear that the wife had to work or the family would be out on the streets. He earned more than she did, and her work was defined as more menial and unskilled than his. Constructing women's work as unskilled frequently required cultural gymnastics, so that nurse's aides were somehow less skilled than the hospital's male janitors, who in turn were more skilled than the female janitors known as cleaning ladies. Running a sewing machine in a sewing factory was somehow less skilled than cutting the cloth to be sewn.

The ability to spend money unnecessarily was—and still is—a mark of success, even if the wife's income was needed to permit the spending. As television in commercials, soap operas, and children's programming made abundantly clear, having "nice" stuff is the key to happiness; the wrong toothpaste can ruin your love life, and the right car can fix it. The wrong salad dressing on a sandwich can consign your child to loneliness; and obviously anyone who is anyone has new furniture. Confronted head-on with such statements, nearly everyone denies they believe them; but their lives are often testimony to the contrary. Attempting to keep up with the Joneses is widely regarded as a sign of self-respect. Families who don't are correspondingly disrespected; the threat of disrespect is a powerful motivator fueling consumerism. White trash—then and now—are often identified by their apparent rejection of the importance of competing.[33] Having a broken-down car up on blocks in front of your house is seen by the middle class as thumbing your nose at basic consumerist values. A satellite dish adds to middle-class ire. If women in such homes have jobs, and particularly if their jobs are steadier than those of the men, the men are derided in middle-class circles as no-good freeloaders.

But by the 1990s many white families were in or headed for the same boat. They could no longer compete; successful consumerism was beyond reach even with two incomes. The fiction that a wife's wages are less critical to survival than her husband's has become harder to maintain. If her income begins to approach his, or if her work is steadier than his, or if she can get a job and he can't, he moves closer to "freeloader" status, and his male honor becomes harder and harder to save; fewer and fewer are able to live up to the standards they learned from their fathers.

Even worse, many young men have little security to offer to attract a wife; their position is much more like the one women have long been in. A young man in this position has little to offer a wife except sexual services, household work, and companionship. Even his half of a household income may be little more than she can offer him. His income isn't necessarily critical to a family's survival, and in some situations his wife and children may be financially better off without him, particularly if he spends his own income on himself, letting his wife spend her income to buy the family necessities, a not unusual pattern. With little but their sexuality to offer, some young men now are turning to muscle shirts, perming their hair and dying it to disguise the gray, and primping in front of a mirror, according to some of their mothers. Like many women, they are working to display what they have to best advantage. Since working-class men's earnings are now unlikely to rise significantly with age they, like women, are beginning to define youth as their greatest asset.

As the sugar-coated contract breaks down elderly white working-class men and women no longer count on a comfortable retirement. Instead they may find themselves bagging or checking out groceries, working under the thumb of much younger supervisors to whom they have to appeal for bathroom privileges. Wal-Mart runs TV ads implying that selling fishing gear in Wal-Mart's sporting goods department is as much fun as going fishing during retirement. Such ads perhaps draw some with inadequate retirement pensions, or who are lonely, but more importantly, they perform the ideological task of reassuring other viewers that the contract isn't in trouble. Elderly workers are there for the "fun" of it.[34]

JUSTIFICATION AND THE AMERICAN DREAM

The "middle class" of the sugar-coated contract had included a new group, workers who had become relatively secure through unionization. But they didn't have the same devotion to the interests of the elite that could be expected of the older managerial and social control branches of the middle class. And along with many of the newly enfranchised Blacks and poor Whites, they were voters. These were the first people targeted for demotion by elites who wanted to wring more sweat out of their employees as global competition heated up. If they were to accept demotion quietly they needed justification, an explanation for the decline of their American Dream.

The American Dream had always been a bit of an illusion for people at the bottom of the drainage system. Nevertheless, a combination of force, propaganda, and the reality that some people actually achieved it allowed it to function, hiding the responsibility of an ever more wealthy elite for the policies that have worsened the conditions we live under. It helped to turn people away from collective solutions to their problems and focused instead on individual merit—or lack of it—to explain why some "succeeded" and others did not. Emphasizing "correct values" and individual responsibility makes collective solutions appear immoral, like cheating on the individual achievement test. But just as in the days of the civil rights movement or of the Tobacco Wars or the People's Party or of the coal mine union wars or of slavery and indenture, the context in which lives are set cannot be changed by working-class individuals. If the drainage system is to be readjusted by working-class people to provide greater equality, the only possible route is collective. In reality the American Dream and the sugar-coated contract on which it was based had come as a buyout after generations of bitter and often bloody *collective*—not *individual*—struggle, granted by the elite to secure industrial peace. But that fact was conveniently forgotten in the teaching of history and sociology, and in media representations of the past. Novels and movies played their part too in denying the reality of the working-class world, promoting individualism and describing capitalism as a system in which anyone can rise.

But in the New World Order this old ideological formula contradicts reality too blatantly. New formulas are needed to justify the elite decisions that are destroying people's lives and hopes, and to deal with the bitterness of the "angry white men" these decisions produced. As in the 1920s the elite have worked to direct that anger away from their own policies into an exclusionary nativist reaction against people toward the bottom of the drainage system—in this case particularly toward Spanish-speaking immigrants, inner-city residents, and poor women with children and no husband—trying to deflect the potential revolt that is an inherent danger of the resort to fascist processes.

AVERTING AN INCLUSIVIST REVOLT AGAINST FASCIST POLICIES

The decision to move toward fascist policies indicates sufficient competition among corporate elites that they want lower wages or cheaper resources badly enough to risk provoking revolt or serious questions about their right to rule.[35] Enormous and continuing effort on the part of the elite is required to make sure people don't realize that change is possible, that the misery they are experiencing is not part of nature, that "economic forces" themselves are not part of nature, but are all a result of human policies. Exclusionary nativism reduces the likelihood of such a realization, but nevertheless that danger remains real. To avert that danger, media and politicians have produced a powerful nativist racialized and gendered rhetoric in a massive propaganda campaign designating people being pushed into the unfree end as "Other," people whose behavior marks them as not true Americans.[36] The rhetoric claims that the renewal of America depends on controlling their behavior.[37] So "community aliens" have been created—the Spanish speakers, the inner-city residents, the poor single women with children, all at the bottom of the drainage system—focusing anger away from the elite. As nativist attitudes are more commonly aired they begin to appear mainstream, gradually shifting the center of political discourse toward a position more in line with the needs of dominant capital.[38] This "normalizes everyday injustice" so that, for instance, much of the population will accept as natural the jailing of enormously disproportionate numbers of black and Latino and Native American men.[39] The stage is set for escalating the use of unfree and semi-free labor. Those still free will be unlikely to connect their own dropping standard of living with their acquiescence in such policies; thus many will support those policies, blind to the fact that in so doing they are damaging themselves.

Nevertheless, the danger of an inclusivist revolt remains real. Many of those reacting to nativist rhetoric are not themselves nativists, although they do participate in "big guy/little guy" analysis. Many, like a friend of mine, see a conspiracy on the part of the big guys, who are out to get the little guys, and that is why times are so hard. She objects to the way tobacco companies profit from moving production and processing to Third World countries, to the way the milk company overworks its truck drivers, to how the price pickle companies pay for cucumbers is so low it hardly pays to grow them, to the gap between the price farmers receive for milk and the price for which cheese is sold, and to the cost of health care for her uninsured elderly parents. Producer egalitarians like my friend are widespread in North and South County. Most of them are poor or near-poor; and most see the elite, not other poor people, as the source of their problems. This is not to say they are free of racism and sexism; if that were so they couldn't be derailed by the nativist rhetoric of productivity and national renewal. But this response often sits uncomfortably beside their understanding that their poverty comes from a failure of wages, not of personal responsibility, and that it is unrelated to the behavior of Blacks, white trash, or Latino immigrants. History has shown over and over that these people are inclined to cross the artificial lines constructed for purposes of divide and rule.

The capability to cross those lines still exists in North and South County. Under black church leadership, for instance, some of the poorest of Blacks and Whites in a nearby tiny town came together for several years in the mid-1990s to run a food bank. Every week there was a long line of Blacks and Whites, a few of them Amish, waiting amicably for the basement door to open under a church that clearly needed a new coat of paint and major repairs. Inside the basement work was organized by the minister's wife, and the people working behind the makeshift counters were about evenly divided by race. Some were related by marriage across racial lines.

The threat to elites of inclusivist anger comes through clearly in the comments of a student I interviewed who had grown up in a coal-mining community in eastern Kentucky. He doesn't for a moment buy the legitimacy of the exploitation corporate capitalism inflicted on his community. As a young man he became peripherally involved in theft, was caught and imprisoned. He was offered the "opportunity" to leave prison if he would join the military and "volunteer" for special forces doing dangerous undercover operations. Jim found prison vicious and dangerous; he talked about guards beating prisoners, arranging "accidental" deaths, and putting them in "the Hole" for any attempt at resistance, as well as about unsafe working conditions. So he agreed. He never told me what he did undercover, although he had clearly been in many parts of Europe and Asia. But, he said, by the time the military was done with him, his back was so destroyed that he was about five inches shorter. He could no longer meet military weight requirements for his shrunken height, and was kicked out of the military. He was bitterly angry at the military, interpreting it as a tool by which big guys used little guys to make the world safe for profiteering. He joined a protest on campus over the acquittal of white policemen shown on national TV brutally beating black motorist Rodney King. Jim saw the acquittal as elite protection of their agents, the police, who were engaged in the usual business of the justice system, the control and intimidation of the poor.

A similarly inclusivist reaction came from another man I interviewed who used to identify himself as a racist. He says he now realizes that "Blacks and Whites shouldn't be fighting *against* each other, they should be fighting *with* each other; the real enemy is poverty and starvation in our streets."

It is in the context of delegitimizing such a response that controlling media reports becomes critical. Stereotypes about rednecks and white trash encourage liberals and black, feminist, and leftist radicals to disdain possible allies by lumping producer egalitarians, who are willing to forgo racism and sexism, with nativists who are not. Equally important, such stereotypes insulate liberals in the middle class from knowledge of producer egalitarians and poor leftists. If liberals listened to those voices they would learn that true oppression is built into the drainage system itself, not into individual members of the elite, and will continue so long as the drainage system remains intact, regardless of who is at the top of the system. And perhaps the voices of black radicals, communists, Wobblies, and socialists might again be heard.

It is no accident that few middle-class people know such voices exist, and that few producer egalitarians feel their views are legitimate. This lack of knowledge results from selective reporting in the media. Producer egalitarians are rarely interviewed on TV or in newspapers; neither are leftist radicals. Views that are claimed to represent the left are generally barely left of center and do not challenge capitalism itself. When there is a true challenge to elite policy it is frequently censored out of the news. The *New York Times,* for instance, barely mentioned an alternative welfare summit, conducted in opposition to President Clinton's welfare summit in the 1990s. Reporting in other papers was distorted. Although most readers of such papers would never know it, thousands of dissidents, social workers, and activists all came together around issues of social justice across a wide range of ethnic, racial, sexual orientation, and class divides to protest Clinton's plans for revising welfare. They conducted their own discussion of how welfare should be fixed.[10]

Disenfranchising the poor yet again

Historically in moments of crisis the elite have manipulated voting rights, granting them or withholding them, to control challenges to their right to rule. At present those most likely to object to the institution of fascist processes are being disenfranchised. But this time much of the disenfranchisement *appears* to be voluntary. Some, however, is not.

"Voluntary" disenfranchisement is enormous. It is highest among those with the least power; they are also the people for whom voting is likely to be extremely inconvenient due to work schedules or lack of transportation. Media reports predicting low voter turnout may validate people's feeling that it isn't worth the effort. Political parties seem bent on increasing such "political apathy," so that those most damaged by the drainage system are less likely to vote.[11] Such "apathy" is widespread in North and South

County. As John Gaventa points out, however, political apathy results from people's accurate perception of the strength of forces arrayed against them. The more powerful those forces, the less difference people can make through voting or through other forms of political activity.[42] One woman I interviewed said she doesn't know anyone who voted in the last election. Her explanation was that "[V]oting makes no difference. . . . Politicians just do what they want." As another put it, "Every time I hear the word 'democracy,' I want to choke because there is no such thing. I'd like to have it, but the elite run everything, nothing is left for little people but to pay taxes to fatten politicians and rich [people's] wallets."[43]

For many in at least the more rural sections of South County, the failure to vote is much more than apathy. It is an active, often religious, refusal to choose between politicians they see as hopelessly immoral, both of whose policies are at odds with poor people's interests. They refuse to validate the drainage system with their votes.

Legal, involuntary disenfranchisement is also on the rise in the United States. People in prison can't vote, and if convicted of a vastly expanding list of federal crimes they may never be allowed to vote again. Technically, some ex-prisoners could have their voting rights restored, but the process they must initiate to do so is intimidating or cumbersome. Thus the rising rate of imprisonment in the United States, the highest in the world, is producing a significant, and growing, number of disenfranchised people. Legal disenfranchisement is most likely to affect people at the bottom of the drainage system. Poor men, particularly poor young minority men, are disproportionately imprisoned and thus disproportionately disenfranchised; 15 percent of black men have been legally denied the right to vote.[44] And then, of course, there is the debacle of the 2000 election, which apparently disenfranchised thousands of poor, mainly minority, voters in Florida.

The future

It is my fear of what I see on the horizon as drainage is ratcheted up, the middle class is demoted, and the U.S. veers toward the exclusionary scapegoating policies that normally accompany fascist processes that has kept me writing—fear, and the hope that we can still avert that future.

17

WHITENESS: THE CONTINUING EVOLUTION OF A SMOKESCREEN

There is nothing new about what is happening to the United States these days. Legal and illegal violence is not new; nor is racialized politics new; neither is a divisive, exclusionary reaction to loss of privilege new. Dying wages, unfree labor, the upward trickle of sweat, and the framing of the suffering they cause as natural and for the good of the country—all of these have been at the basis of the U.S. social structure since the earliest colonial days. In one way or another, they are basic to all stratified societies. But just as continuous as the efforts to drain people has been people's resistance to drainage. Our histories downplay the strength of that resistance, which at times has threatened to overturn the system, or at least to limit the amount of drainage. At such moments the elite have faced a fork in the road; they have consistently chosen the road of continued exploitation, reorganizing the drainage system to co-opt and force those below them into submission. Such moments have frequently come about when elite competition has heated up and the elite have tried to increase the flow of sweat to provide the profits they need as one level of capital takes over from another.

We are at present in such a period of intense competition, this time between elites around the world struggling to control the global economy. The consequences of that struggle are now filtering into the middle class, although they have been affecting people lower in the drainage system since the late 1970s. Whiteness no longer provides protection from the consequences of policies that make larger and larger portions of the United States into a Third World labor force. Nor does middle-class status provide complete protection. The results are similar to those of the 1920s and 1930s in the United States and Germany when the middle class began losing privilege as a result of intense competition among national elites. As usual, when faced with widespread anger at their policies, the elite has been encouraging nativist, exclusionary reactions to facilitate divide and rule. The previous chapter discusses the pervasiveness of the propaganda that blames people at the bottom of the drainage system for the loss of security being felt by people slightly higher, a security they once felt was theirs by virtue of white privilege and male privilege. And, in a racialized society, it is not surprising that many people buy into the nativist reaction.

REDEFINING WHITENESS IN THE NEW WORLD ORDER

The content of racialization has changed somewhat; categories have been redefined or invented to correspond to the power relationships created by shifts in elite strategies. There are now, for instance, "biracial" people who claim ties to two different racial groups. Middle-class Blacks have been to some extent whitened, as have well-to-do immigrant Japanese and Japanese Americans.[1] Some people identified by their African ancestry live their lives as "honorary Whites." Still, most people identified by Native American or Latino/a ancestry, like most Blacks, are not white and don't qualify for white privilege, although they too are sometimes whitened by middle-class status. And welfare trash and trailer trash, like white trash, have been removed from the roles of true whiteness. Anger against welfare recipients is no longer exclusively anger against Blacks, as it was in the days of Reagan's "welfare queen."

Whiteness is less and less the automatic property of people identified by claiming European ancestry. Helán Enoch Page describes whiteness as a set of practices designed to keep resources in elite hands. In the process it has conveyed varying degrees of privilege to all people identified as "white."[2] For some Whites that privilege has been partially an illusion, as it was for white sharecroppers. But it was only *partially* an illusion. Whites actually were less likely to be lynched, less likely to find themselves on chain gangs, and more likely to have jobs that paid a living wage. Looking at the United States as a whole, even in the worst of times Whites were less likely to be among the most seriously oppressed. Since the earliest days of European settlement, however, Kentucky has been an exception that proves the rule. Whiteness here has provided less protection for a larger percentage of people identified by their European ancestry than in other parts of the country. Since the reorganization of the drainage system that accompanied the end of slavery, a far larger percentage of the people at the very bottom of the drainage system in Kentucky has been white than in most other states. The state as a whole ranks low on a wide range of indicators of social well-being. Kentucky has some of the poorest counties in the United States, counties that produce coal and tobacco, the resources on which massive financial empires have been built. The inhabitants of those counties are predominantly white.

Whiteness hasn't worked well for many Kentucky Whites. But like Blacks in Kentucky and elsewhere, they are poor because of elite exploitation, not because of their racial characteristics. Their failure to exhibit the privilege supposedly conveyed by whiteness threatens to expose the structure of the drainage system, threatening the illusions of whiteness itself. Those illusions are essential to the elite ability to use race to divide and rule, to drain Blacks and poor Whites. Without them the white middle class might not go along with the oppression of those below them in the drainage system.

It has not been possible to pretend that white poverty in Kentucky is anything else. And conceptions about white trash haven't been quite adequate to lay to rest the threat presented by Kentucky's white poverty. Talking about white trash works best when Whites who are being drained to within an inch of their lives are a fairly small percentage of the white population, and where a large percentage of killing poverty occurs among people of color. That a large percentage of "ordinary" white people in Kentucky are poor threatens the illusion of whiteness itself. So whenever this fact has bubbled into middle-class white consciousness, additional explanations have been crafted. This happened, for example, when the mountains were initially taken over by timbering and coal-mining operators, or when tobacco farmers rose in revolt, or when coal miners battled in bloody Harlan. The reality of poor white revolt in cases like these triggered cruel myths about white Kentuckians—the familiar stereotypes about hillbillies, rednecks, and incest-prone "barbarians." These stereotypes are applied to Whites in other states with sections of white poverty, but they are far more pervasive about Kentucky. White people from other states are rarely greeted by strangers commenting with surprise that they are wearing shoes.

As the drainage system is reorganized for the New World Order, more Whites in the United States are joining the ranks of the severely exploited. Whiteness across the country is becoming more like whiteness in Kentucky. Whiteness now provides less immunity from unfree labor than it has since its invention, and less immunity from semi-free labor than it has since the decline of sharecropping, although still more immunity than for Blacks and other people of color. Welfare reform, prison labor, indenture-like arrangements: they all apply to Whites as well as to Blacks. At the same time that Whites are *beginning* to lose their immunity to unfree and semi-free labor, such labor for Blacks and Latinos is reaching epidemic proportions. In a mere five years, between 1990 and 1995, the number of young black men under the control of the criminal "justice" system went from one in four to one in three.[3] As imprisonment rises, so does enslaved labor in prisons. As the numbers of people on parole, probation, and work release increases, so does semi-free labor.

It is against those most vulnerable to unfree and semi-free labor that the racialized nativist reaction is now directed. In nativist perceptions none of these people are "true Americans," although they are the people who provide the cheap labor needed at the bottom to keep the sweat flowing up the drainage system. This attitude is not so different from the days of the 1920s white-sheeted Ku Klux Klan. As in the 1920s, much of this nativist reaction comes not from poor Whites, despite their stereotyping as redneck racists, and despite the fact that poor white racists do exist. Instead it comes largely from middle-class wannabes, people who feel their position of slight privilege threatened, or who identify with elite interests, or who expect to become part of the buffer social control class.

Just as the nativist reaction has been a permanent feature of American life, although gaining power or dying back in accordance with elite production of propaganda to feed it, so too has the *inclusionary* anti-elite reaction among poorer people been a permanent fixture. It has hung on against enormous odds, fermenting like yeast toward the bottom of the drainage system. At times it has bubbled up into prominence, and at other times, punched back down, it has waited under the sink to rise again when given half a chance. Many poor Whites who partake of the view from under the sink are far more anti-elite, far more focused on class inequities, than they are anti-Black, anti-Mexican, or anti-welfare. But because their view is given no legitimacy, because they never hear a reflection of their voices in news analysis, or in textbooks, or on talk shows, they often discount their own analysis. They may be pulled into nativism by talk show hosts, politicians, and religious leaders who speak just enough of their language to attract them. But this doesn't mean that the other reaction isn't there, awaiting its chance.

In North and South County oppositional "big guy vs. little guy" analysis is decidedly alive and well. It is held by bony-fingered people looking out at the world from under their sinks—people often stigmatized as rednecks and assumed to be far right nativists. They may acknowledge that as people "big guys" are as likely to be nice people as anyone else. Nevertheless, they don't believe in the benevolence of "big guys" toward "little guys" any more than did earlier white Kentuckians in their opposition to colonial landowners' control of their lives, or to American Tobacco Company, or to coal magnates, or to sharecropping landlords. As I have learned more and more about Kentucky's past I have become convinced that *enormous* effort has gone into keeping large numbers of poor and near-poor Whites focused on their whiteness. At the same time I have become convinced that whiteness has been critical in permitting the elite to continue draining most of us, White, Black, Latino, Native American, some of us to within an inch of our lives, some of us beyond.

Whiteness has been a continuously evolving smokescreen, adjusted and readjusted to the changing needs of elites as the drainage system has been reorganized, disguising from many of the oppressed the nature of their oppression. Racial attitudes, like patterns of racial violence, and like race itself, are not "natural"; neither race nor racism flow inevitably from "difference." Instead, there are reasons why people define particular "differences" as important at particular times and places, and why at particular moments certain differences are defined as so critical that defending them is believed to justify violence. The definition of important differences since European colonization of this continent has revolved around the evolution of "whiteness" and the continuing restructuring of the drainage system to enlarge the upward flow of sweat and consolidate it in fewer and fewer hands.

A New Psychological Wage? Whiteness on the Cusp

When a nation, and local Kentuckians, can raise songs such as Lee Greenwood's "God Bless the USA" to near-anthem status, we are adopting a new psychological wage. Ronald Reagan claimed the song was evidence of "the New Patriotism" and Greenwood sang at the inauguration of George Bush, Sr. Those singing the song, often with deep feeling, are saying they "know" that "at least" Americans are "free."[4] "At least I'm white" preceded the fascism of the 1920s in America; "At least I'm Aryan" preceded the fascism of Nazi Germany. Being American can serve to mark off those who deserve privilege in a now globalized economy, as did status as white or Aryan in a national economy. "At least" in all these cases recognizes the speaker's exploitation, but disguises it and relegates it to a position of minimal importance. That exploitation is supposed to be ignored in deference to a higher good, one that actually carries comparatively little material content, but provides apparent psychological comfort in the face of loss of privilege or real deprivation. As in the 1920s, fascist processes, with their corporate control of government, elite welfare, and the ratcheting up of exploitation, are all raising their heads in the United States these days. So too is a vicious nativist response to increased exploitation. If we go down this road we will all lose, as did everyone except the elite in Germany and in the United States the last time around. Claiming that being American guarantees freedom will no longer be true even for Whites.

To avert fascism and nativism, to keep from being bought off by a new psychological wage, to keep from being derailed by whiteness, honorary whiteness, and whitening, we need alternative histories and anthropologies. These alternative analyses must resonate with the view from under the sink, but go beyond it. They can help people at the bottom of the drainage system to combat the seduction of nativist, exclusionary thinking, and to expose its role in perpetuating inequality. These analyses can give those in the middle, threatened by loss of privilege, the tools to interpret their own nativism and racism, and to evaluate their roles as managers of labor, as members of the buffer social control class. Some in the middle subscribe to the belief that "What is good for the elite is good for the country" with a genuine desire to improve the lives of a large range of people. However, they lack knowledge of the alternative views of what elite rule has meant. They may find that their real interests lie in helping to overturn the drainage system or in limiting drainage, preventing the concentration of wealth and power in a few hands that damages them as well as people below them.

None of what is happening now is part of nature; nor is it new. If we can look at the past with the tools of an alternative history and anthropology, this may be evident. If we understand elite strategies of the past we may see ways to derail their present strategies. We don't have to let a new psychological wage substitute for the human necessities of adequate sleep, nutritious food, time to tend to family relationships and nurture children, an income large enough to provide a sense of security, and a sense of oneness with those around us. We don't have to let a new psychological wage claim that some of us are better than those of us who are being described as the new "community aliens." We don't have to agree that the stomachs of people on the other side of an arbitrary border are less important, or hurt less when empty, than those on the U.S. side of that border. We don't need to allow billionaires who have become rich off our sweat and that of people all over the world to keep their wealth while telling us there isn't enough to go around.

We are all part of the same drainage system; what hurts one of us hurts us all. Some of us may hurt less than others; but what goes around comes around. The pain we justify for others will someday come back to haunt us.

Endnotes

Introduction

1. Some of this research, which started in the early 1980s and has continued to the present, involved formal interviews and focused on the lives of the people who surrounded me. I was interested in the economic and legal forces that shaped lives and attitudes, and in the various ways people dealt with those forces. Eventually, I began to focus more directly on the role of race in these processes. Some of the information came out of group discussions in which people were paid for their time, funded by small grants from the Kentucky Humanities Council and the University of Kentucky. Other interviewing was unfunded and was done on an individual basis with people I had previously taught or met who had experience with the particular issue I was pursuing at the time. Many of those interviewed actively wanted their information to be used; they hoped it might alert readers to unfair treatment. All agreed that their words might be quoted, although most requested anonymity; thus all names of local people are pseudonyms. My research also has involved newspaper archives, census materials, and secondary sources. In addition, the fact that I live and work here means that I am constantly learning about people's lives. When my information does not come from formal interviews I have been doubly careful to preserve anonymity, changing details where necessary. I have given pseudonyms to counties and towns and correspondingly changed names of newspapers and of local histories when they reveal county or town identity, although page and date references are correct. I have also "misplaced" certain locations in order to preserve confidentiality, and avoided using exact census numbers that would reveal county identity; these changes do not affect the argument. Names of local corporations and other institutions are also pseudonyms.

2. County names are pseudonyms; see note 1.

3. For a series of film and print examples of these stereotypes see *Strangers and Kin*, produced by Dee Alvin Davis III and directed by Herb Smith, 58 minutes, Appalshop Films, 1984, videocassette; another more recent and more sophisticated version of these stereotypes can be seen in *American Hollow*, produced and directed by Rory Kennedy, 90 minutes, HBO, 1999, videocassette.

4. For documentation of the fight over black lung and workers' compensation see R. Dunlop and Gardiner Harris, "Few Miners Now Qualify for Benefits," Louisville, KY, *Courier-Journal*, April 25, 1998, A1, 6–8 and Gardiner Harris, "Patton-Run Mines in '70's Had Inaccurate Tests," *Courier-Journal*, April 21, 1998, A1, 7.

5. This alternative version of anthropology and history has been built by several generations of scholars, some of who have received little recognition in mainstream scholarship, or whose recognition has been belated or partial. In writing this book, I have relied heavily on their work, pulling it together in applying it to Kentucky.

6. Statistics come from U.S. Bureau of the Census. *Twenty-first Census of the United States, Population and Housing, 1990* (Washington, D.C.: Summary Tape). The presence of a military installation in North County may affect these numbers considerably; many of the people from Japan are connected with Japanese corporations in North County.

1 Organizing First Steps toward Underdevelopment in the U.S. South

1. See, for example, Andre Gunder Frank, *Capitalism and Underdevelopment in Latin America: Historical Studies of Chile and Brazil* (New York: Monthly Review Press, 1967); Immanuel Wallerstein, *The Modern World System* (New York: Academic Press, 1974).

2. Katherine Newman, *Declining Fortunes: The Withering of the American Dream* (New York: Basic Books, 1993); Walden Bello, *Dark Victory: The United States, Structural Adjustment, and Global Poverty* (London: Pluto Press with Food First, 1994), 90–2.

3. Kathleen Brown, *Good Wives, Nasty Wenches, and Anxious Patriarchs: Gender, Race, and Power in Colonial Virginia* (Chapel Hill: University of North Carolina Press, 1996), 56.

4. For the Shawnee see Jerry Clark, *The Shawnee* (Lexington: University Press of Kentucky, 1977), 1–4, 32–9. For the Cherokee see Richard Sattler, "Women's Status among the Muskogee and Cherokee," in Laura Klein and Lillian Ackerman, eds., *Women and Power in Native North America* (Norman: University of Oklahoma Press, 1995), 214–29; Theda Perdue, *Cherokee Women: Gender and Culture Change* (Lincoln: University of Nebraska Press, 1998); Grace Steele Woodward, *The Cherokees* (Norman: University of Oklahoma Press, 1963), 40–3, 88; Wilma Dunaway, *The First American Frontier* (Chapel Hill: University of North Carolina Press, 1996), 23–50.

5. The Cherokee Nation is still organized matrilineally (Perdue, *Cherokee Women*, 2).

6. For Hopewell and Mississippian societies see Lynda Shaffer, *Native Americans before 1492: The Moundbuilding Centers of the Eastern Woodlands* (Armonk, NY: M.E. Sharpe, c. 1992), 62–6, 70; Stuart Fiedel, *Prehistory of the Americas* (Cambridge: Cambridge University Press, 1992, 2nd ed.), 240–50, 255–6; Brian Fagan, *Ancient North America: The Archaeology of a Continent* (London: Thames and Hudson, 1995), 411–52. See Thomas Patterson, *Archaeology: The Historical Development of Civilizations* (Englewood Cliffs: Prentice Hall, 1993), 88–106, 274–90, on interpretation of archaeological evidence of inequality in chiefdoms and states, and on reestablishing more egalitarian relationships.

7. Theodore Allen, *Invention of the White Race*, vol. II, *The Origin of Racial Oppression in Anglo-America* (New York: Verso, 1997), 32–4.

8. This section depends particularly on Dunaway's world-systems framework (*First American Frontier*, 10–50); see also Allen, *Invention of the White Race*, vol. II, 31–45; Brown, *Good Wives*, 42–74.

9. On the English system see Allen, *Invention*, vol. II, 19–29, 97.

10. Audrey Smedley, *Race in North America: Origin and Evolution of a Worldview* (Boulder: Westview Press, 1993), 82; for an early example see Allen, *Invention*, vol. II, 84–96.

11. Theodore Allen, *The Invention of the White Race*, vol. I, *Racial Oppression and Social Control* (New York: Verso, 1994), 50, 74; Smedley, *Race in North America*, 124. St. Clair Drake in *Black Folk Here and There*, vol. II (Los Angeles: Center for African-American Studies, University of California, 1990), 227–28, 13, makes clear that Africans were no more "selling their own people" than were Europeans; both sold captive enemies.

12. Allen, *Invention*, vol. II, 36–7; Dunaway, *First American Frontier*, 28–9, 40–1.

13. Allen, *Invention*, vol. II, 33–45; Smedley, *Race in North America*, 104–106.

14 The rest of this chapter's conception of unfree labor and the creation of whiteness to control rebellion and increase profits is heavily indebted to Lerone Bennett, *The Shaping of Black America* (New York: Penguin Books, 1993 [1975]). Allen, *Invention of the White Race*, vol. II, provides more detail, but likewise is indebted to Bennett.

15. Allen, *Invention*, vol. II, 61, 91–9.

16. Peter Kolchin, *Unfree Labor: American Slavery and Russian Serfdom* (Cambridge: Harvard University Press, 1987), 11–2; Allan Kulikoff, *Tobacco and Slaves: The Development of*

Southern Cultures in the Chesapeake 1680–1800 (Chapel Hill: University of North Carolina Press, 1986), 45–7, 64–76.

17. Bennett, *The Shaping of Black America*, 45–50; for further description see Allen, Invention, vol. II, 119–22.

18. On tightening vagrancy laws see Allen, *Invention*, vol. II, 12, 20, 24, 25, 120; Brown, *Good Wives*, 22–4; Edmund. Morgan, *American Slavery, American Freedom: The Ordeal of Colonial Virginia* (New York: W. W. Norton and Co, 1975), 339.

19. Smedley, *Race*, 105; Brown, *Good Wives*, 114.

20. The following section depends on Allen, *Invention of the White Race*, vol. II, 51–62, 124–38, 182–91; Brown, *Good Wives*, 113–5, 131–3.

21. For further discussion see Smedley, *Race*, 99; Brown, *Good Wives*, 112–3; Allen, *Invention*, vol. II, 177–80, 182, 185; Bennett, *Shaping of Black America*, 11; David Roediger, *The Wages of Whiteness: Race and the Making of the American Working Class* (New York: Verso, 1991), 24–6, 30–1; Eric Williams, *Capitalism and Slavery* (Chapel Hill: University of North Carolina Press, 1994 [1944]), 7.

22. Bennett, *Shaping of Black America*, 10, 44–5.

23. Allen, *Invention*, vol. I, 109.

24. On runaways see Morgan, *American Slavery, American Freedom*, 217; Smedley, *Race*, 103–5; Bennett, *Shaping of Black America*, 55.

25. On the tendency to make common cause, see Allen, *Invention*, vol. II, 148–58; Bennett, *Shaping of Black America*, 19–22, 74. On increasing anger and landlessness see Allen, *Invention*, vol. II, 208–9, 343 n. 33; Ronald Takaki, *A Different Mirror: A History of Multicultural America* (Boston: Little, Brown, 1993), 62.

26. Berkeley is quoted in Takaki, *Different Mirror*, 63.

27. On Bacon's Rebellion see Takaki, *Different Mirror*, 63–5; Morgan, *American Slavery, American Freedom*, 254–70; Allen, *Invention*, vol. II, 163–5, 208–17, 239; Brown, *Good Wives*, 137–86. Although interpretations of the rebellion vary widely, it does seem clear that the frightening aspect of the rebellion for those who controlled the drainage system was its dramatic demonstration of the power of a united opposition to those who monopolized land, labor, and trade with Native Americans.

28. Kulikoff, *Tobacco and Slaves*, 104–17.

29. Morgan, *American Slavery, American Freedom*, 271–9.

30. This section depends particularly on Bennett, *Shaping of Black America*, 63. My interpretation is very different from that taken by many historians who say that shortage of labor "forced" landowners and government to turn to unfree labor (for example, Kolchin, *Unfree Labor*, 30). Gary Nash, in *Race and Revolution* (Madison: Madison House, 1990), maintains that even as late as the Revolutionary War there was strong anti-slavery sentiment in the South, but that slavery was then a national institution and the North was instrumental in defeating abolitionism.

31. Allen, *Invention*, vol. II, 79–81, 125–6.

32. Morgan, *American Slavery, American Freedom*, 297–9.

33. Allen, *Invention*, vol. II, 62, 68–9, 134; Brown, *Good Wives*, 80–2.

34. Bennett, *Shaping of Black America*, 78. For work showing the dependence of capitalism for its early development on forced and enslaved labor see Williams, *Capitalism and Slavery*.

2 Derailing Rebellion: Inventing White Privilege

1. Ronald Takaki, *A Different Mirror: A History of Multicultural America* (Boston: Little, Brown, 1993), 66.

2. Audrey Smedley, *Race in North America: Origin and Evolution of a Worldview* (Boulder: Westview Press, 1993), 98–9.

3. Allan Kulikoff, *Tobacco and Slaves: The Development of Southern Cultures in the Chesapeake 1680–1800* (Chapel Hill: University of North Carolina Press, 1986), 77, 118–9, 131, 262–3.

4. My discussion of the construction of race and racial slavery is deeply indebted to Lerone Bennett, *The Shaping of Black America* (New York: Penguin Books, 1993 [1975]), 1–109. See also Theodore Allen, *Invention of the White Race*, vol. II, *The Origin of Racial Oppression in Anglo-America* (New York: Verso, 1997), 75–109; Smedley, *Race in North America*, 100–1, 109, 142–3, 198; Kathleen Brown, *Good Wives, Nasty Wenches, and Anxious Patriarchs: Gender, Race, and Power in Colonial Virginia* (Chapel Hill: University of North Carolina Press, 1996), 107–244; bell hooks, *Ain't I a Woman: Black Women and Feminism* (Boston: South End Press, 1981), 15–51.

5. Bennett, *Shaping of Black America*, 74–5.

6. Allen, *Invention*, vol. II, 241.

7. Brown, *Good Wives*, pays particular attention to control of women's bodies and status in producing slavery and race (see especially 181, 129–133, 116); also see Allen, *Invention*, vol. II, 128–35, 146–7, 177–88; Bennett, *Shaping of Black America*, 75.

8. For this section see Bennett, *Shaping of Black America*, 72; Edmund Morgan, *American Slavery, American Freedom: The Ordeal of Colonial Virginia* (New York: W. W. Norton and Co, 1975), 311–3; Allen, *Invention*, vol. II, 249–53.

9. Bennett, *Shaping of Black America*, 73–4.

10. The first quote is from Smedley, *Race in North America*, 224; the second is from David Roediger, *The Wages of Whiteness: Race and the Making of the American Working Class* (New York: Verso, 1991), 6.

11. Allen, *Invention*, vol. II, 162, 248–53 emphasizes that elites invented white supremacy to protect their own interests, although working-class Whites did much of the "dirty work" of oppression.

12. Morgan, *American Slavery*, 312–3. On white privileges see Takaki, *Different Mirror*, 67–8; Allen, *Invention*, vol. II, 250–3; Brown, *Good Wives*, 180–3.

13. The quote is from Allen, *Invention*, vol. II, 256, citing a contemporary traveler.

14. Howard Zinn, *A People's History of the United States* (New York: HarperCollins, 1995, 2nd ed.), 58.

15. Smedley, *Race in North America*, 174–5.

16. Takaki, *Different Mirror*, 50, 68–9. See Theodore Allen, *The Invention of the White Race*, vol. I, *Racial Oppression and Social Control* (New York: Verso, 1994), 69, and Allen, *Invention of the White Race*, vol. II, 13, for analysis of an "intermediate buffer social control stratum." See Thomas Patterson and Frank Spencer, "Racial Hierarchies and Buffer Races," *Transforming Anthropology*, vol. 5, no. 1&2 (1994), 20–7, on the creation of "buffer races" to perform this function.

17. Fredrika Johanna Teute, "Land, Liberty, and Labor in the Post-Revolutionary Era: Kentucky as the Promised Land" (Ph.D. diss., Johns Hopkins University, 1988), 172–4. For details of early Kentucky settlement see Craig Thompson Friend, ed., *The Buzzel about Kentuck: Settling the Promised Land* (Lexington: University of Kentucky Press, 1999); Otis Rice, *Frontier Kentucky* (Lexington: University Press of Kentucky, 1975).

18. Quoted in Teute, "Land, Liberty, and Labor," 176; also see 142–3.

19. Richard Slotkin, *The Fatal Environment: The Myth of the Frontier in the Age of Industrialization 1800–1890* (New York: HarperCollins 1994 [1985]), 66–7.

20. On land policy and migration see Teute, "Land, Liberty, and Labor," 60, 185–91, 384–6; Stephen Aron, "Pioneers and Profiteers: Land Speculation and the Homestead Ethic in Frontier Kentucky," *The Western Historical Quarterly*, vol. 23 (1992), 179–98; Daniel Smith, " 'This Idea in Heaven': Image and Reality on the Kentucky

Frontier," in Friend, *The Buzzel about Kentuck*, 77–98; Wilma Dunaway, *The First American Frontier* (Chapel Hill: University of North Carolina Press, 1996), 66–70.

21. C. G. Calloway, "'We Have Always Been the Frontier': The American Revolution in Shawnee Country," *American Indian Quarterly*, vol. 16, no.1 (1992), 39–53; Grace Steele Woodward, *The Cherokees* (Norman: University of Oklahoma Press, 1963), 88–116.

22. Dunaway, *First American Frontier*, 43.

23. Woodward, *Cherokees*, 40, for "petticoat" reference. See Theda Perdue, *Cherokee Women: Gender and Culture Change* (Lincoln: University of Nebraska Press, 1998), for the effect of these policies.

24. Takaki, *Different Mirror*, 47–50.

25. Theda Perdue, *Slavery and the Evolution of Cherokee Society, 1540–1866* (Knoxville: University of Tennessee Press, 1979).

26. Smith, " 'This Idea in Heaven', " 83; Daniel McClure, Jr., *Two Centuries in North County Seat and North County, Kentucky 1776–1976* (North County Seat: North County Historical Society, 1979), 7–9.

27. On the reality of upward mobility see Teute, "Land, Liberty, and Labor," 389.

28. Teute, "Land," 189–94; Dunaway, *First American Frontier*, 68.

29. Dunaway, *First American Frontier*, 52; Bennett, *Shaping of Black America*, 121.

30. Bennett, *Shaping of Black America*, 89–90.

31. Brown, *Good Wives*, 58.

32. Teute, "Land," 192, 161, 237; for further analysis see Dunaway, *First American Frontier*, 52–6; Aron, "Pioneers and Profiteers."

33. Teute, "Land," 146–7, 153.

34. Teute, "Land," 29–36.

35. The description of early settlement in this section depends on McClure, *Two Centuries*; Samuel Haycraft, *A History of North County Seat, Kentucky and Its Surroundings* (North County Seat: North County Historical Society, 1960 [1869]); U.S. Census Office, *Compendium of the Eleventh Census: 1890, Part I, Population* (Washington, D.C.: Government Printing Office, 1892), Table 2, "Aggregate Population by Counties: 1790–1890"; *"Second Census" of Kentucky, 1800*, G. Glenn Clift, compiler (Baltimore: Genealogical Publishing Co, 1970); U.S. Census Office, *Population Schedules of the Fourth Census of the United States, 1820*, manuscript county schedules on microfilm (National Archives, 1959); U.S. Census Office *Census for 1820* (Washington, D.C.: Gales and Seaton, 1821; reprinted, New York: Norman Ross Publishing, 1990). Kentucky's fort system is described in Nancy O'Malley, "Frontier Defenses and Pioneer Strategies in the Historic Settlement Era," in Friend, *The Buzzel about Kentuck*, 57–75.

36. Teute, "Land," 63, 194; Dunaway, *First American Frontier*, 68–70.

37. On Henderson see Rice, *Frontier Kentucky*, 80; Smith, " 'This Idea in Heaven,' " 81; Aron, "Pioneers and Profiteers."

38. Teute, "Land," 59; Aron, "Pioneers and Profiteers," 189.

39. Teute, "Land," 340–1.

40. Teute, "Land," 46, 389.

41. Teute's dissertation, "Land, Liberty, and Labor," is centered around proving this point. See particularly 109–34, 368–90.

3 Life in Black and White

1. See Audrey Smedley, *Race in North America: Origin and Evolution of a Worldview* (Boulder: Westview Press, 1993), 172, 184. Smedley traces the racialization of

human physical variation. Lee Baker, *From Savage to Negro: Anthropology and the Construction of Race, 1864–1954* (Berkeley: University of California Press, 1998), documents anthropology's role in the process. For an overview of the scholarship on race and ethnicity see Faye Harrison, "The Persistent Power of 'Race' in the Cultural and Political Economy of Racism," *Annual Review of Anthropology*, vol. 24 (1995), 47–74; papers collected in Faye Harrison , ed., "Contemporary Issues Forum: Race and Racism," *American Anthropologist*, vol. 100, no. 3 (1998); Brackette Williams, "A Class Act: Anthropology and the Race to Nation across Ethnic Terrain," *Annual Reviews in Anthropology*, vol. 18 (1989), 401–44.

2. Federal Hill information comes from Sarah Smith, *Historic Nelson County: Its Towns and People* (Bardstown, KY: GBA/Delmar, 1983), 463–8; Ida Roberts, *Rising Above It All: A Tribute to the Rowan Slaves of Federal Hill* (Louisville: Harmony House Publishers, 1994), which also includes a copy of John Rowan's will, 17–31; Randall Capps, *The Rowan Story: From Federal Hill to My Old Kentucky Home* (Cincinnati: The Creative Company, 1976); a 1988 interview with the director of the shrine, tours in 1988 and 1999, a pamphlet for visitors, and from Rowan entries in U.S. Census Office, *Population Schedules for Nelson County, 1810, 1820, 1830, 1840,* hand-transcriptions of schedules, on file at Nelson County Library, KY. There is disagreement about the size of the plantation. In 1833 a cholera epidemic killed 23 slaves, and by 1840 the Rowans had only 8 slaves.

3. On Kentucky antebellum agriculture see U.S. Census Office, *Agriculture of the United States in 1860* (Washington, D.C.: Government Printing Office, 1864; reprinted, New York: Norman Ross Publishing, 1990), which also contains 1850 state comparisons; *Seventh Census of the United States, 1850,* (Washington, D.C.: Robert Armstrong, Public Printer, 1853; reprinted, New York: Norman Ross Publishing, 1990); Lowell Harrison and James Klotter, *A New History of Kentucky* (Lexington: University Press of Kentucky, 1997), 134–8; Thomas Clark, "The Antebellum Hemp Trade of Kentucky with the Cotton Belt," *Register of the Kentucky Historical Society*, vol. 27 (1929), 538–4; James Hopkins, *A History of the Hemp Industry in Kentucky* (Lexington: University Press of Kentucky, 1998 [1951]), 68. On tobacco see William Axton, *Tobacco and Kentucky* (Lexington: University Press of Kentucky, 1975).

4. For statistics on production in 1850 and 1860 see U.S. Census Office, *Agriculture of the United States in 1860; Seventh Census of the United States, 1850.*

5. Virginia Davis, *A Glimpse of the Past: A Brief History of South County from Settlement to 1930* (printed with aid of a Kentucky Humanities Council Grant, 1994), 75; Paul McClure, *Nearbytown and Its People: A Brief Record of Nearbytown, KY* (North County Seat: North County Historical Society, 1992), 94; Ellis Hartford and James Hartford, *Green River Gravel* (Utica, KY: McDowell Publications, 1983), 205. The few surviving tax records for South County and postbellum residence patterns (Davis, *A Glimpse of The Past*, 119) also indicate that southern South County was more plantation-like.

6. On Southern antebellum land use patterns generally see Stephen DeCanio, *Agriculture in the Postbellum South: The Economics of Production and Supply* (Cambridge: MIT Press, 1974), 220–9; Thomas Clark, *Agrarian Kentucky* (Lexington: University Press of Kentucky, 1977), 43–4; Ralph Mann, "Diversity in the Antebellum South: Four Farm Communities in Tazewell County, Virginia," in Mary Beth Pudup, Dwight Billings, and Altina Waller, eds., *Appalachia in the Making: The Mountain South in the Nineteenth Century* (Chapel Hill: University of North Carolina Press, 1995), 132–62. On frontier land use generally see Jeremy Atack and Fred Bateman, "Was There Ever an 'Agrarian Democracy' in America? The American Middle West in 1860," in Frederik Carstensen, Morton Rothstein, and Joseph Swanson, eds.,

Outstanding in His Field: Perspectives on American Agriculture in Honor of Wayne D. Rasmussen (Ames: Iowa State University Press, 1993), 85.

7. John Keller, *Power in America: The Southern Question and the Control of Labor* (Chicago: Vanguard Books, 1983); Wilma Dunaway, *The First American Frontier* (Chapel Hill: University of North Carolina Press,1996); Theodore Allen, *The Invention of the White Race*, vol. I, *Racial Oppression and Social Control* (New York: Verso, 1994), 161; most authors assume that colonial relationships are relevant to understanding the South.

8. Lerone Bennett, *The Shaping of Black America* (New York: Penguin Books 1993 [1975]), 74; Smedley, *Race in North America*, 195, 219; on the presence of slavery in the North see Michael Blakey, "The New York African Burial Ground Project: An Examination of Enslaved Lives, A Construction of Ancestral Ties," *Transforming Anthropology*, vol. 7, no. 1 (1998), 53–8; Peter Kolchin, *Unfree Labor: American Slavery and Russian Serfdom* (Cambridge: Harvard University Press, 1987), 20–6.

9. Sidney Mintz, *Sweetness and Power: The Place of Sugar in Modern History* (New York: Penguin Books, 1985), 184.

10. Dunaway, *First American Frontier*, 141; Clark, "The Antebellum Hemp Trade."

11. For media support, see Frank Mathias, "Slavery, the Solvent of Kentucky Politics," *Register of the Kentucky Historical Society*, vol. 70 (1972), 3. For elite control of local government see Robert Ireland, "Aristocrats All: The Politics of County Governments in Antebellum Kentucky," *Review of Politics*, vol. 32 (1970), 365–83; Mary Beth Pudup, "Social Class and Economic Development in Southeast Kentucky, 1820–1880," in Robert Mitchell, ed., *Appalachian Frontiers: Settlement, Society, and Development in the Preindustrial Era* (Lexington: University Press of Kentucky,1991), 235–60; Fredrika Johanna Teute, "Land, Liberty, and Labor in the Post-Revolutionary Era: Kentucky as the Promised Land" (Ph.D. diss., Johns Hopkins University, 1988), 80–94.

12. Nell Irvin Painter, "Soul Murder and Slavery: Toward a Fully Loaded Cost Accounting," in Linda Kerber, Alice Kessler-Harris, and Kathryn Kish Sklar, eds., *US History as Women's History: New Feminist Essays* (Chapel Hill: University of North Carolina Press, 1995), 143; this section depends heavily on her work. See also bell hooks, *Ain't I a Woman: Black Women and Feminism* (Boston: South End Press, 1981); Helen Irvin, *Women in Kentucky* (Lexington: University Press of Kentucky, 1979), 33–4; Alice Abel Kemp, *Women's Work: Degraded and Devalued* (Englewood Cliffs: Prentice Hall, 1994), 146. For discussion of the role of the state in constructing marriage see Nancy Cott, "Giving Character to Our Whole Civil Polity: Marriage and the Public Order in the Late Nineteenth Century," in Linda Kerber, *U.S. History as Women's History*, 107–21.

13. Kemp, *Women's Work*, 145; Mathias, "Slavery, the Solvent of Kentucky Politics," 4; Clark, *Agrarian Kentucky*, 125–6; Michael Tadman, *Speculators and Slaves: Masters, Traders, and Slaves in the Old South* (Madison: University of Wisconsin Press,1996), 121ff., table 2.1, for import/export statistics.

14. James Cobb, *Industrialization, 1877–1984* (Lexington: University Press of Kentucky, 1984), 7.

15. David Corbin, *Life, Work, and Rebellion in the Coal Fields: The Southern West Virginia Miners 1880–1922* (Urbana: University of Illinois Press, 1981), 34; Kolchin, *Unfree Labor*, 136.

16. Cobb, *Industrialization*, 8-9; Marion Lucas, *A History of Blacks in Kentucky*, vol. II, *From Slavery to Segregation, 1760–1891* (Frankfort: Kentucky Historical Society, 1992), 101ff.

17. W. E. B. Du Bois, *Black Reconstruction in America* (New York: Russell & Russell, 1963 [1935]), 26, 32–3.

18. Clark, *Agrarian Kentucky*, 125; also see Teute, "Land, Liberty, and Labor," 149–55.

19. This section depends on Smedley, *Race in North America*, for example, 175–6; Stephanie McCurry, "The Politics of Yeoman Households in South Carolina," in Catherine Clinton and Nina Silber, eds., *Divided Houses: Gender and the Civil War* (New York: Oxford University Press, 1992), 22–8; Steven Hahn, "The Yeomanry of the Nonplantation South: Upper Piedmont Georgia, 1850–1860," in Orville Burton and Robert McMath, eds., *Class, Conflict and Consensus: Antebellum Southern Community Studies* (Westport, CN: Greenwood Press, 1982), 29–56; Kathleen Brown, *Good Wives, Nasty Wenches, and Anxious Patriarchs: Gender, Race, and Power in Colonial Virginia* (Chapel Hill: University of North Carolina Press, 1996), 277–82, 298–318, particularly 306.

20. On landownership and inequality in antebellum Kentucky see in particular Teute, "Land, Liberty, and Labor," 80–94, 272–9; Dwight Billings and Kathleen Blee, "Agriculture and Poverty in the Kentucky Mountains: Beech Creek, 1850–1910," in Pudup, et al., *Appalachia in the Making*, 237–8; Dunaway, *The First American Frontier*; Pudup, "Social Class and Economic Development in Southeast Kentucky, 1820–1880," in Mitchell, *Appalachia Frontier*.

21. The following sections on early tenant farming depend on Teute, "Land, Liberty, and Labor," 194ff., 313–42; Dunaway, *First American Frontier*, 69–70, 87–121.

22. Martin Primack, "Land Clearing under Nineteenth-Century Techniques: Some Preliminary Calculations," *Journal of Economic History*, vol. 22 (1962), 484.

23. Teute, "Land," 390.

24. On early hopes of commercial wealth see Robert Mitchell, *Commercialism and Frontier: Perspectives on the Early Shenandoah Valley* (Charlottesville: University Press of Virginia, 1977), 3; Dunaway, *The First American Frontier*, 123–36; Paul Salstrom, "Newer Appalachia as One of America's Last Frontiers," in Pudup, et al., *Appalachia*, 82; Elizabeth Perkins, "The Consumption Frontier: Household Consumption in Early Kentucky," *Journal of American History*, vol. 78 (Sept. 1991), 486–510.

25. The following description is based on Hahn, "The Yeomanry of the Nonplantation South"; McCurry, "The Politics of Yeoman Households in South Carolina"; Jacqueline Jones, *The Dispossessed: America's Underclasses from the Civil War to the Present* (New York: Basic Books, 1992), 55; Altina Waller, *Feud: Hatfields, McCoys, and Social Change in Appalachia, 1860–1900* (Chapel Hill: University of North Carolina Press, 1988), 22–3; Teute, "Land, Liberty, and Labor"; Billings and Blee, "Agriculture and Poverty in the Kentucky Mountains"; Clark, *Agrarian Kentucky*, 42–63; Gavin Wright, *The Political Economy of the Cotton South: Households, Markets, and Wealth in the Nineteenth Century* (New York: W. W. Norton and Co., 1978), 43–74; *Seventh Census of the United States, 1850*; U.S. Census Office, *Agriculture of the United States in 1860*. See also surviving newspapers—in South County these are spotty, as are other records, because the courthouse burned in 1928. Note that these counties display a less commercial pattern than that documented by Dunaway for Appalachia in *The First American Frontier*.

26. On Knob Creek see Albert Beveridge, *Abraham Lincoln*, vol. 1 (Boston: Houghton Mifflin, 1928), 13.

27. David Mauer, *Kentucky Moonshine* (Lexington: University Press of Kentucky, 1974), 16–9; Mary K. Tachau, "The Whiskey Rebellion in Kentucky: A Forgotten Episode of Civil Disobedience," *Journal of the Early Republic*, vol. 2 (Fall 1982), 239–59; for North County see Samuel Haycraft, *A History of North County Seat, Kentucky and Its Surroundings* (North County Seat: North County Historical Society, 1960 [1869]), 130; Daniel McClure, Jr., *Two Centuries in North County Seat and North County, Kentucky 1776–1976* (North County Seat: North County Historical Society,1979), 82–5; Beveridge, *Lincoln*, 35.

28. Haycraft, *History of North County Seat*, 18, 35, 100–1; Clark, *Agrarian Kentucky*, 24–36.

29. Beveridge, *Lincoln*, 27; David Donald, *Lincoln* (New York: Simon & Schuster, 1995), 23.

30. Dunaway, *First American Frontier*, 115–7.
31. There are major disagreements on the issue of gender relations in subsistence, diversified subsistence, and commercial farming families; many authors do not clearly distinguish between these types, adding more confusion. There does seem to be significant evidence that equality decreases in commercial families. For various time periods and perspectives see Helen Lewis, Sue Kobak, and Linda Johnson, "Family, Religion and Colonialism in Central Appalachia, or: Bury My Rifle at Big Stone Gap," in Jim Axelrod, ed., *Grown' Up Country* (Clintwood, VA: Resource and Information Center, Council of the Southern Mountains, 1973), 131–53; Waller, *Feud*, 58; Dunaway, *First American Frontier*, 117; Joan Jensen, "Cloth, Butter, and Boarders: Women's Household Production for the Market," *Review of Radical Political Economics*, vol. 12, no. 2 (1980), 14–24; Leith Mullings, "Uneven Development: Class, Race, and Gender in the United States before 1900," in Eleanor Leacock and Helen Safa, eds., *Women's Work: Development and the Division of Labor by Gender* (South Hadley, Mass: Bergin and Garvey, 1986), 48; McCurry, "The Politics of Yeoman Households in South Carolina"; Kemp, *Women's Work*, 142, 150–1; Jeanette Keith, *Country People in the New South: Tennessee's Upper Cumberland* (Chapel Hill: University of North Carolina Press, 1995), 27; Allen Tullos, *Habits of Industry: White Culture and the Transformation of the Carolina Piedmont* (Chapel Hill: University of North Carolina Press, 1989), 75–7; Mary Anglin, "Lives on the Margin: Rediscovering the Women of Antebellum Western North Carolina," in Pudup, et al., *Appalachia in the Making*, 185–209; Suzanne Hall, "Working in the Black Patch: Tobacco Farming Traditions," *Register of the Kentucky Historical Society*, vol. 89 (1991), 266–86. For an English comparison see Jane Humphries, "Enclosures, Common Rights, and Women: The Proletarianization of Families in the Late Eighteenth and Early Nineteenth Centuries," *Journal of Economic History*, vol. 50 (1990), 17–43.
32. Haycraft, *History of North County Seat*, 111–2; Perkins, "The Consumption Frontier."
33. Nancy Bonvillain, *Women and Men: Cultural Constructs of Gender*, 2nd ed. (Upper Saddle River, NJ: Prentice Hall, 1998), 91–3.
34. Dunaway, *First American Frontier*, 117–9.
35. For selling oneself piecemeal see Noel Ignatiev, *How the Irish Became White* (New York: Routledge, 1995), 132.
36. O. M. Mather, "Aetna Furnace, South County, KY," *Register of the Kentucky Historical Society*, vol. 39, no. 127 (1941), 95–105; J. Winston Coleman, "Old Kentucky Iron Furnaces," *The Filson Club History Quarterly*, vol. 31(1957), 227–42.
37. Dunaway, *The First American Frontier*, 111–4.
38. David Roediger, *The Wages of Whiteness: Race and the Making of the American Working Class* (New York: Verso, 1991), 50.
39. Roediger Wages, 65–87.
40. Kemp, *Women's Work*, 141, 149–54.
41. Edward Royce, *The Origins of Southern Sharecropping* (Philadelphia: Temple University Press, 1993), 122.
42. Kemp, *Women's Work*, 153.
43. or Irish conditions in United States and Ireland see Allen, *Invention of the White Race*, vol. I; Ignatiev, *How the Irish Became White*; Roediger, *The Wages of Whiteness*, 133–156.
44. Information for this section comes from Beveridge, *Lincoln*, 1–37; Donald, *Lincoln*, 9–32; McClure, *Two Centuries*, 33, 81–103.
45. Otis Rice, *Frontier Kentucky* (Lexington: University Press of Kentucky, 1975), 37–110, describes the violence that accompanied invasion.
46. Gerald Mullin, *Flight and Rebellion: Slave Resistance in Eighteenth-Century Virginia* (New York: Oxford University Press, 1972), 83ff., 160–1.
47. Coleman, "Old Kentucky Iron Furnaces."

48. William Pusey, "Grahamton and the Early Textile Mills of Kentucky," *The Filson Club History Quarterly*, vol. 5, no. 3 (1931), 131–2.

49. Beveridge, *Lincoln*, 20; Haycraft, *History of North County Seat*, 27, 63–4; Teute, "Land, Liberty, and Labor," 286, refers to frontier counties and extensive lawlessness in the 1790s.

50. Beveridge, *Lincoln*, 13–14.

51 Teute, "Land," 262.

52. Quotation is cited in Hahn, "The Yeomanry of the Nonplantation South," 46; Jones, *The Dispossessed*, 57.

53. Quotes are from Du Bois, *Black Reconstruction in America*, 27–8, 13; for runaway rates see Howard Zinn, *A People's History of the United States*, 2nd ed. (New York: HarperCollins, 1995), 171; Mathias, "Slavery, the Solvent of Kentucky Politics," 7–8.

54. Teute, "Land," 385; Royce, *The Origins of Southern Sharecropping*, 123.

55. Atack and Bateman, "Was There Ever an 'Agrarian Democracy' in America?" 83.

56. Ignatiev, *How the Irish Became White*, 109.

4 Resisting Trickle-up While Accommodating Whiteness

1. Gerald Mullin, *Flight and Rebellion: Slave Resistance in Eighteenth-Century Virginia* (New York: Oxford University Press, 1972), 125, 161.

2. On this shift and its consequences see Mullin, *Flight and Rebellion*; Theodore Allen, *The Invention of the White Race*, vol. I, *Racial Oppression and Social Control* (New York: Verso, 1994), 160–2; Gavin Wright, *The Political Economy of the Cotton South: Households, Markets, and Wealth in the Nineteenth Century* (New York: W.W. Norton and Co, 1978), 164–80.

3. On local transportation see Samuel Haycraft, *A History of North County Seat, Kentucky, and Its Surroundings* (North County Seat: North County Historical Society, 1960 [1869]), 98.

4. Allen, *Invention*, vol. I, 160; Mullin, *Flight and Rebellion*, 161.

5. Mullin, *Flight and Rebellion*, ix, 128.

6. Mullin, *Flight*, 40–63; Howard Zinn, *A People's History of the United States*, 2nd ed. (New York: HarperCollins, 1995), 169–70.

7. Haycraft, *History of North County Seat*, 36.

8. Lerone Bennett, *The Shaping of Black America* (New York: Penguin Books, 1993 [1975]), 150. On slave revolts and resistance for the following section see Peter Kolchin, *Unfree Labor: American Slavery and Russian Serfdom* (Cambridge: Harvard University Press, 1987), 155–60; Zinn, *People's History*, 169–70; Audrey Smedley, *Race in North America: Origin and Evolution of a Worldview* (Boulder: Westview Press, 1993), 215.

9. Smedley, *Race*, 231.

10. Anthony Bimba, *The History of the American Working Class* (New York: International Publishers, 1927), 66–80.

11. The rest of this section draws largely on Zinn, *People's History*, 206–28; Bimba, *History of the American Working Class*, 80–114; Rosalyn Baxandall, Linda Gordon, and Susan Reverby, *America's Working Women: A Documentary History—1600 to the Present* (New York. Vintage Books, 1976), 57–68; and Albert Fried, ed., *Except to Walk Free: Documents and Notes in the History of American Labor* (New York: Anchor Press, 1974), 15–71. For unionization in Kentucky see *Labor History in Kentucky: A Teaching Supplement* (Kentucky Department of Education Labor, 1986), II, 17–8.

12. Zinn, *People's History*, 206, 220.

13. Jacqueline Jones, *The Dispossessed: America's Underclasses from the Civil War to the Present* (New York: Basic Books, 1992), 56.

14. Spencer Albright, "Electoral Qualifications," *Encyclopedia Americana*, vol. 10 (New York: Americana Corporation, 1956), 75–6.
15. Bimba, *History*, 78–80; Zinn, *People's History*, 234–5.
16. Zinn, *People's History*, 214.
17. *Labor History*, II, 17, 23–4; also see James Cobb, *Industrialization and Southern Society, 1877–1984* (Lexington: University Press of Kentucky, 1984), 9.
18. U.S. Census Office, *Manufactures of the United States in 1860* (Washington, D.C.: Government Printing Office, 1865). See Wilma Dunaway, *The First American Frontier* (Chapel Hill: University of North Carolina Press,1996), 191–4, on the Appalachian situation.
19. Charles Dew, *Bond of Iron: Master and Slave at Buffalo Forge* (New York: W.W. Norton, 1994).
20. Jones, *The Dispossessed*, 57; Steven Hahn, "The Yeomanry of the Nonplantation South: Upper Piedmont Georgia, 1850–1860," in Orville Burton and Robert McMath, eds., *Class, Conflict and Consensus: Antebellum Southern Community Studies* (Westport, CN: Greenwood Press, 1982).
21. W. E. B. Du Bois, *Black Reconstruction in America* (New York: Russell & Russell, 1963 [1935]), 700.
22. See David Roediger, *The Wages of Whiteness: Race and the Making of the American Working Class* (New York: Verso, 1991), 13–4, 65–87, for a discussion of white attitudes toward "wage slavery" and "white slavery."
23. For discussion of elite manipulation of attitudes see particularly Alexander Saxton, *The Rise and Fall of the White Republic: Class Politics and Mass Culture in Nineteenth-Century America* (New York: Verso, 1990); Smedley, *Race in North America*; Allen, *Invention of the White Race*, vol. I, 163–5.
24. Allen, *Invention*, vol. I, 192–9, critiques the common assumption that the focus on "job competition" was natural as opposed to manipulated by elites.
25. Noel Ignatiev, *How the Irish Became White* (New York: Routledge, 1995), 112, 115; Allen, *Invention*, vol. I, 195. On "Marketplace Man" see Michael Kimmel, "Masculinity as Homophobia: Fear, Shame, and Silence in the Construction of Gender Identity," in Harry Brod and Michael Kaufman, eds., *Theorizing Masculinities* (Thousand Oaks: Sage Publications, 1994), 123; Jonathan Edmonds, " 'Meat vs. Rice': Euro-American Labor and the Feminization of the Chinese American Working Class" (term paper, Seminar on Chinese American Labor, Oberlin College, 1997).
26. On independence and labor as a free man's own property see Lacy Ford, "Frontier Democracy: The Turner Thesis Revisited," *Journal of the Early Republic*, vol. 13 (1993), 158–9; McCurry, "The Politics of Yeoman Households in South Carolina"; Smedley, *Race in North America*, 47–8; Hahn, "The Yeomanry of the Nonplantation South," 33.
27. For issues raised in this section see Karen Brodkin, *How Jews Became White Folks, and What That Says about Race in America* (New Brunswick: Rutgers University Press, 1998), 77–102; Julie Matthaei, *An Economic History of Women in America: Women's Work, the Sexual Division of Labor, and the Development of Capitalism* (New York: Schocken Books, 1982), 124–40; Alice Abel Kemp, *Women's Work: Degraded and Devalued* (Englewood Cliffs: Prentice Hall, 1994), 149–59.
28. Leith Mullings, "Uneven Development: Class, Race, and Gender in the United States before 1900," in Eleanor Leacock and Helen Safa, eds., *Women's Work: Development and the Division of Labor by Gender* (South Hadley, MA: Bergin and Garvey, 1986), 50–1.
29. Du Bois, *Black Reconstruction*, 80.
30. Ignatiev, *How the Irish Became White*, 117, 109; more generally see Roediger, *The Wages of Whiteness*, 144–56.
31. Ignatiev, *How the Irish Became White*, 129–30.

32. Ignatiev, *How the Irish*, 132.
33. George Yater, *Two Hundred Years at the Falls of the Ohio: A History of Louisville and Jefferson County* (Louisville: The Heritage Foundation, 1979), 66–71; Harrison and Klotter, *A New History of Kentucky* (Lexington: University of Kentucky Press, 1997), 123; Germans were a secondary focus of this riot.
34. Ignatiev, *How the Irish*, 44–51; Roediger, *Wages of Whiteness*, 134.
35. Allen, *Invention*, vol. I, 178.
36. For the role of the Irish leaders see Roediger, *Wages of Whiteness*, 109, 136; Allen, *Invention*, vol. I, 198–99.
37. Smedley, *Race in North America*, 218–9; Allen, *Invention*, vol. I, 195.
38. Allen, *Invention*, vol. I, 169–99.
39. Ignatiev, *How the Irish*, 163.
40. On shedding blood, citizenship, and manhood see Brackette Williams, "A Class Act: Anthropology and the Race to Nation across Ethnic Terrain," *Annual Reviews in Anthropology*, vol. 18 (1989), 436–9; Jim Cullen, " 'I's a Man Now': Gender and African American Men," in Catherine Clinton and Nina Silber, eds., *Divided Houses*, 76–91; Leeann Whites, "The Civil War as a Crisis in Gender," in Clinton and Silber, *Divided Houses: Gender and the Civil War* (New York: Oxford University Press, 1992), 12; Ira Berlin, "Fighting on Two Fronts: War and the Struggle for Racial Equality in Two Centuries," in Gabor S. Boritt, ed., *War Comes Again: Comparative Vistas on the Civil War and World War II* (New York: Oxford University Press, 1995), 125–41; Du Bois, *Black Reconstruction*, 104.
41. The following discussion of the Civil War follows the approach of Du Bois, *Black Reconstruction*, 55–127.
42. For discussion of Northern attitudes see Ignatiev, *How the Irish Became White*, 164–5; Allen, *Invention of the White Race*, vol. I, 161–2; John Keller, *Power in America: The Southern Question and the Control of Labor* (Chicago: Vanguard Books, 1983), 55; Bennett, *The Shaping of Black America*, 178–94.
43. For poorer Southern Whites' attitudes see Stephanie McCurry, "The Politics of Yeoman Households in South Carolina," in Clinton and Silber, *Divided Houses*, 36–7; Hahn, "The Yeomanry of the Nonplantation South," 45–7; Altina Waller, *Feud: Hatfields, McCoys, and Social Change in Appalachia, 1860–1900* (Chapel Hill: University of North Carolina Press, 1988), 30–1; Jones, *The Dispossessed*, 57. Even most abolitionists had no interest in equality between Blacks and Whites (Smedley, *Race in North America*, 210ff.).
44. Harrison and Klotter, *New History of Kentucky*, 193.
45. Yater, *Two Hundred Years at the Falls of the Ohio*, 70, 83.
46. James Copeland, "Where Were the Kentucky Unionists and Secessionists?" *Register of the Kentucky Historical Society*, vol. 71 (Oct. 1973), 344–63.
47. For the military situation see James McDonough, *War in Kentucky: From Shiloh to Perryville* (Knoxville: University of Tennessee Press, 1994), 319. For Louisville's role in transportation see Yater, *Two Hundred Years at the Falls of the Ohio*, 95; Keller, *Power in America*, 28.
48. Du Bois, *Black Reconstruction*, 55–83. Also see Bennett, *The Shaping of Black America*, 178–83. One-tenth of Union and one-fourth of all Confederate soldiers died (D'Ann Campbell and Richard Jensen, "Gendering Two Wars," in Gabor S. Boritt, ed., *War Comes Again*, 120).
49. Jeremy Atack and Fred Bateman, "Was There Ever an 'Agrarian Democracy' in America? The American Middle West in 1860," in Frederik Carstensen, Morton Rothstein, and Joseph Swanson, eds., *Outstanding in His Field: Perspectives on American Agriculture in Honor of Wayne D. Rasmussen* (Ames: Iowa State University Press, 1993), 83; Zinn, *People's History*, 233; Allen, *Invention of the White Race*, vol. I, 198.

50. See Du Bois, *Black Reconstruction,* 55–127; Zinn, *People's History,* 184–9.

51. Du Bois, *Black Reconstruction,* 103–4.

52. On Blacks and military initiation see Reid Mitchell, *The Vacant Chair: The Northern Soldier Leaves Home* (New York: Oxford University Press, 1993), 3–18, 64–8; Cullen, " 'I's a Man Now,' " 84ff.; Whites, "The Civil War as a Crisis in Gender," 12–3.

53. Du Bois, *Black Reconstruction,* 106–14.

54. Cullen, " 'I's a Man Now,' " 81; Jones, *The Dispossessed,* 20; Copeland, "Where Were the Kentucky Unionists and Secessionists?" 345.

55. Jones, *The Dispossessed,* 58–9; Eric Foner, *A Short History of Reconstruction, 1863–1877* (New York: Harper & Row, 1990), 6–7.

56. On riots see Jones, *The Dispossessed*, 61; Drew Faust, "Altars of Sacrifice: Confederate Women and the Narratives of War," in Clinton and Silber, eds., *Divided Houses,* 182, 194–7; Campbell and Jensen, "Gendering Two Wars," 108–9.

57. Cullen, " 'I's a Man Now,' " 88–9.

58. Du Bois, *Black Reconstruction,* 121.

59. Du Bois, *Black Reconstruction,* 121; Richard Beringer, Herman Hattaway, Archer Jones, and William Still, Jr., *Why the South Lost the Civil War* (Athens: University of Georgia Press, 1986), 339–51, 436–8, describes the reluctance of Southern generals to use guerilla tactics, which could lead to Northern defeat, much as the United States suffered in Vietnam. Their overriding fear was guerilla war's inevitable disruption of social controls over poor Whites and Blacks.

5 Forks in the Road

1. Audrey Smedley, *Race in North America: Origin and Evolution of a Worldview* (Boulder: Westview Press, 1993), 255–72, and Lee Baker, *From Savage to Negro: Anthropology and the Construction of Race, 1864–1954* (Berkeley: University of California Press, 1998), 26–53, document the development of this belief.

2. I have adopted this phrase from David Roediger, *The Wages of Whiteness: Race and the Making of the American Working Class* (New York: Verso, 1991), 6.

3. Thaddeus Stevens, "Extracts of Speech in Lancaster, Pa.," *New York Tribune,* Sept. 11, 1865, n.p. For discussion of his proposal see W. E. B. Du Bois, *Black Reconstruction in America* (New York: Russell & Russell, 1963 [1935]), 197–9, 221, 273–6; Stephen DeCanio, *Agriculture in the Postbellum South: The Economics of Production and Supply* (Cambridge, MA: MIT Press, 1974), 236–9.

4. For discussion of these federal wartime experiments see Eric Foner, *A Short History of Reconstruction, 1863–1877* (New York: Harper & Row, 1990), 23–32; Leon Litwack, *Been in the Storm So Long: The Aftermath of Slavery* (New York: Vintage Books, 1980), 399–408; Julie Saville, *The Work of Reconstruction: From Slave to Wage Labor in South Carolina, 1860–1870* (Cambridge, MA: Cambridge University Press, 1994).

5. Edward Royce, *The Origins of Southern Sharecropping* (Philadelphia: Temple University Press, 1993), 97–8, 109; John Strickland, "Traditional Culture and Moral Economy: Social and Economic Change in the South Carolina Low Country, 1865–1910," in Steven Hahn and Jonathan Prude, eds., *The Countryside in the Age of Capitalist Transformation* (Chapel Hill: University of North Carolina Press, 1985), 153; Du Bois, *Black Reconstruction,* 352.

6. For crop choice see Strickland, "Traditional Culture and Moral Economy," 162–6.

7. Foner, *Short History of Reconstruction,* 27.

8. Most authors attribute the condition of the South to its colonial situation, but disagree on details. For examples see Lerone Bennett, *The Shaping of Black America* (New

York: Penguin Books, 1993 [1975]), 208–29; John Keller, *Power in America: The Southern Question and the Control of Labor* (Chicago: Vanguard Books, 1983), 1–70; Steven Hahn, "Class and State in Post-Emancipation Societies: Southern Planters in Comparative Perspective," *The American Historical Review*, vol. 95, no. 1 (1990), 92–8; Jacqueline Jones, *The Dispossessed: America's Underclasses from the Civil War to the Present* (New York: Basic Books, 1992), 130; Lowell Harrison and James Klotter, *A New History of Kentucky* (Lexington: University Press of Kentucky, 1997), 302; Paul Salstrom, "Newer Appalachia as One of America's Last Frontiers," in Mary Beth Pudup, Dwight Billings, and Altina Waller, eds., *Appalachia in the Making: The Mountain South in the Nineteenth Century* (Chapel Hill: University of North Carolina Press, 1995), 76–102; Foner, *Short History*, 120.

9. Foner, *Short History*, 122.

10. On slavery in prison see Lennox Hinds, *Illusions of Justice: Human Rights Violations in the United States* (Iowa City: University of Iowa Press, 1978), 328.

11. Du Bois, *Black Reconstruction*, 273–4.

12. Litwack, *Been in the Storm So Long*, 407.

13. Du Bois, *Black Reconstruction*, 276.

14. From an illustration of a Democratic broadside following p. 48 in Foner, *Short History*; also see Du Bois, *Black Reconstruction*, 225; Steven Hahn, "The 'Unmaking' of the Southern Yeomanry: The Transformation of the Georgia Upcountry, 1860-1890," in Hahn and Prude, *The Countryside in the Age of Capitalist Transformation*, 185–6.

15. See Frances Piven and Richard Cloward, *Regulating the Poor: The Functions of Public Welfare*, 2nd ed. (New York: Vintage, 1993), 3–41, 343–99, for a summary of their analysis of welfare.

16. Harrison and Klotter, *New History of Kentucky*, 239; Du Bois, *Black Reconstruction*, 568.

17. Robert Ireland, *Little Kingdoms, The Counties of Kentucky, 1850-1891* (Lexington: University Press of Kentucky, 1977), 69–70. For an example of a white sale, see *South County News*, March 2, 1887, 2; for general analysis see Mark Colvin, *Penitentiaries, Reformatories, and Chain Gangs: Social Theory and the History of Punishment in Nineteenth-Century America* (New York: St. Martin's Press, 1997), 233; Jones, *The Dispossessed*, 11–70; for Kentucky see Victor Howard, *Black Liberation in Kentucky: Emancipation and Freedom, 1862-1884* (Lexington: University Press of Kentucky, 1983), 96–101.

18. Gavin Wright, *Old South, New South: Revolutions in the Southern Economy since the Civil War* (New York: Basic Books, 1986), 100–1.

19. Harrison and Klotter, *New History of Kentucky*, 237.

20. Foner, *Short History*, 26.

21. Howard, *Black Liberation in Kentucky*, 102–105; Jones, *Dispossessed*, 50–3.

22. Jones, *The Dispossessed*, 44, 46, 53; Noel Ignatiev, *How the Irish Became White* (New York: Routledge, 1995), 164.

23. Foner, *Short History of Reconstruction* , 38; Leith Mullings, "Uneven Development: Class, Race, and Gender in the United States before 1900," in Eleanor Leacock and Helen Safa, eds., *Women's Work: Development and the Division of Labor by Gender* (South Hadley, MA: Bergin and Garvey, 1986), 53.

24. For effects of the war see Michael Adams, "Retelling the Tale: Wars in Common Memory," in Gabor S. Boritt, ed., *War Comes Again: Comparative Vistas on the Civil War and World War II* (New York: Oxford University Press, 1995), 201–7; Russell Weigley, "The Necessity of Force: The Civil War, World War II, and the American View of War," in Boritt, *War Comes Again*, 226; Jones, *The Dispossessed*, 47, 62–5; Jim Cullen, " 'I's a Man Now': Gender and African American Men," in Catherine Clinton and Nina Silber, eds., *Divided Houses: Gender and the Civil War* (New York: Oxford University Press, 1992), 86; Drew Faust, "Altars of Sacrifice: Confederate

Women and the Narratives of War," in Clinton and Silber, *Divided Houses*, 182; D'Ann Campbell and Richard Jensen, "Gendering Two Wars," in Boritt, *War Comes Again*, 120. Before the Civil War Whites picked only one-tenth of all cotton; by about 1875 Whites picked two-fifths of the cotton crop, mostly as sharecroppers (Jones, *The Dispossessed*, 48).

25. Du Bois, *Black Reconstruction*, 80, 700. Smedley, *Race in North America*, 28, 226, 250ff., demonstrates the increase in the importance of race as a worldview after the Civil War, and points out the complementary roles played by academics, historians, local elites, poor and working class Whites in its development. Baker, *From Savage to Negro*, documents the role of anthropology in this process.

26. Jones, *The Dispossessed*, 127–66.

27. *Rufus v.Commonwealth of Virginia* (1871), quoted in Hinds, *Illusions of Justice*, 333.

28. Colvin, *Penitentiaries, Reformatories, and Chain Gangs*, 233; Bennett, *The Shaping of Black America*, 255.

29. Colvin, *Penitentiaries*, 244; see also Jones, *The Dispossessed*, 148–52.

30. Harrison and Klotter, *New History of Kentucky*, 260–1; see also Colvin, *Penitentiaries*, 246–249.

31. Colvin, *Penitentiaries*, 245; Pem Davidson Buck, "Arbeit Macht Frei: Racism and Bound, Concentrated Labor in U.S. Prisons," *Urban Anthropology*, vol. 23, no. 4 (1994), 331–72.

32. Ireland, *Little Kingdoms*, 64–70; Marion Lucas, *A History of Blacks in Kentucky*, vol. II, *From Slavery to Segregation, 1760–1891* ([Frankfort]:Kentucky Historical Society, 1992), 273.

33. Pete Daniel, *The Shadow of Slavery: Peonage in the South, 1901–1969* (Urbana: University of Illinois Press, 1972); Jones, *The Dispossessed*, 127–66.

34. Steven Hahn, "The Yeomanry of the Nonplantation South: Upper Piedmont Georgia, 1850–1860," in Orville Burton and Robert McMath, eds., *Class, Conflict and Consensus: Antebellum Southern Community Studies* (Westport, CN: Greenwood Press, 1982); Jones, *The Dispossessed*, 44, 68, and 73–126 on sharecropping in general; Wright, *Old South, New South*, 108–15; Michael Schwartz, *Radical Protest and Social Structure: The Southern Farmers' Alliance and Cotton Tenancy, 1880–1890* (New York: Academic Press, 1976), 6–71. On Kentucky tobacco sharecropping see Tracy Campbell, *The Politics of Despair: Power and Resistance in the Tobacco Wars* (Lexington: University Press of Kentucky, 1993), 6–20; Lucas, *History of Blacks in Kentucky*, vol. II, 270–2; John van Willigen and Susan Eastwood, *Tobacco Culture: Farming Kentucky's Burley Belt* (Lexington: University Press of Kentucky, 1998), 25–37.

35. Campbell, *Politics of Despair*, 8.

36. Pete Daniel, *Standing at the Crossroads: Southern Life since 1900* (New York: Hill and Wang, 1986), 84.

37. Daniel, *Standing*, 22–4.

38. Wages from the report on tobacco included in U.S. Census Office, *Report on the Productions of Agriculture as Returned at the Tenth Census, 1880* (Washington, D.C.: Government Printing Office, 1883), 57[651].

39. Thomas Clark, *Agrarian Kentucky* (Lexington: University Press of Kentucky, 1977), 53.

40. George Wright, "By the Book: Legal Executions of Kentucky Blacks," in W. Fitzhugh Brundage, ed., *Under Sentence of Death: Lynching in the South* (Chapel Hill: University of North Carolina Press, 1997), 250–70; Terence Finnegan, "Lynching and Political Power in Mississippi and South Carolina," Brundage, *Under Sentence*, 189–215.

41. On lynching in Kentucky see George Wright, *Racial Violence in Kentucky, 1865–1940: Lynchings, Mob Rule, and "Legal Lynchings"* (Baton Rouge: Louisiana State University Press, 1990); also see Stewart Tolnay and E. M. Beck, *A Festival of Violence: An Analysis*

of Southern Lynchings (Chicago: University of Illinois Press, 1995); Finnegan, "Lynching and Political Power in Mississippi and South Carolina."

42. On mule ownership see Wright, *Old South, New South*, 100.

43. Campbell, *Politics of Despair*, 12, 39; one owner had 260 acres of tobacco; at 5 acres per family that is about 50 families.

44. Jones, *The Dispossessed*, 118; Litwack, *Been in the Storm So Long*, 448; Bennett, *The Shaping of Black America*, 249–50.

45. Daniel, *Shadow of Slavery*, 190.

46. Jones, *The Dispossessed*, 27–8; for examples see Ellis Hartford and James Hartford, *Green River Gravel* (Utica, KY: McDowell Publications, 1983), 205; Howard, *Black Liberation in Kentucky*, 102.

47. Jones, *The Dispossessed*, 77; Litwack, *Been in the Storm So Long*, 429–30.

48. Foner, *Short History of Reconstruction*, 123.

6 Gender, Whiteness, and the Psychological Wage

1. Ellis Hartford and James Hartford, *Green River Gravel* (Utica, KY: McDowell Publications, 1983), 146–169; Paul McClure, *Nearbytown and Its People: A Brief Record of Nearbytown, KY* (North County Seat: North County Historical Society, 1992), 93.

2. *South County News*, February 22, 1934, 1.

3. Derived from U.S. Census Office, *Report on the Statistics of Agriculture in the United States at the Eleventh Census:1890* (Washington. D.C.: Government Printing Office, 1895).

4. *South County Democrat*, January 19, 1882, 3; September 7, 1922, 3.

5. From the report on tobacco included in U.S. Census Office, *Report on the Productions of Agriculture as Returned at the Tenth Census, 1880* (Washington, D.C.: Government Printing Office, 1883), 55[649].

6. Tracy Campbell, *The Politics of Despair: Power and Resistance in the Tobacco Wars* (Lexington: University Press of Kentucky, 1993), 8–13; Steven Hahn, "The 'Unmaking' of the Southern Yeomanry: The Transformation of the Georgia Upcountry, 1860–1890," in Steven Hahn and Jonathan Prude, eds., *The Countryside in the Age of Capitalist Transformation* (Chapel Hill: University of North Carolina Press, 1985), 189ff.

7. *Kentucky Intelligencer*, July 29, 1868, 3. On trade using country produce see Jeanette Keith, *Country People in the New South: Tennessee's Upper Cumberland* (Chapel Hill: University of North Carolina Press, 1995), 89; Suzanne Hall, "Working in the Black Patch: Tobacco Farming Traditions," *Register of the Kentucky Historical Society*, vol. 89 (1991), 281; Hahn, "The 'Unmaking' of the Southern Yeomanry," 193; Gavin Wright, *Old South, New South: Revolutions in the Southern Economy since the Civil War* (New York: Basic Books, 1986), 107–15; Campbell, *Politics of Despair*, 6–20; Susan Strasser, *Satisfaction Guaranteed: The Making of the American Mass Market* (New York: Pantheon Books, 1989), 73; Edward Ayers, *The Promise of the New South: Life After Reconstruction* (New York: Oxford University Press, 1992), 81–103. Some country produce, particularly eggs, was accepted into the 1920s.

8. *South County News*, May 25, 1887, 1; on egalitarian sentiments see also Helen Lewis, Sue Kobak, and Linda Johnson, "Family, Religion and Colonialism in Central Appalachia, or: Bury My Rifle at Big Stone Gap," in Jim Axelrod, ed., *Growin' Up Country* (Clintwood, VA: Resource and Information Center, Council of the Southern Mountains, 1973).

9. Richard Robbins. *Global Problems and the Culture of Capitalism* (Boston, MA: Allyn and Bacon, 1999), 179–207; Jon Bennett, *The Hunger Machine: The Politics of Food* (Cambridge, MA: Polity Press/Basil Blackwell, 1987).

10. From the report on tobacco included in U.S. Census Office, *Report on the Productions of Agriculture as Returned at the Tenth Census, 1880* (Washington, D.C.: Government Printing Office, 1883), 58[652].

11. See Chapter 3, note 31, on the disagreements about the prior degree of equality between men and women in diversified subsistence farming. Hall, "Working in the Black Patch," describes women's lack of autonomy in commercial family farming in western Kentucky.

12. Julie Matthaei, *An Economic History of Women in America: Women's Work, the Sexual Division of Labor, and the Development of Capitalism* (New York: Schocken Books, 1982), 31ff.; Susan Mann, "Slavery, Sharecropping, and Sexual Inequality," *Signs*, vol. 14, no. 4 (1989), 797; Alice Abel Kemp, *Women's Work: Degraded and Devalued* (Englewood Cliffs: Prentice Hall, 1994), 142.

13. Michael Kimmel, "Masculinity as Homophobia: Fear, Shame, and Silence in the Construction of Gender Identity," in Harry Brod and Michael Kaufman, eds., *Theorizing Masculinities* (Thousand Oaks: Sage Publications, 1994), 135–7; Allen Tullos, *Habits of Industry: White Culture and the Transformation of the Carolina Piedmont* (Chapel Hill: University of North Carolina Press, 1989), 57, 78.

14. The following section depends on Eric Foner, *A Short History of Reconstruction, 1863–1877* (New York: Harper & Row, 1990), 52–4; bell hooks, *Ain't I a Woman: Black Women and Feminism* (Boston: South End Press, 1981); Jacqueline Dowd Hall, "'The Mind that Burns in Each Body': Women, Rape, and Racial Violence," in Margaret Andersen and Patricia Hill Collins, eds., *Race, Class, and Gender: An Anthology* (Belmont: Wadsworth, 1995), 434–9; Nancy Cott, "Giving Character to Our Whole Civil Polity: Marriage and the Public Order in the Late Nineteenth Century," in Linda Kerber, Alice Kessler-Harris, and Kathryn Kish Sklar, eds., *US History as Women's History: New Feminist Essays* (Chapel Hill: University of North Carolina Press, 1995); Mann, "Slavery, Sharecropping, and Sexual Inequality"; Victor Howard, *Black Liberation in Kentucky: Emancipation and Freedom, 1862–1884* (Lexington: University Press of Kentucky, 1983), 126–7; Catherine Clinton, "Reconstructing Freedwomen," in Catherine Clinton and Nina Silber, eds., *Divided Houses: Gender and the Civil War* (New York: Oxford University Press, 1992), 306–19; Peter Bagdaglio, *Reconstructing the Household: Families, Sex, and the Law in the Nineteenth Century South* (Chapel Hill: University of North Carolina Press, 1995).

15. hooks, *Ain't I a Woman*, 15–49; Nell Irvin Painter, "Soul Murder and Slavery: Toward a Fully Loaded Cost Accounting," in Kerber, et al., *US History as Women's History*, 125–46.

16. Leith Mullings, "Uneven Development: Class, Race, and Gender in the United States before 1900," in Eleanor Leacock and Helen Safa, eds., *Women's Work: Development and the Division of Labor by Gender,* (South Hadley, MA: Bergin and Garvey, 1986), 54; Hall, " 'The Mind that Burns in Each Body.' "

17. Foner, *Short History*, 39.

18. Cott, "Giving Character to Our Whole Civil Polity," 118.

19. Jacqueline Jones, *The Dispossessed: America's Underclasses from the Civil War to the Present* (New York: Basic Books, 1992), 44, 46; W. E. B. Du Bois, *Black Reconstruction in America* (New York: Russell & Russell, 1963 [1935]), 630–5.

20. Jones, *The Dispossessed*, 127–66, provides a description of working conditions, pay, and the varying racial compositions of jobs in different industries and locations.

21. *South County News*, May 18, 1887, 1.

22. See David Roediger, *The Wages of Whiteness: Race and the Making of the American Working Class* (New York: Verso, 1991) for a thorough analysis, focused on the North, growing out of W. E. B. Du Bois's conception of the psychological wage.

23. *South County News*, October 13, 1886, 1.

7 Jim Crow, Underdevelopment, and the Reinforcement of the Tottering Drainage System

1. Howard Zinn, *A People's History of the United States*, 2nd ed. (New York: HarperCollins, 1995) makes this clear, but see also J. Morgan Kousser, *The Shaping of Southern Politics: Suffrage Restriction and the Establishment of the One-Party South, 1880–1910* (New Haven: Yale University Press, 1974).

2. Pete Daniel, *Standing at the Crossroads: Southern Life since 1900* (New York: Hill and Wang, 1986), 37–8; Kousser, *The Shaping of Southern Politics*, 260–1.

3. Tracy Campbell, *The Politics of Despair: Power and Resistance in the Tobacco Wars* (Lexington: University Press of Kentucky, 1993), 72.

4. Eric Foner, *Short History, 1863–1877* (New York: Harper & Row, 1990), 10. For an analysis of this process see W. E. B. Du Bois, *Black Reconstruction in America* (New York: Russell & Russell, 1963 [1935]), 580–635.

5. Foner , *Short History*, 120.

6. John Keller, *Power in America: The Southern Question and the Control of Labor* (Chicago: Vanguard Books, 1983), 45; Alexander Saxton, *The Rise and Fall of the White Republic: Class Politics and Mass Culture in Nineteenth-Century America* (New York: Verso, 1990), 365; Mary Beth Pudup, "Social Class and Economic Development in Southeast Kentucky, 1820–1880," in Robert Mitchell, ed., *Appalachian Frontiers: Settlement, Society, and Development in the Preindustrial Era* (Lexington: University Press of Kentucky, 1991), 259–60.

7. Gavin Wright, *Old South, New South: Revolutions in the Southern Economy since the Civil War* (New York: Basic Books, 1986), 182–3; Jones, *The Dispossessed: America's Underclasses from the Civil War to the Present* (New York: Basic Books, 1992), 147.

8. Jones, *The Dispossessed*, 106–26.

9. Keller, *Power in America*, 87–8. For analysis of this process in Georgia see David Weiman, "The Economic Emancipation of the Non-Slaveholding Class: Upcountry Farmers in the Georgia Cotton Economy," *Journal of Economic History*, vol. XLV, no. 1 (1985), 71–93.

10. Susan Strasser, *Satisfaction Guaranteed: The Making of the American Mass Market* (New York: Pantheon Books, 1989), 20–5; Zinn, *People's History*, 247–58; see Campbell, *Politics of Despair*, 21–9, for the tobacco industry.

11. Lowell Harrison and James Klotter, *A New History of Kentucky* (Lexington: University Press of Kentucky, 1997), 268–9.

12. On railroads and increased market dependence see Robert Ireland, *Little Kingdoms: The Counties of Kentucky, 1850–1891* (Lexington: University Press of Kentucky, 1977), 101–23; Jeanette Keith, *Country People in the New South: Tennessee's Upper Cumberland* (Chapel Hill: University of North Carolina Press, 1995), 76–86, 103–17; Ronald Lewis, "Railroads, Deforestation, and the Transformation of Agriculture in the West Virginia Back Counties, 1880–1920," in Mary Beth Pudup, Dwight Billings, and Altina Waller, eds., *Appalachia in the Making: The Mountain South in the Nineteenth Century* (Chapel Hill: University of North Carolina Press, 1995), 297–320; Steven Hahn, "The 'Unmaking' of the Southern Yeomanry: The Transformation of the Georgia Upcountry, 1860–1890," in Steven Hahn and Jonathan Prude, eds., *The Countryside in the Age of Capitalist Transformation* (Chapel Hill: University of North Carolina Press, 1985); Alan Banks, "Class Formation in the Southeastern Kentucky Coalfields, 1890–1920," in Pudup, et al., *Appalachia in the Making*, 321–46.

13. Campbell, *Politics of Despair*, 35.

14. Campbell, *Politics*, 35–6; J. Abramowitz, "The Negro in the Populist Movement," *The Journal of Negro History*, vol. 38 (1953), 257–89; Lawrence Goodwyn, *Democratic Promise: the Populist Moment in America* (New York: Oxford University Press, 1976), 294.

15. Julie Jeffrey, "Women in the Southern Farmers' Alliance: A Reconsideration of the Role and Status Of Women in the Late Nineteenth Century South," *Feminist Studies*, vol. 3 (Fall 1975), 72–91.

16. Zinn, *People's History*, 258–89; Harrison and Klotter, *New History of Kentucky*, 257–69.

17. Campbell, *Politics of Despair*, 34–7. For analysis of the Subtreasury Plan see Goodwyn, *Democratic Promise*, 567–9; on the Alliance economic program generally see Michael Schwartz, *Radical Protest and Social Structure: The Southern Farmers' Alliance and Cotton Tenancy, 1880–1890* (New York: Academic Press, 1976).

18. Goodwyn, *Democratic Promise*, 292; William Holmes, "The Demise of the Colored Farmers' Alliance," *Journal of Southern History*, vol. 41, no. 2 (1975), 187–200; on class contradiction in the Alliance see Michael Schwartz, Naomi Rosenthal, and Laura Schwartz, "Leader-Member Conflict in Protest Organizations: The Case of the Southern Farmers' Alliance," *Social Problems*, vol. 29, no. 1 (1981), 22–36.

19. Norman Pollack, *The Humane Economy: Populism, Capitalism, and Democracy* (New Brunswick: Rutgers University Press, 1990), 57–60; Bruce Palmer, *"Man over Money": The Southern Populist Critique of American Capitalism* (Chapel Hill: University of North Carolina Press, 1980).

20. Sheldon Hackney, *Populism to Progressivism in Alabama* (Princeton: Princeton University Press, 1969), 69.

21. Schwartz, *Radical Protest and Social Structure*, 207ff.; James Cobb, *Industrialization and Southern Society, 1877–1984* (Lexington: University Press of Kentucky, 1984), 23–4.

22. For example, *West County Herald*, April 8, 1892; Goodwyn, *Democratic Promise*, 660, #6; these are commonly used tactics all over the world used to derail people's resistance to underdevelopment (see e.g., Pem Davidson Buck, "Colonized Anthropology: Cargo-Cult Discourse," in Faye V. Harrison, ed., *Decolonizing Anthropology* [Washington, D.C.: American Anthropological Association]), 24–41.

23. *West County Herald*, April 18, 1892, June 9, 1892; George Wright, *A History of Blacks in Kentucky*, vol. II: *In Pursuit of Equality, 1890–1980* ([Frankfort]:Kentucky Historical Society, 1992), 94–7; Mark Colvin, *Penitentiaries, Reformatories, and Chain Gangs: Social Theory and the History of Punishment in Nineteenth-Century America* (New York: St. Martin's Press, 1997), 241–3.

24. Audrey Smedley, *Race in North America: Origin and Evolution of a Worldview* (Boulder: Westview Press, 1993), 226; Terence Finnegan, "Lynching and Political Power in Mississippi and South Carolina," in W. Fitzhugh Brundage, ed., *Under Sentence of Death: Lynching in the South* (Chapel Hill: University of North Carolina Press, 1997), 194–5; Abramowitz, "The Negro in the Populist Movement."

25. George Wright, "By the Book: Legal Executions of Kentucky Blacks," in Brundage, *Under Sentence of Death*; *North County Seat News*, March 20, 1891, 4, and November 13, 1891, 4.

26. Kousser, *Shaping of Southern Politics*, 68–72, 246–50. See also Numan Bartley and Hugh Graham, *Southern Politics and the Second Reconstruction* (Baltimore: Johns Hopkins University Press, 1975), 5–20, 109–10; Chandler Davidson, *Biracial Politics: Conflict and Coalition in the Metropolitan South* (Baton Rouge: Louisiana State University Press, 1972), 82.

27. Kousser, *Shaping of Southern Politics*, 63–4; calculated using Kousser's income figures.

28. Kousser, *Shaping*, 28–9, 41–3.

29. Jasper Shannon, *Toward a New Politics in the South* (Knoxville, TN: University of Tennessee Press, 1949), 23, 31. Wright, *A History of Blacks in Kentucky*, vol. II, 46–102, documents violence and black political resistance. A local black union organizer remembers fearing to vote in the '60s in Kentucky, despite the fact that voting was legal.

30. Stewart Tolnay and E. M. Beck, *A Festival of Violence: An Analysis of Southern Lynchings* (Chicago: University of Illinois Press, 1995), 25–8.

248 WORKED TO THE BONE

31. Quoted in Campbell, *Politics of Despair*, 21.
32. See Kousser, *The Shaping of Southern Politics*, on the effects of disfranchisement in diminishing left-leaning politics; Davidson, *Biracial Politics*, 205–7, analyzes a continuing tendency of poor Whites to vote with Blacks when economic issues were emphasized. See also Smedley, *Race in North America*, 270; Lee Baker, *From Savage to Negro: Anthropology and the Construction of Race, 1864–1954* (Berkeley: University of California Press, 1998), 54–80; Davidson, *Biracial Politics*, 159–80.
33. Smedley, *Race in North America*, 228.
34. Wright, *Old South, New South*, 182–94; Jones, *The Dispossessed*, 86, 127–66.
35. Leith Mullings, "Uneven Development: Class, Race, and Gender in the United States before 1900," in Eleanor Leacock and Helen Safa, eds., *Women's Work: Development and the Division of Labor by Gender* (South Hadley, MA: Bergin and Garvey, 1986), 53.

8 Critiquing Capital: The Wannabes

1. Tracy Campbell, *The Politics of Despair. Power and Resistance in the Tobacco Wars* (Lexington: University Press of Kentucky, 1993) argues that the name "Tobacco Wars" should replace the older "Black Patch War." My discussion is based on local newspaper accounts, descriptive accounts, and on what little social structural (rather than descriptive) analysis there is, particularly Campbell's *Politics of Despair*; Pem Davidson Buck, "Racial Representations and Power in the Dependent Development of the United States South," in George C. Bond and Angela Gilliam, eds., *The Social Construction of the Past: Representation as Power* (New York: Routledge, 1994), 29–43; George Wright, *Racial Violence in Kentucky 1865–1940: Lynchings, Mob Rule, and "Legal Lynchings"* (Baton Rouge: Louisiana State University Press, 1990). For the postbellum history of tobacco production see William Axton, *Tobacco and Kentucky* (Lexington: University Press of Kentucky, 1975).
2. Resolution adopted by a farmers' meeting, quoted in Ellis Hartford and James Hartford, *Green River Gravel* (Utica, KY: McDowell Publications, 1983), 220.
3. For Duke's monopolizing tactics see Campbell, *Politics of Despair*, 21–9; Bill Cunningham, *On Bended Knees: The True Story of the Night Rider Tobacco War in Kentucky and Tennessee* (Kuttawa, KY: McClanahan Publishing House, 1983), 13–7.
4. Campbell, *Politics of Despair*, 91.
5. Campbell, *Politics of Despair*, 16–8.
6. Quote is from *South County Democrat*, September 7, 1922, 3.
7. Derived from U.S. Bureau of the Census, *Thirteenth Census of the United States, Supplement for Kentucky: Population, Agriculture, Manufactures, Mines and Quarries, 1910* (Washington, D.C.: Government Printing Office, n.d.); U.S. Census Office, *Compendium of the Eleventh Census: 1890, Part I, Population* (Washington, D.C.: Government Printing Office, 1892); U.S. Census Office, *Report on the Statistics of Agriculture in the United States at the Eleventh Census: 1890* (Washington, D.C.: Government Printing Office, 1895).
8. U.S. Bureau of the Census, *Thirteenth Census…, Supplement for Kentucky*.
9. Campbell, *Politics of Despair*, 111, 116.
10. Information in this paragraph comes from Campbell, *Politics of Despair*, 39, 62 ff., 67, 111, 135 ff.
11. Campbell, *Politics*, 67.
12. Wright, *Racial Violence in Kentucky*, 135; Cunningham, *On Bended Knees*, 143–4, says a higher percentage of Blacks joined.
13. Fred Shannon, *American Farmers' Movements* (Princeton: Van Nostrand, 1957), 77.

14. Wright, *Racial Violence in Kentucky*, 134–43. Campbell's appendix of incidents does not specify race, although he does discuss night-riding violence against Blacks (Campbell, *Politics*, appendix and 171–80; 90–7).

15. Campbell, *Politics*, 166ff. Mainstream interpretations, however, emphasize overproduction, for example, Lowell Harrison and James Klotter, *A New History of Kentucky* (Lexington: University Press of Kentucky, 1997), 295.

16. Virginia Davis, *A Glimpse of the Past: A Brief History of South County from Settlement to 1930* (printed with aid of a Kentucky Humanities Council Grant, 1994), 130; U.S. Bureau of the Census, *Thirteenth Census…, Supplement for Kentucky*.

17. For examples of Blacks "adopted" by white elites, see Hal Cox, *Had to Tell Someone: A Collection of His Poems*, ed. Celia McDonald and David Buck (Hodgenville, KY: The West County Herald News, 1986); Davis, *Glimpse of the Past*, 115, 117, 120.

18. Campbell, *Politics Of Despair*, 133.

19. For examples see Hartford and Hartford, *Green River Gravel*, 212; *West County Herald*, November 29, 1906, 8; Theodore Saloutos, *Farmer Movements in the South, 1865–1933* (Lincoln: University of Nebraska Press, 1960), 174.

20. For Kentucky stereotypes see Altina Waller, *Feud: Hatfields, McCoys, and Social Change in Appalachia, 1860–1900* (Chapel Hill: University of North Carolina Press, 1988), 1–13; Henry Shapiro, *Appalachia on Our Mind: The Southern Mountains and Mountaineers in the American Consciousness, 1870–1920* (Chapel Hill: University of North Carolina Press, 1978); *Strangers and Kin*, produced by Dee Alvin Davis III and directed by Herb Smith, 58 min., Appalshop Films, 1984, videocassette; for examples of state and national reporting see Cunningham, *On Bended Knees*, 107, 110, 147.

21. Quote is from Cunningham, *On Bended Knees*, 114; see also Harrison and Klotter, *New History of Kentucky*, 281.

22. Theodore Allen, *Invention of the White Race*, vol. II: *The Origin of Racial Oppression in Anglo-America* (New York: Verso, 1997), 219.

23. Nancy MacLean, *Behind the Mask of Chivalry: The Making of the Second Ku Klux Klan* (New York: Oxford University Press, 1994), 43. See Pete Daniel, *Standing at the Crossroads: Southern Life since 1900* (New York: Hill and Wang, 1986), 31, for a similar interpretation.

24. Cunningham, *On Bended Knees*, 136.

25. Alexander Saxton, *The Rise and Fall of the White Republic: Class Politics and Mass Culture in Nineteenth-Century America* (New York: Verso, 1990), 360, describes the producer ethic. However, his use of the term apparently includes both my nativists and producer egalitarians. In earlier papers I used the term "populist" to refer to producer egalitarians. However, in talking to activists I began to realize that the word "populist" conjured up connotations I did not intend, and which did not characterize the people I am talking about in this category. Many readers, like many of the activists I have spoken with, because they have never met people like those I am describing here, will assume that their image of populists as White supremacists or as close-minded rednecks is correct, and that I am defending potential members of the KKK, and may therefore be unable to hear what I am saying. While not free of racism, the people I am describing as producer egalitarians are opposed to the KKK and to much of what it stands for. However, there are other people on the far right, many of them nativists, who are white supremacists, or whose views are directly inimical to the welfare of minority men and women and white women. So, in order to avoid the confusion brought about by my former use of the word "populist," I have changed my language.

9 National Capital and the Waning of Independence

1. Mary Harris Jones, *The Autobiography of Mother Jones* (Chicago, IL: Charles H. Kerr, 1996 [1925]), 247.

2. Quoted in Albert Fried, ed., *Except to Walk Free: Documents and Notes in the History of American Labor* (New York: Anchor Press, 1974), 174.

3. Bill Haywood, *Bill Haywood's Book: The Autobiography of William Haywood* (New York: International Publishers, 1929), 187.

4. Haywood, *Haywood's Book.*, 246.

5. Edward Herman and Noam Chomsky, *Manufactoring Consent: The Political Economy of the Mass Media* (New York: Pantheon Books, 1988), xi, 298–307.

6. Howard Zinn, *A People's History of the United States*, 2nd ed. (New York: HarperCollins, 1995), 354, discussing Du Bois's approach; Priscilla Long, *Where the Sun Never Shines: A History of America's Bloody Coal Industry* (New York: Paragon House, 1989), 305ff.

7. For "left"-leaning politics see James Weinstein, *The Decline of Socialism in America 1912–1925* (New Brunswick: Rutgers University Press, 1984 [1967]); Zinn, *People's History*, 314–49; J. Morgan Kousser, *The Shaping of Southern Politics: Suffrage Restriction and the Establishment of the One-Party South, 1880–1910* (New Haven: Yale University Press, 1974); Long, *Where the Sun Never Shines*, 201–71, 306; for somewhat later see Robin Kelley, *Hammer and Hoe: Alabama Communists during the Great Depression* (Chapel Hill: University of North Carolina Press, 1990); Anthony Dunbar, *Against the Grain: Southern Radicals and Prophets, 1929–1959* (Charlottesville: University Press of Virginia, 1981); on the flood of immigrants into eastern Kentucky mining areas see Doug Cantrell, "Immigrants and Community in Harlan County, 1910–1930," *Register of the Kentucky Historical Society*, vol. 86, no. 2 (1988), 119–41; Doug Cantrell, "Aliens and Appalachia: Immigrants in the Southern Mountain Coalfields, 1870–1940" (unpublished manuscript, c. 1997).

8. Anthony Bimba, *The History of the American Working Class* (New York: International Publishers, 1927), 215.

9. Haywood, *Haywood's Book*, 241–2.

10. Harry Braverman, *Labor and Monopoly Capital: The Degradation of Work in the Twentieth Century* (New York: Monthly Review Press, 1974), 90ff.

11. Zinn, *People's History*, 327, 331, 338–9.

12. Lynne Taylor, "Food Riots Revisited," *Journal of Social History*, vol. 30, no. 2 (1996), 487.

13. Nancy Maclean, *Behind the Mask of Chivalry: The Making of the Second Ku Klux Klan* (New York: Oxford University Press, 1994), 23.

14. Haywood, *Haywood's Book*, 87.

15. Jonathond Edmunds, " 'Meat vs. Rice:' Euro-American Labor and the Feminization of the Chinese American Working Class" (term paper, seminar on Chinese American Labor, Oberlin College, 1997), 10.

16. Haywood, , *Haywood's Book*, 164–6; Zinn, *People's History*, 346–9.

17. Patrick Renshaw, *The Wobblies: The Story of Syndicalism in the United States* (New York: Doubleday, 1967), 187–8.

18. Zinn, *People's History*, 348.

19. For example, the *New York Times* downplayed the Rockefellers' Ludlow Massacre (Zinn, *People's History*, 348).

20. James Cobb, *Industrialization and Southern Society, 1877–1984* (Lexington: University Press of Kentucky, 1984), 24.

21. Zinn, *People's History*, 342–6.

22. James Klotter, *Kentucky: Portrait in Paradox, 1900–1950* (Frankfort: Kentucky Historical Society, 1996). 127, 131.

23. Klotter, *Kentucky*, 133–4; Cobb, *Industrialization and Southern Society*, 81. John Gaventa, *Power and Powerlessness: Quiescence and Rebellion in an Appalachian Valley* (Urbana: University of Illinois Press, 1980), 213–4.

24. Dwight Billings and Kathleen Blee, "Family Strategies in a Subsistence Economy: Beech Creek, Kentucky, 1850–1942," *Sociological Perspectives*, vol. 33, no. 1 (1990), 69–70.

25. For further discussion of each of these see Klotter, *Kentucky: Portrait in Paradox*, 136ff.; David Corbin, *Life, Work, and Rebellion in the Coal Fields: The Southern West Virginia Miners 1880–1922* (Urbana, IL: University of Illinois Press, 1981); John Hevener, *Which Side Are You On?: The Harlan County Coal Miners, 1931–1939* (Urbana: University of Illinois Press, 1978); Long, *Where the Sun Never Shines*.

26. U.S. Bureau of the Census, *Thirteenth Census of The United States, Supplement for Kentucky: Population, Agriculture, Manufactures, Mines and Quarries, 1910* (Washington, D.C.: Government Printing Office, n.d.), 683.

27. The rest of this paragraph and the next draw on Helen Irvin, *Women in Kentucky* (Lexington: University Press of Kentucky, 1979), 67–89; Lowell Harrison and James Klotter, *A New History of Kentucky* (Lexington: University Press of Kentucky, 1997), 258, 284–5, 303–5; George Yater, *Two Hundred Years at the Falls of the Ohio: A History of Louisville and Jefferson County* (Louisville: Heritage Foundation, 1979), 155–6; *Labor History in Kentucky: A Teaching Supplement* (Kentucky Department of Education and Labor, 1986), III, 27–8.

28. Dunbar, *Against the Grain*, 143–4.

29. Jacqueline Jones, *The Dispossessed: America's Underclasses from the Civil War to the Present* (New York: Basic Books, 1992), 127–66; Daniel, *The Shadow of Slavery: Peonage in the South, 1901–1969* (Urbana: University of Illinois Press, 1972).

30. Harrison and Klotter, *New History of Kentucky*, 307–9; Corbin, *Life, Work, and Rebellion*, 25–34, 92.

31. Harrison and Klotter, *New History of Kentucky*, 300; Altina Waller, *Feud: Hatfields, McCoys, and Social Change in Appalachia, 1860–1900* (Chapel Hill: University of North Carolina Press, 1988), 151–2.

32. This section depends on Weinstein, *The Decline of Socialism in America*, 134–62; Zinn, *People's History*, 350–67; Jeanette Keith, *Country People in the New South: Tennessee's Upper Cumberland* (Chapel Hill: University of North Carolina Press, 1995), 143–69; Klotter, *Kentucky: Portrait in Paradox*, 236; Haywood, *Haywood's Book*, 300–5; Harrison and Klotter, *New History of Kentucky*, 290.

33. Weinstein, *Decline of Socialism*, 139–40.

34. Figured from Harrison and Klotter, *New History of Kentucky*, 290, and U.S. Bureau of the Census, *Thirteenth Census...*, *Supplement for Kentucky*, 591.

35. Weinstein, *Decline of Socialism*, 157–9.

36. Harrison and Klotter, *New History of Kentucky*, 290; Charles Alexander, *The Ku Klux Klan in the Southwest* (Norman: University of Oklahoma Press, 1995 [1965]), 12.

37. Klotter, *Kentucky: Portrait in Paradox*, 240; Lee Baker, *From Savage to Negro: Anthropology and the Construction of Race, 1864–1954* (Berkeley: University of California Press, 1998), 135–8.

38. Pete Daniel, *Standing at the Crossroads: Southern Life since 1900* (New York: Hill and Wang, 1986), 45.

39. Jones, *The Dispossessed*, 136, 148–155.

40. On the control instituted by corporations, see Corbin, *Life, Work, and Rebellion*, 10, 116–54; Gaventa, *Power and Powerlessness*, 85–96; Maclean, *Behind the Mask of Chivalry*, 38–9; Cobb, *Industrialization and Southern Society*, 68–77; Cantrell, *Aliens and Appalachia*, 142–88; David Ashley, *History without a Subject: The Postmodern Condition* (Boulder: Westview Press, 1997), 97–8.

41. Klotter, *Kentucky: Portrait in Paradox*, 238, 245; Gavin Wright, *Old South, New South: Revolutions in the Southern Economy since the Civil War* (New York: Basic Books, 1986), 199.

42. Cobb, *Industrialization and Southern Society*, 73–4; Zinn, *People's History*, 372–3.

43. On the rising interest in communism see Kelley, *Hammer and Hoe*; Dunbar, *Against the Grain*; Hevener, *Which Side Are You On?*, 50–88; Zinn, *People's History*, 376, 438.

44. Dunbar, *Against the Grain*, 110, 184, 256.

45. Robert Ireland, *Little Kingdoms: The Counties of Kentucky, 1850–1891* (Lexington: University Press of Kentucky, 1977); see also Keith, *Country People in the New South*, 143–69; Mary Beth Pudup, "Social Class and Economic Development in Southeast Kentucky, 1820–1880," in Robert Mitchell, ed., *Appalachian Frontiers: Settlement, Society, and Development in the Preindustrial Era* (Lexington: University Press of Kentucky, 1991).

46. Kenneth Corder, " 'You Can't Get a Gold Mine for a Pocket of Change': The Struggle for Local Funding of Agriculture Extension in Breckinridge County, Kentucky, 1918–1939," *Filson Club Historical Quarterly*, vol. 69, no. 3 (1995), 312–3. For discussion of mechanization see Pete Daniel, *Breaking the Land: The Transformation of Cotton, Tobacco, and Rice Cultures since 1880* (Chicago: University of Illinois Press, 1985), particularly 290–8; Keith, *Country People in the New South*, 153, 177; Lawrence Goodwyn, *Democratic Promise: The Populist Moment in America* (New York: Oxford University Press, 1976), 568–9.

47. Maclean, *Behind the Mask of Chivalry*, 23–51; Jones, *The Dispossessed*, 84.

10   The Redefinition of the Producer Egalitarian Ethic

1. See Ruth Cowan, *More Work for Mother: The Ironies of Household Technology from the Open Hearth to the Microwave* (New York: Basic Books, 1983), 71–8; Harry Braverman, *Labor and Monopoly Capital: The Degradation of Work in the Twentieth Century* (New York: Monthly Review Press, 1974), 271–83; Susan Strasser, *Satisfaction Guaranteed: The Making of the American Mass Market* (New York: Pantheon Books, 1989), 5–28. Pete Daniel, *Standing at the Crossroads: Southern Life since 1900* (New York: Hill and Wang, 1986), 44, discusses the use of consumerism by mill town owners to control employees.

2. Audrey Smedley, *Race in North America: Origin and Evolution of a Worldview* (Boulder: Westview Press, 1993), 270–1. On "racial agents" see Helán Enoch Page, "The 'Black' Public Sphere in White Public Space: Racialized Information and Hi-Tech Cultural Production in the Global African Diaspora" (paper presented at the New York Academy of Sciences workshop "Post-Boasian Studies of Whiteness and Blackness: Towards an Anthropological Conception of Racial Practices," March 1997).

3. Quoted and discussed in Howard Zinn, *A People's History of the United States*, 2nd ed. (New York: HarperCollins, 1995), 321, 354.

4. On wages see Gavin Wright, *Old South, New South: Revolutions in the Southern Economy since the Civil War* (New York: Basic Books, 1986), 182–3, 197; Jacqueline Jones, *The Dispossessed: America's Underclasses from the Civil War to the Present* (New York: Basic Books, 1992), 147.

5. George Wright, *A History of Blacks in Kentucky*, vol. II: *In Pursuit of Equality, 1890–1980* ([Frankfort]:Kentucky Historical Society, 1992), 6–7.

6. On the paycheck and proper use of it see Karen Brodkin, *How Jews Became White Folks, and What That Says about Race in America* (New Brunswick: Rutgers University Press, 1998), 86–94; Jeanette Keith, *Country People in the New South: Tennessee's Upper Cumberland* (Chapel Hill: University of North Carolina Press, 1995), 190–1, 201. The increased importance of the term "white trash" grew from eugenics studies,

which claimed that poor Whites were genetically defective (Annalee Newitz and Matt Wray, "Introduction," in Matt Wray and Annalee Newitz, eds., *White Trash: Race and Class in America* [New York: Routledge, 1997], 2–3). As I use it, "white trash" refers to people defined by European descent who don't meet the standards expected of "Whites." It does not imply that such people really were (or are) "trashy."

7. Altina Waller, "Feuding in Appalachia: Evolution of a Cultural Stereotype," in Mary Beth Pudup, Dwight Billings, and Altina Waller, eds., *Appalachia in the Making: The Mountain South in the Nineteenth Century* (Chapel Hill: University of North Carolina Press, 1995), 367; James Cobb, *Industrialization and Southern Society, 1877–1984* (Lexington: University Press of Kentucky, 1984), 74–5.

8. On the intensification of work generally and on conditions at Ford see Braverman, *Labor and Monopoly Capital*, 107–21, 146–51; for textile mills see Daniel, *Standing at the Crossroads*, 103–6.

9. Braverman, *Labor and Monopoly Capital*, 148–9.

10. Altina Waller, *Feud: Hatfields, McCoys, and Social Change in Appalachia, 1860–1900* (Chapel Hill: University of North Carolina Press, 1988), 203–5; Nancy MacLean, *Behind the Mask of Chivalry: The Making of the Second Ku Klux Klan* (New York: Oxford University Press, 1994), 35–40; Alan Banks, "Class Formation in the Southeastern Kentucky Coalfields 1890–1920" (1995), Cobb, *Industrialization and Southern Society*, 137–8 discuss relatively open –for whites– social structures becoming more stratified.

11. MacLean, *Behind the Mask of Chivalry*, 23, 44; Keith, *Country People in the New South*, 144.

12. Keith, *Country People*, 106, 210.

13. Veblen, quoted in Braverman, *Labor and Monopoly Capital*, 266; the strategies followed are described in Strasser, *Satisfaction Guaranteed*.

14. James Klotter, *Kentucky: Portrait in Paradox, 1900–1950* (Frankfort: Kentucky Historical Society, 1996), 134; George Yater, *Two Hundred Years at the Falls of the Ohio: A History of Louisville and Jefferson County* (Louisville: The Heritage Foundation, 1979), 221.

15. See Thomas Arcury, "Household Composition and Economic Change in a Rural Community, 1900–1980: Testing Two Models," *American Ethnologist*, vol. 11 (1984), 677–98, for a similar pattern in another Kentucky county.

16. Braverman, *Labor and Monopoly Capital*, 150–1; David Ashley, *History without a Subject: The Postmodern Condition* (Boulder: Westview Press, 1997), 100. David Corbin, *Life, Work, and Rebellion in the Coal Fields: The Southern West Virginia Miners 1880–1922* (Urbana: University of Illinois Press, 1981), 121, shows coal operators promoting consumerism to encourage hard work.

17. I am indebted to Helán Enoch Page for the conception of whiteness as behavioral.

18. Daniel, *Standing at the Crossroads*, 56; George Wright, "By the Book: Legal Executions of Kentucky Blacks," in W. Fitzhugh Brundage, ed., *Under Sentence of Death: Lynching in the South* (Chapel Hill: University of North Carolina Press, 1997), 250–1; Stewart Tolnay and E. M. Beck, *A Festival of Violence: An Analysis of Southern Lynchings* (Chicago: University of Illinois Press, 1995), ix, 37–8.

19. George Wright, *Racial Violence in Kentucky 1865–1940: Lynchings, Mob Rule, and "Legal Lynchings"* (Baton Rouge: Louisiana State University Press, 1990).

11 The Klan and the Manufacture of Middle-Class Consent: Splitting the White Working Class, Terrorizing the Black

1. James Klotter, *Kentucky: Portrait in Paradox, 1900–1950* (Frankfort: Kentucky Historical Society, 1996), 242; George Wright, *A History of Blacks in Kentucky*, vol. II, *In Pursuit of Equality, 1890–1980* ([Frankfort]:Kentucky Historical Society, 1992), 992,

85–6; Thomas Matijasic, "The Ku Klux Klan in the Big Sandy Valley of Kentucky," *Journal of Kentucky Studies*, vol. 10 (1993), 75–80; E. H. Lougher, *The Kall of the Klan in Kentucky* (Knights of the Ku Klux Klan, 1924), 63–77. My overall interpretation of the Klan draws particularly on Nancy MacLean, *Behind the Mask of Chivalry: The Making of the Second Ku Klux Klan* (New York: Oxford University Press, 1994) and Kathleen Blee, *Women of the Klan: Racism and Gender in the 1920s* (Berkeley: University of California Press, 1991).

2.   Blee, *Women of the Klan*, 7, 17, 172; MacLean, *Behind the Mask of Chivalry*, xi–xv, 3–12, 52–74; Matijasic, "The Ku Klux Klan in the Big Sandy Valley of Kentucky," 76; see Michael Omi and Howard Winant, *Racial Formation in the United States: From the 1960s to the 1990s*, 2nd ed. (New York: Routledge, 1994) on the racial state.

3.   MacLean, *Behind the Mask of Chivalry*, 52–74; William Jenkins, *Steel Valley Klan: The Ku Klux Klan in Ohio's Mahoning Valley* (Kent, OH: Kent State University Press, 1990), 86; Chandler Davidson, *Biracial Politics: Conflict and Coalition in the Metropolitan South* (Baton Rouge: Louisiana State University Press, 1972), 163.

4.   Paul McClure, *Nearbytown and Its People: A Brief Record of Nearbytown, KY* (North County Seat: North County Historical Society, 1992), 91–2.

5.   Daniel McClure, Jr., *Two Centuries in North County Seat and North County, Kentucky 1776–1976* (North County Seat: North County Historical Society, 1979), 341, 490.

6.   Harry Braverman, *Labor and Monopoly Capital: The Degradation of Work in the Twentieth Century* (New York: Monthly Review Press, 1974), 403–9.

7.   MacLean, *Behind the Mask*, 19–22; Blee, *Women of the Klan*, 20–2, 123–53, 165–73.

8.   MacLean, *Behind the Mask*, 47, 86–91.

9.   MacLean, *Behind the Mask*, 62.

10.   MacLean, *Behind the Mask*, 82–3, 160; Charles Alexander, *The Ku Klux Klan in the Southwest* (Norman: University of Oklahoma Press, 1995 [1965]), 24.

11.   Lougher, *The Kall of the Klan*, 20.

12.   Sanford Cohen, *Labor in the United States*, 3rd ed. (Columbus: Charles E. Merrill Publishing, 1970 [1960]), 99–101; Alexander, *Ku Klux Klan in the Southwest*, 61–3.

13.   MacLean, *Behind the Mask*, 74, 182.

14.   On Klan attitudes toward Catholics see MacLean, *Behind the Mask*, 95–7; Blee, *Women of the Klan*, 86–93. On white trash see Annalee Newitz and Matt Wray, "Introduction," in Matt Wray and Annalee Newitz, eds., *White Trash: Race and Class in America* (New York: Routledge, 1997), 1–8. On racialized distinctions between people of European descent see Audrey Smedley, *Race in North America: Origin and Evolution of a Worldview* (Boulder: Westview Press, 1993), 264–71; Lee Baker, *From Savage to Negro: Anthropology and the Construction of Race, 1864–1954* (Berkeley: University of California Press, 1998), 81–98.

15.   Lougher, *Kall of the Klan*, 13–4.

16.   Estimates vary; see Pete Daniel, *Standing at the Crossroads: Southern Life since 1900* (New York: Hill and Wang, 1986), 77–9; Stewart Tolnay and E. M. Beck, *A Festival of Violence: An Analysis of Southern Lynchings* (Chicago: University of Illinois Press, 1995), 241–2.

17.   Jacqueline Jones, *The Dispossessed: America's Underclasses from the Civil War to the Present* (New York: Basic Books, 1992), 178, 187; Anthony Dunbar, *Against the Grain: Southern Radicals and Prophets, 1929–1959* (Charlottesville: University Press of Virginia, 1981), 105–7, 124; MacLean, *Behind the Mask*, 85.

18. Blee, *Women of the Klan*, 147–153; Lee Shai Weissbach, "Kentucky's Jewish History in National Perspective: The Era of Mass Migration," *Filson Club History Quarterly*, vol. 69, no. 3 (1995), 258.

19.   Lougher, *Kall of the Klan*, 47; percentage figured from his numbers.

20.   Jones, *The Dispossessed*, 114–26; Daniel, *Standing at the Crossroads*, 43–4.

21. Quoted in Lowell Harrison and James Klotter, *A New History of Kentucky* (Lexington: University Press of Kentucky, 1997), 256.

22. Matijasic, "The Ku Klux Klan in the Big Sandy Valley of Kentucky," 76, quoting Frost, president of Berea College.

23. For documentation of such claims see *Strangers and Kin*, producer Dee Alvin Davis III and director Herb Smith, 58 min., Appalshop Films, 1984, videocassette. Also see Helen Lewis, Sue Kobak, and Linda Johnson, "Family, Religion and Colonialism in Central Appalachia, or: Bury My Rifle at Big Stone Gap," in Jim Axelrod, ed., *Growin' Up Country* (Clintwood, VA: Resource and Information Center, Council of the Southern Mountains, 1973), 145; David Corbin, *Life, Work, and Rebellion in the Coal Fields: The Southern West Virginia Miners 1880–1922* (Urbana: University of Illinois Press, 1981), 121.

24. Corbin, *Life, Work, and Rebellion*, 33–4, 121–6.

25. For discussion see Karen Brodkin, *How Jews Became White Folks, and What That Says about Race in America* (New Brunswick: Rutgers University Press, 1998), 86–102.

26. Quoted in Alexander, *Ku Klux Klan in the Southwest*, 64. On violence against white men see also Matijasic, "The Ku Klux Klan in the Big Sandy Valley of Kentucky," 79; Alexander, *Ku Klux Klan in the Southwest*, 58–68, 92; MacLean, *Behind the Mask*, 153. On patriarchal support and control of white women see Jacqueline Dowd Hall, " 'The Mind that Burns in Each Body': Women, Rape, and Racial Violence," in Margaret Andersen and Patricia Hill Collins, eds., *Race, Class, and Gender: An Anthology* (Belmont: Wadsworth, 1995), 434–9; MacLean, *Behind the Mask*, 114, 123; Blee, *Women of the Klan*, 84–6.

27. Matijasic, "The Ku Klux Klan in the Big Sandy Valley of Kentucky," 79; Blee, *Women of the Klan*, 103–9.

28. MacLean, *Behind the Mask*, 114–24; Blee, *Women of the Klan*, 85.

29. Lougher, *Kall of the Klan*, 75.

30. Victor Howard, *Black Liberation in Kentucky: Emancipation and Freedom, 1862–1884* (Lexington: University Press of Kentucky, 1983), 105–6, 178.

31. Tolnay and Beck, *Festival of Violence*, 212–3; Wright, *History of Blacks in Kentucky*, vol. II, 83.

32. Alexander, *Ku Klux Klan in the Southwest*, 9–10.

33. MacLean, *Behind the Mask*, 7.

34. Quoted in Baker, *From Savage to Negro*, 132–4; see also MacLean, *Behind the Mask*, 12–3.

35. James Ridgeway, *Blood in the Face: The Ku Klux Klan, Aryan Nations, Nazi Skinheads, and the Rise of a New White Culture* (New York: Thunder's Mouth Press, 1990), 37–44; Roger Biles, *The South and the New Deal* (Lexington: University Press of Kentucky, 1994), 140.

36. Dunbar, *Against the Grain*; Robin Kelley, *Hammer and Hoe: Alabama Communists during the Great Depression* (Chapel Hill: University of North Carolina Press, 1990).

37. MacLean, *Behind the Mask*, 129; on the New Negro see Baker, *From Savage to Negro*, 127–42.

38. On employer attitudes see Jenkins, *Steel Valley Klan*, 22–3; Baker, *From Savage to Negro*, 62; James Cobb, *Industrialization and Southern Society, 1877–1984* (Lexington: University Press of Kentucky, 1984), 29.

39. For discussion of business positions see Cobb, *Industrialization and Southern Society*, 27–30; Priscilla Long, *Where the Sun Never Shines: A History of America's Bloody Coal Industry* (New York: Paragon House, 1989), 305ff.

40. Wright, *History of Blacks in Kentucky*, vol. II, 1–6, describes the "cleansing" of certain Kentucky counties. On the elite position see MacLean, *Behind the Mask*, 182–3; Tolnay and Beck, *Festival of Violence*, 213–33.

41. Wright, *History of Kentucky*, vol. II, 83; see Tolnay and Beck, 250–1, for a summary of their findings on the economic factors in lynching; Lougher, *Kall of the Klan*, describes being arrested for giving Klan speeches in Kentucky.

42. Sarah Smith, *Historic Nelson County: Its Towns and People* (Bardstown, KY: GBA/Delmar, 1983), 469–70.

43. Quoted in Dunbar, *Against the Grain*, 14.

44. Kelley, *Hammer and Hoe*.

45. Cobb, *Industrialization and Southern Society*, 92; the second phrase was used by my husband's grandfather.

46. On the miners see Corbin, *Life, Work, and Rebellion in the Coal Fields*. On the Ford incident see Saul Alinsky, *John L. Lewis: An Unauthorized Biography* (New York: G. P. Putnam's Sons, 1949), 102–3. On mill workers see Daniel, *Standing at the Crossroads*, 105–7; Cobb, *Industrialization and Southern Society*, 73.

12 Brown Shirts/White Sheets: Fascism and Middle-Class Demotion

1. For the Klan's anti-big business stance see for instance Nancy MacLean, *Behind the Mask of Chivalry: The Making of the Second Ku Klux Klan* (New York: Oxford University Press, 1994), 77–97; for the early Nazis see Henry Turner, *German Big Business and the Rise of Hitler* (New York: Oxford University Press, 1985), 64–7,75; Daniel Guerin, *Fascism and Big Business* (New York: Pathfinder Press, 1973 [1939]), 85–8.

2. Arthur Schweitzer, *Big Business in the Third Reich* (Bloomington: Indiana University Press, 1964), 35–7.

3. John Gillingham, *Industry and Politics in the Third Reich: Ruhr Coal, Hitler, and Europe* (New York: Columbia University Press, 1985), 50–1; Guerin, *Fascism and Big Business*, 39; see Schweitzer, *Big Business in the Third Reich*, 197–238, 538–9, 239–96, for big business's takeover of economic policy and for the Nazi party's relationship with big business.

4. Bruce Catton, *The War Lords of Washington* (New York: Harcourt, Brace, 1948), 34.

5. Bernard Bellon, *Mercedes in Peace and War: German Automobile Workers, 1903–1945* (New York: Columbia University Press, 1990), 83–214; Turner, *German Big Business and the Rise of Hitler*, 19–47.

6. See James Cobb, *Industrialization and Southern Society, 1877–1984* (Lexington: University Press of Kentucky, 1984), 92; David Corbin, *Life, Work, and Rebellion in the Coal Fields: The Southern West Virginia Miners 1880–1922* (Urbana: University of Illinois Press, 1981); Bill Haywood, *Bill Haywood's Book: The Autobiography of William Haywood* (New York: International Publishers, 1929), 290–309; Anthony Dunbar, *Against the Grain: Southern Radicals and Prophets, 1929–1959* (Charlottesville: University Press of Virginia, 1981), 1–8; Robin Kelley, *Hammer and Hoe: Alabama Communists during the Great Depression* (Chapel Hill: University of North Carolina Press, 1990). Howard Zinn, *A People's History of the United States*, 2nd ed. (New York: HarperCollins, 1995), 346–97, provides an overall description of this period.

7. James Weinstein, *The Decline of Socialism in America 1912–1925* (New Brunswick: Rutgers University Press, 1984 [1967]), 327, 249–50.

8. Harry Braverman, *Labor and Monopoly Capital: The Degradation of Work in the Twentieth Century* (New York: Monthly Review Press, 1974), 90–9; Bellon, *Mercedes in Peace and War*, 37, 260; John Keller, *Power in America: The Southern Question and the Control of Labor* (Chicago: Vanguard Books, 1983), 56–62.

9. Claudia Koonz, *Mothers in the Fatherland: Women, the Family, and Nazi Politics* (New York: St. Martin's Press, 1987); Edward Homze, *Foreign Labor in Nazi Germany* (Princeton: Princeton University Press, 1967); Jeremy Noakes, "Social Outcasts in the Third

Reich," in Richard Bessel, ed., *Life in the Third Reich* (New York: Oxford University Press, 1987), 83–96; Tilly Siegel, "Wage Policy in Nazi Germany," *Politics and Society*, vol. 1 (1985), 1–51.

10. Tim Mason, "Labor in the Third Reich, 1933–1939," *Past and Present*, vol. 33 (1966), 140.

11. Gisela Bock, "Racism and Sexism in Nazi Germany: Motherhood, Compulsory Sterilization, and the State," in Renate Bridenthal, Atina Grossmann, and Marion Kaplan, eds., *When Biology Became Destiny: Women in Weimar and Nazi Germany* (New York: Monthly Review Press, 1984), 271–96; Koonz, *Mothers in the Fatherland*, 189.

12. Mason, "Labor in the Third Reich," 120–3; Gillingham, *Industry and Politics in the Third Reich*, 24–6, 41.

13. Sanford Cohen, *Labor in the United States,* 3rd ed. (Columbus: Charles E. Merrill Publishing, 1970 [1960]), 110; for examples see Roger Biles, *The South and the New Deal* (Lexington: University Press of Kentucky, 1994), 45, 83–99; Patrick Renshaw, *The Wobblies: The Story of Syndicalism in the United States* (New York: Doubleday, 1967), 160–7, 174–87, 190–1.

14. Michael Adams, "Retelling the Tale: Wars in Common Memory," in Gabor Boritt, ed., *War Comes Again: Comparative Vistas on the Civil War and World War II* (New York: Oxford University Press, 1995), 208.

15. *South County News,* April 8, 1943, 2.

16. Quotes are from *South County News,* February 4, 1943, 2, 4; February 18, 1943, 2. Remnants of little-guy objections continued well into the 1950s; an editorial refers in passing to sentiment against Rockefeller for president as a result of the "remnant of the bitter feeling against the financial Moloch of a giant monopoly" (*North County Seat News,* November 11, 1958, 2).

17. Pete Daniel, *Standing at the Crossroads: Southern Life since 1900* (New York: Hill and Wang, 1986), 138–9; Jacqueline Jones, *The Dispossessed: America's Underclasses from the Civil War to the Present* (New York: Basic Books, 1992), 172–3.

18. Gillingham, *Industry and Politics in the Third Reich,* 85; more generally see Mary Nolan, *Visions of Modernity: American Business and the Modernization of Germany* (New York: Oxford University Press, 1994).

19. On Rockefeller see Priscilla Long, *Where the Sun Never Shines: A History of America's Bloody Coal Industry* (New York: Paragon House, 1989), 330; David Simon, *Elite Deviance,* 5th ed. (Boston: Allyn and Bacon, 1996), 65; Michael Hirsh, "The Hunt Hits Home," *Newsweek,* December 14, 1998, 48; Michael Dobbs, "Whose Side Were They On?" *Washington Post National Weekly Edition,* vol. 16, no. 6, December 7, 1998, 6–7.

20. Bock, "Racism and Sexism in Nazi Germany," 273–5; Audrey Smedley, *Race in North America: Origin and Evolution of a Worldview* (Boulder: Westview Press, 1993), 281; Koonz, *Mothers in the Fatherland,* 189ff.

21. Keller, *Power in America,* 79.

22. There is an enormous theoretical literature but no real consensus on the definition and meaning of fascism. For discussions of the confusion surrounding fascism see Roger Griffin, ed., *Fascism* (Oxford: Oxford University Press, 1995), 1–2; Stanley Payne, *Fascism: Comparison and Definition* (Madison: University of Wisconsin Press, 1980); Alan Brinkley, *Voices of Protest: Huey Long, Father Coughlin, and the Great Depression* (New York: Vintage Books, 1983), 276–83. In the context of Western fascism the power-holding group has in fact been "white." However, this should not be construed to imply that fascism or adherence to it is a naturally "white" phenomenon.

23. According to mainstream assumptions, the United States was not fascist in the 1920s, but was merely pursuing normal corporate profiteering. Despite a few marginalized extremists, goes the assumption, Americans have always been too level-

headed and believe too thoroughly in fairness to allow fascism to gain a foothold. These assumptions exonerate the elite from responsibility in the nativist rise to power in both the U.S. and German cases. The control that Nazi rule gave German elites over the entire labor hierarchy is played down, and concentration camp labor is rarely described as a direct benefit to corporations. These assumptions don't correspond with my view of American history from under the sink.

24. Kelley, *Hammer and Hoe*, xii–xiii.
25. Lerone Bennett, *The Shaping of Black America* (New York: Penguin Books, 1993 [1975]), 61–80.

13 National Capital, the Retreat from Fascist Processes, and the Sugar-Coated Contract

1. Fred Hartley, *Our New National Labor Policy* (New York: Funk and Wagnalls, 1948), 210, 137.
2. However, see John Schwarz and Thomas Volgy, *The Forgotten Americans* (New York: W.W. Norton & Company, 1992), 61–3, for a critique of official figures. See Frances Piven and Richard Cloward, *Regulating the Poor: The Functions of Public Welfare*, 2nd ed. (New York: Vintage, 1993), 3–41, 343–99, for a summary of their analysis of welfare and revolt.
3. Harvey Swados, "The Myth of the Happy Worker," in Robert Purruci and Marc Pilisuk, eds., *The Triple Revolution: Social Problems in Depth* (Boston: Little, Brown, 1968), 234–40, describes 1950s attitudes and conditions in factories; Chandler Davidson, *Biracial Politics: Conflict and Coalition in the Metropolitan South* (Baton Rouge: Louisiana State University Press, 1972), 237–9.
4. Anthony Dunbar, *Against the Grain: Southern Radicals and Prophets, 1929–1959* (Charlottesville: University Press of Virginia, 1981), 225–58.
5. *Rosie the Riveter*, produced and directed by Connie Fields, 65 min., Clarity Production, Direct Cinema Limited, Inc., c. 1987, videocassette, displays a *New York Times* headline for February 21,1944, giving comparative numbers of deaths. See David Corbin, *Life, Work, and Rebellion in the Coal Fields: The Southern West Virginia Miners 1880–1922* (Urbana: University of Illinois Press, 1981), 181, for mining deaths in relation to World War I military deaths. For examples of wartime films see *Rosie the Riveter* and *Strangers and Kin*, produced by Dee Alvin Davis III and directed by Herb Smith, 58 min., Appalshop Films, 1984, videocassette. For the World War I beginnings of corporate public relations to portray themselves as saviors, see Priscilla Long, *Where the Sun Never Shines: A History of America's Bloody Coal Industry* (New York: Paragon House, 1989), 308–13, 329–31.
6. Pete Daniel, *Standing at the Crossroads: Southern Life since 1900* (New York: Hill and Wang, 1986), 116–7, 121–3; Roger Biles, *The South and the New Deal* (Lexington: University Press of Kentucky, 1994), 154–5.
7. David Simon, *Elite Deviance*, 5th ed. (Boston: Allyn and Bacon, 1996), 151.
8. See David Ashley, *History without a Subject: The Postmodern Condition* (Boulder: Westview Press, 1997), 113–4, for a concise theoretical treatment of this shift.
9. John Keller, *Power in America: The Southern Question and the Control of Labor* (Chicago: Vanguard Books, 1983), 154–8. James Cobb, *Industrialization and Southern Society, 1877–1984* (Lexington: University Press of Kentucky, 1984), 115–6, points out how superficial incoming industries' interest in improving race relations was.
10. Howard Zinn, *A People's History of the United States,* 2nd ed. (New York: HarperCollins, 1995), 416, 428–9. Daniel, *Standing at the Crossroads,* 136–7, talks about huge military spending in the South.

11. Zinn, *People's History*, 571; Edward Herman and Noam Chomsky, *Manufacturing Consent: The Political Economy of the Mass Media* (New York: Pantheon Books, 1988), 29–31.
12. Hermann and Chomsky, *Manufacturing Consent*.
13. The House Un-American Activities Committee was supposed to investigate both fascist and communist underground activity; in fact it heard essentially only one witness concerning fascism (Dunbar, *Against the Grain*, 225). Also see Zinn, *People's History*, 422–3.
14. Zinn, *People's History*, 374–6.
15. Dunbar, *Against the Grain*, 217–58, carefully documents the stifling of radical organizations by the use of the accusation of communism. Robert Botsch, *We Shall Not Overcome: Populism and Southern Blue-Collar Workers* (Chapel Hill: University of North Carolina Press, 1980), 188, highlights the role of churches.
16. Daniel, *Standing at the Crossroads*, 163–4.
17. Daniel, *Standing*, 204.
18. Cobb, *Industrialization and Southern Society*, 83–5.
19. Dunbar, *Against the Grain*, 258.
20. Quoted in Chandler Davidson, *Biracial Politics*, 162–3.
21. Daniel, *Standing*, 181–219, is the basis for the rest of this section.
22. See Daniel, *Standing*, 8, for a summary of his study. See Botsch, *We Shall Not Overcome*, 4–5, 54–5, for a review of the literature on white working-class racism; one line of interpretation sees Blacks and poor Whites as being further apart in the 1970s than they were in the 1950s, implying that local elite strategies have been successful. See Cobb, *Industrialization and Southern Society*, 151–3, for a discussion of White Citizens Councils that supports the contention that white supremacist politicians may have been reflecting not the majority, but the threatened middle class. Much of the financial support for the fight against integration came from wealthy Northerners (Douglas Blackmon, "Silent Partner: How the South's Fight to Uphold Segregation Was Funded Up North," *The Wall Street Journal*, June 11, 1999, A1, 8).
23. Numan Bartley and Hugh Graham, *Southern Politics and the Second Reconstruction* (Baltimore: Johns Hopkins University Press, 1975), 50–1, 109–10; Davidson, *Biracial Politics*, 52–82; Botsch, *We Shall Not Overcome*, 122–3.
24. Cobb, *Industrialization and Southern Society*, 43.
25. Cobb, *Industrialization*, 159.
26. On strategies of whitening see Karen Brodkin, *How Jews Became White Folks, and What That Says about Race in America* (New Brunswick: Rutgers University Press, 1998); Helán Enoch Page, "The 'Black' Public Sphere in White Public Space: Racialized Information and Hi-Tech Cultural Production in the Global African Diaspora" (paper presented at the New York Academy of Sciences workshop "Post-Boasian Studies of Whiteness and Blackness: Towards an Anthropological Conception of Racial Practices," March 1997).
27. Jacqueline Jones, *The Dispossessed: America's Underclasses from the Civil War to the Present* (New York: Basic Books, 1992), 172–201.
28. Jasper Shannon, *Toward a New Politics in the South* (Knoxville: University of Tennessee Press, 1949), 65, cites articles translated from *Izvestia* published in *Harpers* Magazine; Ashley, *History without a Subject*, 237. See Daniel, *Standing at the Crossroads*, 143–50, for Nazi and Japanese use of the same argument and the diplomatic problems it caused after the war.
29. M. Brinton Lykes et al., "Introduction" in M. Brinton Lykes et al., eds., *Myths about the Powerless: Contesting Social Inequalities* (Philadelphia: Temple University Press, 1996), 3, point out that there was a "core assumption" that guaranteeing a minimum standard of living for all citizens was a fundamental task of government.

30. Bennett Harrison and Barry Bluestone, *The Great U-Turn: Corporate Restructuring and the Polarizing of America* (New York: Basic Books, 1988), 4–5.

31. Karen Brodkin, *How Jews Became White Folks*, 41–2, 53–76.

32. See Anne Francis Okongwu, "Looking Up from the Bottom to the Ceiling of the Basement Floor: Female Single-Parent Families Surviving on $22,000 or Less a Year," *Urban Anthropology*, vol. 24, no. 3–4 (1995), 344, on comparative white security; Harrison and Bluestone, *The Great U-Turn*, 5. Swados, "The Myth of the Happy Worker," points out that even supposedly well-paid factory jobs often left families struggling.

33. Mercer Sullivan, *Getting Paid: Youth, Crime and Work in the Inner City* (Ithaca: Cornell University Press, 1989), 52–4; my thanks to Anne Okongwu for highlighting the role of parental class in this study.

34. See *Strangers and Kin* for examples of the gendered construction of poverty in the stereotyping of poor white Kentuckians.

35. However, for discussions of voter apathy see Botsch, *We Shall Not Overcome*, 91, 121; John Gaventa, *Power and Powerlessness: Quiescence and Rebellion in an Appalachian Valley* (Urbana: University of Illinois Press, 1980).

14 Local Elite Choices and the Reorganized Drainage System: "Old South" and "New South"

1. See Daniel, *Breaking the Land: The Transformation of Cotton, Tobacco, and Rice Cultures since 1880* (Chicago: University of Illinois Press, 1985) and Roger Biles, *The South and the New Deal* (Lexington: University Press of Kentucky, 1994), 36–57, for the effects of New Deal agricultural policies.

2. Numan Bartley, *The New South 1945–1980* (Baton Rouge: Louisiana State University Press, 1995), 105.

3. Calculated from U.S. Bureau of the Census, *Census of Population: 1950*, vol. II, *Characteristics of the Population, part 17, Kentucky* (Washington, D.C.: Government Printing Office, 1952); U.S. Bureau of the Census, *1970 Census of Population*, vol. 1, *Characteristics of the Population, part 19: Kentucky* (Washington, D.C.: Government Printing Office, 1973).

4. For discussion of 1950s studies of two nearby counties that showed a similar pattern of business leader control see Ernest L Hill, "Leadership Identification by Newspaper Analysis: The Development and Testing of a Method" (Master's thesis, University of Kentucky, 1954), 4, 66. See also Robert Ireland, *Little Kingdoms: The Counties of Kentucky, 1850–1891* (Lexington: University Press of Kentucky, 1977).

5. See Robert Botsch, *We Shall Not Overcome: Populism and Southern Blue-Collar Workers* (Chapel Hill: University of North Carolina Press, 1980), 9–10, for a similar pattern in another Southern community.

6. Daniel McClure, Jr., *Two Centuries in North County Seat and North County, Kentucky, 1776–1976* (North County Seat: North County Historical Society, 1979), 493, identifies the early 1970s as the point at which business moved to the outskirts of the county seat. This is confirmed by Bureau of the Census, *County Business Patterns*, volumes for 1949–1994 (Washington, D.C.: Government Printing Office); local newspapers (e.g. *North County Enterprise*, January 12, 1970, 1; U.S. Bureau of the Census, *1970 Census of Population, Kentucky* (Washington, D.C.: Government Printing Office, 1973); U.S. Bureau of the Census, *1980 Census of Population*, vol.1, *Characteristics of the Population, Chapter C, General Social and Economic Characteristics, part 19: Kentucky* (Washington, D.C.: Government Printing Office, 1983); U.S. Bureau of the Census, *1990 Census Lookup*, Summary Tape File 3.

http://venus.census.gov/cdrom/lookup; U.S. Bureau of the Census, *1970 Census of Housing, Housing Characteristics for States, Cities, and Counties, part 19: Kentucky* (Washington, D.C.: Government Printing Office, 1973).

7. U.S. Bureau of the Census, *1970 Census of Population, Kentucky,* Tables 107 and 137; "Rich Man, Poor Man," Staff article, (Louisville, KY) *Courier-Journal,* Jan. 19, 2000. Record Number 200011912131104. The 1990 census is the first to give the total dollars held by those with incomes over $150,000; in both counties this is less than 1 percent of households. In North County these households' average income is 10.7 times the median county household income; in South County it is 19.5 times the median. Furthermore in South County there are no households in the next lower category of $125, 000 to $149,000, while North County has many in that category.

8. Bartley, *The New South 1945–1980,* 130.

9. U.S. Bureau of the Census, *Thirteenth Census of the United States, Supplement for Kentucky: Population, Agriculture, Manufactures, Mines and Quarries, 1910* (Washington, D.C.: Government Printing Office, n.d.); McClure, *Two Centuries,* 384–5. This appears to have been a fairly common pattern for sections of Kentucky that were neither coalmining nor former plantation areas: see Thomas Arcury, "Household Composition and Economic Change in a Rural Community, 1900–1980: Testing Two Models," *American Ethnologist,* vol. 11 (1984), 684, 690; Dwight Billings and Kathleen Blee, "Family Strategies in a Subsistence Economy: Beech Creek, Kentucky, 1850–1942," *Sociological Perspectives,* vol. 33, no. 1 (1990), 69. Jeanette Keith, *Country People in the New South: Tennessee's Upper Cumberland* (Chapel Hill: University of North Carolina Press, 1995), 173–178, describes a similar nearby section of Tennessee.

10. Henry Sommers, *History of North County Seat 1869–1921* (Owensboro KY: McDowell Publications, 1981), 49–50.

11. The North County seat was involved in several attempts, some successful, to connect it by rail and road to other Kentucky cities, while South County's seat apparently found its north-south tie to Louisville and Nashville sufficient, implying quite different economic orientations (Ireland, *Little Kingdoms,* 102–7).

12. The county seat had a population of about 2,500 in 1920 and 3,500 in 1940, but between 1940 and 1943 increased 100 percent (*North County Seat News,* January 8, 1943, 1); McClure, *Two Centuries,* 311, 405; Sommers, *History of North County Seat,* 154.

13. Paul McClure, *Nearbytown and Its People: A Brief Record of Nearbytown, KY* (North County Seat: North County Historical Society, 1992), 94.

14. McClure, *Two Centuries,* 311.

15. Newspapers, in referring to community leaders, generally mention their business connections in North County, while in South County such identification is rarely made. The control of South County by a few huge landowners/lawyers was frequently mentioned in conversations when we arrived here.

16. Sommers, *History of North County Seat,* 154–6, provides information on numbers of banks, the makeup of the town council; quote is McClure, *Two Centuries,* 311.

17. Editorials in *North County Seat News* (August 22, 1958, 2; August 8, 1958, 2); see James Cobb, *Industrialization and Southern Society, 1877–1984* (Lexington: University Press of Kentucky, 1984), 51–52, on massive military investment during the Second World War in Southern communities.

18. *North County Seat News* (October 28, 1958, 2) refers to the increase in rural industrial workers. For quote see August 8, 1958, 3. For depiction of the continued importance of tenant farming for a landlord's wealth in the 1970s and 1980s, see *Lord and Father,* produced and directed by Joe Gray, Jr., 45 min., Appalshop Films, 1983, videocassette.

19. *1950, 1970, and 1990 Census of Population. North County Seat News,* January 8, 1943, 2, cites a survey of manufacturing in Kentucky for 1939 showing the small numbers of manufacturing employees in most Kentucky counties, including North and South

Counties. In 1950, 23 percent of North County's population was classed as "rural farm," as compared with 69 percent in South County.

20. Ireland, *Little Kingdoms*, 36, 53, 60, 150.

21. Robert Mier and Scott Gelzer, "State Enterprise Zones: The New Frontier?" *Urban Affairs Quarterly*, vol. 18, no. 1 (1982), 47. See James Cobb, *The Selling of the South: The Southern Crusade for Industrial Development, 1936–1990*, 2nd ed. (Chicago: University of Illinois Press, 1993) and Cobb, *Industrialization and Southern Society*, 32–41, for the logic and strategy of attracting industry. For local examples see *South County News*, August 23, 1951, 9; *North County Seat News*, June 22, 1951, 2. Politicians campaigned for governor on the basis of their ability to "sell businesses on the advantages of locating [in Kentucky]" (*North County Seat News*, April 7, 1959, 3). On Southern elite organization to resist unions and other strategies to keep a low-wage industrial and agricultural workforce see Cobb, *Industrialization and Southern Society*, 90–8, 149–50.

22. See John Keller, *Power in America: The Southern Question and the Control of Labor* (Chicago: Vanguard Books, 1983), 83–97, for old Northern industries moving south. For more specifics see Cobb, *Industrialization and Southern Society*, 63–4; Werner Hochwald, "Interregional Income Flows and the South," in Melvin Greenhut and W. Tate Whitman, eds., *Essays in Southern Economic Development* (Chapel Hill: University of North Carolina Press, 1964), 325–6.

23. Pete Daniel, *Standing at the Crossroads: Southern Life since 1900* (New York: Hill and Wang, 1986), 48–9, shows Northern control of industry with Southerners in intermediate positions. On the lack of prosperity and relative income drop see Cobb, *Industrialization and Southern Society*, 136. For an example of local elite interest in bringing in industry, see *North County Enterprise*, January 5, 1970, 14. See also Robert Cromley and Thomas Leinbach, "External Control of Nonmetropolitan Industry in Kentucky," *Professional Geographer*, vol. 38, no. 4 (1986), 339.

24. *South County News*, February 27, 1958, 1. According to an interview with the executive director of the South County Chamber of Commerce, this group successfully held off industrialization until they died.

25. Cynthia Mitchell, "Tobacco Farmers Growing Uneasy," *The Atlanta Journal and the Atlanta Constitution*, December 27, 1992, R/01, 3, NewsBank Record No. AJC*12*27*930030058; John van Willigen and Susan Eastwood, *Tobacco Culture: Farming Kentucky's Burley Belt* (Lexington: University Press of Kentucky, 1998), 25–7.

26. Women held a bigger percentage of manufacturing jobs than men. This pattern was reversed in North County (figured from Kentucky Department of Commerce, *Kentucky Directory of Manufacturers*, [Frankfort: Kentucky Department of Commerce, 1979]). See *1950, 1970 Censuses of Population* for racial patterns.

27. For a comparable variation between counties in solicitation of industry during the early 1950s in two nearby counties see Hill, "Leadership Identification by Newspaper Analysis," 4, 61.

28. *North County Seat News*, November 4, 1958, 2, worries about large numbers of people leaving Kentucky; *North County Enterprise*, January 6, 1955, 2, refers to tractors doing the work formerly done by several men and teams.

29. McClure, *Two Centuries*, 542–3, refers to the effort to bring in manufacturing plants. *North County Seat News*, April 13, 1951, 1, headlines "another new business," a retail business. Retail businesses were beginning to consolidate, including buy outs by Louisville corporations, e.g. *North County Enterprise*, December 18, 1950, 1.

30. Examples come from *South County News*, February 19, 1949, 8; *North County Seat News*, June 12, 1951, 4, 9; June 22, 1951, 10; *North County Enterprise*, November 14, 1955, 1.

31. Cobb, *Industrialization and Southern Society*, 104–9.

32. Cobb, *Industrialization*, 99–104. For the Chamber's development program see *North County Seat News*, November 7, 1958, 9; *North County Enterprise*, August 8, 1960, 1;

August 18, 1960, 1; September 12, 1960, section 2, 1; September 15, 1960, section 2, 1.

33. For examples see captions and articles in *North County Enterprise*, November 17, 1955, 11; January 10, 1955, 1. Cobb, *Industrialization and Southern Society*, 82, discusses post–Second World War national industry wanting women.

34. McClure, *Two Centuries*, 547, lists the dates of major incoming industries; starting in 1960 references to attracting industry in the North County papers become extremely frequent.

35. McClure, *Two Centuries*, 544.

36. According to McClure, 548, unions came in the 1960s and 70s as industry moved in.

37. Cobb, *The Selling of the South*, 113–21; for descriptions of Southern working conditions see Jacqueline Jones, *The Dispossessed: America's Underclasses from the Civil War to the Present* (New York: Basic Books, 1992).

38. *South County News*, March 10, 1948, 8.

39. *South County News*, September 1, 1949, 8.

15 Hooking in the Rest of the World: The Reorganization of Drainage in the New World Order

1. Anuradha Vittachi, "The World's Seven Richest Men Could Wipe Out Poverty," *One World News Service*, June 12, 1997, www.oneworld.org/news/reports/rich.html, referring to *Forbes* Magazine's 1997 listing on billionaires and the UN 1997 Human Development Report. On general concentration of wealth see Howard Zinn, *A People's History of the United States*, 2nd ed. (New York: HarperCollins, 1995), 567–9; Walden Bello, *Dark Victory: The United States, Structural Adjustment, and Global Poverty* (London: Pluto Press with Food First, 1994), 89; Frances Piven and Richard Cloward, "Welfare Reform and the New Class War," in M. Brinton Lykes et al., eds., *Myths about the Powerless: Contesting Social Inequalities* (Philadelphia: Temple University Press, 1996), 75.

2. Vittachi, "The World's Seven Richest Men Could Wipe Out Poverty."

3. James Gross, *Broken Promise: The Subversion of U.S. Labor Relations Policy, 1947–1994* (Philadelphia: Temple University Press, 1995), 9–10, 285.

4. For this section see Sumner Rosen, "Dismantling the Postwar Social Contract," in Lykes et al., *Myths about the Powerless*, 337–47; Bennet Harrison and Barry Bluestone, *The Great U-Turn: Corporate Restructuring and the Polarizing of America* (New York: Basic Books, 1988), 4–7; David Ashley, *History Without a Subject: The Postmodern Condition* (Boulder: Westview Press, 1997), 140, 245; S. M. Miller, "Equality, Morality, and the Health of Democracy," in Lykes et al., *Myths about the Powerless*, 17–33; Piven and Cloward, "Welfare Reform and the New Class War."

5. Both phrases are quoted in Zinn, *People's History*, 416.

6. This section draws on David Simon, Elite Deviance, 5th ed. (Boston: Allyn and Bacon, 1996), 105–7, 94–6, 161–97; Harry Braverman, Labor and Monopoly Capital: The Degradation of Work in the Twentieth Century (New York: Monthly Review Press, 1974), 255; Zinn, People's History, 565, 571.

7. Quoted in Simon, *Elite Deviance*, 164.

8. This and the following paragraphs draw on Gross, *Broken Promise*, 200–36, 365–71.

9. For the processes described in this section, see Ashley, *History without a Subject*, 95–183; Harrison and Bluestone, *The Great U-Turn*; Braverman, *Labor and Monopoly Capital*; Bello, *Dark Victory*; Robert Schaeffer, *Understanding Globalization: The Social Consequences of Political, Economic, and Environmental Change* (New York: Rowman and Littlefield, 1997).

10. John Bodley, *Anthropology and Contemporary Human Problems*, 3rd ed. (Moutain View, CA: Mayfield Publishing Co., 1996), 21, discussing a study by Thomas Dye saying that "just 5,778 individuals 'ran' the giant corporations, the federal government, the news media, and the primary cultural institutions in the country as a whole."

11. National Labor Committee Education Fund in Support of Worker and Human Rights in Central America, *Paying to Lose Our Jobs*, Preliminary Report (National Labor Committee Education Fund in Support of Worker and Human Rights in Central America, 15 Union Square West, New York, NY, 1992), 20. My thanks to Deborah D'Amico for bringing this study to my attention.

12. James Cobb, *Industrialization and Southern Society, 1877–1984* (Lexington: University Press of Kentucky, 1984), 58–9.

13. Ashley, *History without a Subject*, 129.

14. Bello, *Dark Victory*, 94; Piven and Cloward, "Welfare Reform and the New Class War," 81. In 1980 the poverty line for a family of four was $8,414, in 1990 $13,360; the minimum wage was $4.25 in 1992 (John Schwarz and Thoman Volgy, *The Forgotten Americans* [New York: W. W. Norton & Company, 1992], 34, 134).

15. Gross, *Broken Promise*, 246–71, describes the role of the Reagan administration in empowering employers.

16. Zinn, *People's History*, 555, 580–8. Television coverage of the 1991 Gulf War emphasized American technology, talking over and over about "smart bombs," for instance.

17. Ashley, *History without a Subject*, 99.

18. For summaries see Jon Bennett, *The Hunger Machine: The Politics of Food* (Cambridge: Polity Press/Basil Blackwell, 1987); Bodley, *Anthropology and Contemporary Human Problems*; Bello, *Dark Victory*; Frances Lappe and Joseph Collins, "Why People Can't Feed Themselves," in *Anthropology 95/96* (annual editions, Guilford, CN: Duskin Publishing Group, Brown and Benchmark Publishers, 1995 [1977]), 202–6.

19. Forty percent of South County workers commute to a job outside the county. Only 10 percent of North County workers work outside the county. That South County employees are primarily low-wage is demonstrated by their low per capita and median family income (U.S. Bureau of the Census, *1990 Census Lookup*, Summary Tape File 3. http://venus.census.gov/cdrom/lookup).

20. Ann Kingsolver, "Tobacco, Toyota, and Subaltern Development Discourses: Constructing Livelihoods and Community in Rural Kentucky" (Ph.D. diss., University of Massachusetts, 1991) describes an outer Bluegrass county that has an economy in many ways similar to that of South County. See also Rhoda Halperin, *The Livelihood of Kin: Making Ends Meet "The Kentucky Way"* (Austin: University of Texas Press, 1990) for Appalachian Kentucky.

21. I am indebted to Ann Kingsolver for this phrase; see also Halperin, *The Livelihood of Kin*. For a description of the social economy now built around tobacco see Kingsolver, "Tobacco, Toyota, and Subaltern Development Discourses"; John van Willigen and Susan Eastwood, *Tobacco Culture: Farming Kentucky's Burley Belt* (Lexington: University Press of Kentucky, 1998).

22. On the continuing importance of kin in quite different sections of Kentucky see Kingsolver, "Tobacco, Toyota, and Subaltern Development Discourses"; Halperin, *The Livelihood of Kin*.

23. Cynthia Mitchell, "Tobacco Farmers Growing Uneasy," *The Atlanta Journal and the Atlanta Constitution*, December 27, 1992. R/01, 3, NewsBank Record No. AJC*12*27*930030058; World Health Organization, "Tobacco or Health in Brazil," Fact Sheet No. 195, May 1998. www.who.int/inffs/en/fact195.html; Frank Swoboda and Martha Hamilton, "Two on Top of the World," *Washington Post*, July 7, 1997, F10, NewsBank Record No. 008670D1D2E07E9ED9795. Kingsolver, "Tobacco, Toyota,

and Subaltern Development Discourses," 35, points out that the tobacco industry as a whole has long been multinational.

24. Stephen Evans, "Where Now?" *Herald-Courier* (Bristol,VA), September 21, 1997, 4, NewsBank Record No. 009470D1CD7E4E2E89B40.

25. Letter form Bale Tobacco Marketing, Inc, an agent of Philip Morris, USA, received February 2001.

26. Joseph Gerth, "Hospitality for Hispanic Laborers," *Courier-Journal,* July 20, 1998, 1A, 2, NewsBank Record No. 003460D6D7FF089152B5; Kingsolver, "Tobacco, Toyota, and Subaltern Development Discourses," 246–7; Ann Kingsolver, "Passing the Word on NAFTA: Policy and 'the Public' in Mexican, U.S., and Canadian Contexts" (paper presented at the annual meeting of the American Anthropological Association, Washington, D.C., November 1993). Local people talk about Hispanic workers on larger farms, while often expressing outrage at the housing such farmers provide. See van Willigan and Eastwood, *Tobacco Culture*, 32–3.

27. The Executive director of the South County Chamber of Commerce sees this change taking off in the mid-1980s (interview, 1999).

28. Interview in 1999 with Executive Director, South County Chamber of Commerce.

29. See Kentucky Department of Commerce, *Kentucky Directory of Manufacturers, 1995* (Frankfort: Kentucky Department of Commerce); interview with Executive Director, South Country Chamber of Commerce; Bureau of Census, *County Business Patterns, 1994* (Washington, D.C.: Government Printing Office). Osha Davidson, *Broken Heartland: The Rise of America's Rural Ghetto* (Iowa City: University of Iowa Press, 1996), describes a similar process in the rural Midwest.

30. Kingsolver, "Passing the Word on NAFTA"; Van Willigan and Eastwood, *Tobacco Culture*, 30; Cobb, *Industrialization and Southern Society*, 80, says earlier agricultural labor "shortage" complaints were really objections to having to pay higher wages to get workers.

31. Kentucky Department of Commerce, *Kentucky Directory of Manufacturers, 1979* (Frankfort: Kentucky Department of Commerce).

32. Calculated from a list produced by the North County Seat Industrial Foundation.

33 For instance, "Why Kentucky," produced for Commonwealth of Kentucky (Coral Springs, FL: Location Strategies Marketing Group, 1993), 19–27, 53–9, outlines the new laws, incentive program, and employer reactions to incentives and to the workforce. See Kingsolver, "Tobacco, Toyota, and Subaltern Development Discourses," 273–354, for the recruitment of Toyota to Kentucky and labor at the plant.

34. "What a Hundred New Manufactory Jobs Mean to North County Seat and North County," pamphlet produced by North County Seat-North County Chamber of Commerce and Industrial Foundation, 1995.

35. For effects in Kentucky generally see Jason Bailey and Liz Natter, *Kentucky's Low Road to Economic Development: What Corporate Subsidies Are Doing to the Commonwealth* (Lexington: Democracy Resource Center, 2000).

36. "Why Kentucky," 71, shows the cost of living in two towns close to the North County seat (one of which is similar to that town) as 92 percent of the national average. For wages see "Working Hard, Earning Less: The Story of Job Growth in Kentucky," Kentucky Fact Sheet, *Grassroots Factbook 1* (Series 2) (Northampton, MA: National Priorities Project, 1998).

37. "Why Kentucky" shows manufacturing firms in North County to be 22.4 percent unionized in 1993, one of the higher rates in Kentucky.

38. Interviewees, labor leaders, and students frequently mention anti-union tactics; the county's largest manufacturing employer has been under court injunction for its anti-organizing tactics. For general low-wage strategies also see Harrison and Bluestone, *The Great U-Turn*, 48–52; Andrew Mair, Richard Florida, and Martin Kenney, "The

New Geography of Automobile Production: Japanese Transplants in North America," *Economic Geography*, vol. 64, no. 4 (1989), 366.

39. Ashley, *History without a Subject*, 162–3; Harrison and Bluestone, *The Great U-Turn*, 53–63; R. C. Longworth, "Nationhood Under Siege," *Chicago Tribune*, Perspective, October 25, 1998, 1, 6. For a list comparing countries and corporations see David Newman, *Sociology: Exploring the Architecture of Everyday Life* (Thousand Oaks: Pine Forge Press, 1997), 352–3.

40. Jim Hightower, "Newt Buddies Up to the Other Bill," *Detroit Sunday Journal*, September 27, 1998, 6.

41. Bello, *Dark Victory*.

42. Holly Sklar, *Trilateralism: The Trilateral Commission and Elite Planning for World Management* (Boston: South End Press, 1980), 76–82.

43. Quotations are from the report, quoted in Sklar, *Trilateralism*, 299.

44. The effects of the switch to capitalism are still reverberating in former communist countries as their citizens adjust to the fact that health care, jobs, and food are no longer rights, but belong only to those who have money, luck, or connections. They are rapidly becoming more stratified, and the rich are becoming richer while the poor become poorer, as shocked American reporters observe.

45. Quoted in Sklar, *Trilateralism*, 3.

46. See Don Robotham, "The Wealth of Races: The Political Economy of Race and Globalization" (paper presented at the New York Academy of Sciences workshop "Post-Boasian Studies of Whiteness and Blackness: Towards an Anthropological Conception of Racial Practices," March 1997) for a view of globalization not constrained by the assumption of American hegemony.

47. Maria Patricia Fernandez Kelly used this phrase in a panel sponsored by the Overseas Development Network at Oberlin College in which we both participated in 1988.

16 The Resumption of Fascist Processes

1. Most of these comments, made in the 1990s, came from formal interviews; a few are comments by neighbors or students.

2. For the decline in wages, downsizing, increases in part-time and temporary work and overtime, see Bennett Harrison and Barry Bluestone, *The Great U-Turn: Corporate Restructuring and the Polarizing of America* (New York: Basic Books, 1988), 3–52, 109–38; Juliet Schor, *The Overworked American: The Unexpected Decline of Leisure* (New York: Basic Books, 1991); "The Downsizing of America," *New York Times* Special Report (Random House/Times Books, 1996); Walda Katz-Fishman and Jerome Scott, "Diversity and Equality: Race and Class in America," *Sociological Forum*, vol. 9, no. 4 (1994), 569–81; Jeremy Rifkin, *The End of Work: The Decline of the Global Labor Force and the Dawn of the Post-Market Era* (New York: Tarcher/Putnam, 1995).

3. Kentucky workers were rated first in the South and among the top five most productive nationally (John Calhoun Wells, "The Kentucky Experience: State Government as a Partner in Labor-Management Relations," *Journal of State Government*, vol. 60, no. 1 (1987), 44); state boosters put their productivity per dollar of wages above the national average ("Why Kentucky," 19–20).

4. See Anne Francis Okongwu and Joan Mencher, "The Anthropology of Public Policy: Shifting Terrains," *Annual Review of Anthropology* vol. 29 (2000), 107–24, for the social policy changes that have resulted around the world as nations come under the sway of international capital. See George Lipsitz, *The Possessive Investment in Whiteness: How White People Profit from Identity Politics* (Philadelphia: Temple University Press, 1998), for a discussion of efforts to maintain whiteness in the face of these conditions.

5. Ty Tagami, "Garment Maker to Lay Off 1,035," *Lexington Herald-Leader*, November 12, 1997, A1; Kirsten Haukebo, "Fruit of the Loom to Close Campbellsville Plant," (Louisville, KY) *Courier-Journal*, April 16, 1998, 1A. Kentucky Long-Term Policy Research Center, "Emerging Issues for Kentucky," Winter 1998, http://www.lrc.state.ky.us/LTPRC/scan_w98.htm. For the globalization of the clothing industry see Edna Bonacich et al., eds., *Global Production: The Apparel Industry in the Pacific Rim* (Philadelphia: Temple University Press, 1994); National Labor Committee Education Fund in Support of Worker and Human Rights in Central America, *Paying to Lose Our Jobs*, Preliminary Report (National Labor Committee Education Fund in Support of Worker and Human Rights in Central America, 15 Union Square West, New York, NY, 1992).

6. Central Labor Council officials, interviews, and innumerable student comments all indicate that this is in fact done; there are macabre jokes about one particularly unsafe corporation.

7. Written comments by an anonymous unemployment office employee in a nearby county.

8. "Working Hard, Earning Less: The Story of Job Growth in Kentucky," Kentucky Fact Sheet, *Grassroots Factbook 1*(Series 2) (Northampton, MA: National Priorities Project, 1998).

9. Sumner Rosen, "Dismantling the Postwar Social Contract," in M. Brinton Lykes et al., eds., *Myths about the Powerless: Contesting Social Inequalities* (Philadelphia: Temple University Press, 1996), 337–47.

10. *ABC Evening News,* October 29, 1997; also see Richard Dudman, "Mixed Emotions: China Was a Friend, Then a Demon, Now . . .?" *St. Louis Post-Dispatch,* October 26, 1997, 4B, NewsBank Record No 004550D1ADD992CEC3D0A.

11. Louis Uchitelle and N. R. Kleinfield, "The Price of Jobs Lost," in "The Downsizing of America," *New York Times* Special Report, 8; Katherine Newman, *Declining Fortunes: The Withering of the American Dream* (New York: Basic Books, 1993).

12. *The News-Enterprise* (North County Seat, KY), December 18, 1995, 3C. The perception of increased workload is widespread in the two counties. Supporting statistics showing a 5 percent real wage drop and a 6 percent increase in hours of work per job were calculated from U.S. Department of Labor, Bureau of Labor Statistics, *Geographic Profile of Employment and Unemployment,* Bulletins 2216, 2446 (Washington, D.C., 1983, 1993) and Kentucky Cabinet for Human Resources, *Unemployment Insurance Covered Employment and Wages, Employer Contributions and Benefits Paid by Industry,* 1983, 1994. These bulletins do not show multiple job holding. Real-dollar comparisons were made using the Consumer Price Index.

13. My approach to the meaning of poverty is based on the discussion of Townsend's definition, cited in Anne Francis Okongwu, "Looking Up from the Bottom to the Ceiling of the Basement Floor: Female Single-Parent Families Surviving on $22,000 or Less a Year," *Urban Anthropology,* vol. 24, no. 3–4 (1995), 345–6.

14. The following description is built on interviews, on discussions with neighbors, students, a local social worker, domestic violence counselors, and on what students who have come to see me in my capacity as liaison with the local domestic violence program have told me about their lives. See also Okongwu, "Looking Up from the Bottom"; John Schwarz and Thomas Volgy, *The Forgotten Americans* (New York: W.W. Norton & Company, 1992); U.S. Census Bureau, "Poverty Thresholds" 2001, www.census.gov/hhes/poverty/threshld.html.

15. Uchitelle and Kleinfield, "The Price of Jobs Lost," 18.

16. Tagami, "Garment Maker to Lay Off 1,035"; Haukebo, "Fruit of the Loom to Close Campbellsville Plant"; Jon Fortt, "Amazon Rates Job Recruiting Successful," *Lexington Herald-Leader,* June 8, 1999, D1.

17. Calculated from Bureau of the Census, *County Business Patterns*, 1968, 1980, 1993 (Washington, D.C.: Government Printing Office). This pattern holds true for Kentucky generally ("Working Hard, Earning Less").

18. Figured for 1970 from U.S. Employment Standards Administration, *Federal Minimum Wage Rates: 1955–1997*. nd. www.dol.gov/esa/public/minwage, and Schwarz and Volgy, *The Forgotten Americans*, 34.

19. See Frances Piven and Richard Cloward, "Welfare Reform and the New Class War," in Lykes et al., eds., *Myths about the Powerless*, 77–8, for welfare reform in terms of the reserve labor force; also see Paul Street, "The Poverty of Workfare: Dubious Claims, Dark Clouds, and a Silver Lining," *Dissent*, vol. 45, no. 4 (1998), 6, http://www.igc.org/dissent/archive/fall98/street.html. A labor activist says that in a nearby county wages and benefits began to decline within a few months of implementing welfare reform.

20. For analysis of the concept of the underclass and its relationship to social scientific explanations of this supposed failure see Andrew Maxwell, "The Underclass, 'Social Isolation' and 'Concentration Effects': The Culture of Poverty Revisited," *Critique of Anthropology*, vol. 13, no. 3 (1993), 231–45; Joan Vincent, "Framing the Underclass," *Critique of Anthropology*, vol. 13, no. 3 (1993), 215–30.

21. Note that these (Center on Budget and Policy Priorities, Press Release: *Poverty Despite Work—Many Working Families with Children in Kentucky Remain Poor*. April 7,1999, 1, http://www.cborg/4-7-99sfhtm; Kentucky Long-Term Policy Research Center, "Emerging Issues for Kentucky," 1) are official estimates; for a more activist approach see Street, "The Poverty of Workfare."

22. Gardiner Harris, "Making Welfare Work," *Courier-Journal*, December 15, 1996, 1A, NewsBank Record No. 003460D1D02395B2235CA; Street, "The Poverty of Workfare," 9. For the consequences of welfare reform see Alisse Waterston, "The Facts of the Matter: Consequences of Welfare 'Reform' for Poor Women in the U.S." (paper presented at the annual meeting of the American Anthropological Association Meeting, Philadelphia, December 3, 1998); Anne Francis Okongwu, "Living on the Edge: Economically Marginal Families and Welfare Reform" (paper presented in panel on Homelessness, Welfare, and Public Policy in New York City, New York Academy of Sciences, October 24, 1997); Barbara Sands, "A Wobbly Asks: 'So . . . How's the Family?'–A Workfare Review," *Industrial Worker*, July/August 1999, 12. For analyses of welfare that make it clear that these issues are far from straight-forward, and link female poverty with the economy rather than directly with their childbearing, see Frances Piven and Richard Cloward, "Welfare Reform and the New Class War," in Lykes et al., *Myths about the Powerless*, 79; Michael Katz, *The Undeserving Poor: From the War on Poverty to the War on Welfare* (New York: Pantheon Books, 1989), 215–35; Arline Geronimus, "Clashes of Common Sense: On the Previous Child Care Experience of Teenage Mothers-to-Be," *Human Organization*, vol. 51, no. 4 (1992), 318–29.

23. This section is based on a 1998 telephone interview with an employee of the Flint Hill, Kansas, Job Corps, two copies of *Job Corps in Action*, and a background information packet provided by Alexis Buss, IWW activist.

24. *Job Corps in Action*, Spring 1997, 18. Presumably this is not the norm for Job Corps programs. My letter and phone calls requesting further information on this particular program went unanswered.

25. Dennis Culhane, "The Homeless Shelter and the Nineteenth-Century Poorhouse: Comparing Notes from Two Eras of 'Indoor Relief,' " in Lykes et al., *Myths about the Powerless*, 55–6.

26. Mark Dunlea, "The Poverty Profiteers Privatize Welfare," *Covert Action Quarterly*, vol. 59 (n.d.), 8, http://caq.com/CAQ59.PrivateWelfare.html.

27. Harris, "Making Welfare Work," 5.
28. Pem Davidson Buck, "Arbeit Macht Frei: Racism and Bound, Concentrated Labor in U.S. Prisons," *Urban Anthropology*, vol. 23, no. 4 (1994), 331–72.
29. Anonymous communication from an activist, who referred to it as indenture.
30. Kenneth Noble, "Thai Workers Held Captive, Officials Say," *New York Times*, August 4, 1995, A1, A20; William Branigin, "Sweatshops Are Back," *Washington Post National Weekly Edition*, February 24, 1997, 6–7.
31. For more on the issues raised in this section see Buck, "Arbeit Macht Frei"; John Cole Vodicka, "Striking a Blow Against Slave Labor," *Freedomways*, #42, July/August 1999, 1–3 (newsletter of the Prison and Jail Project, PO Box 6749, Americus, GA). For Microsoft see Daniel Levine, "For Prison Workers, It's Low Tech or No Tech," *Wired News*, 1997, barnesandnoble.com.
32. See Michael Kimmel and Michael Kaufman, "Weekend Warriors: The New Men's Movement," in Harry Brod and Michael Kaufman, eds., *Theorizing Masculinities* (Thousand Oaks: Sage Publications, 1994), 261–3. Michael Kimmel, "Masculinity as Homophobia: Fear, Shame, and Silence in the Construction of Gender Identity," in Brod and Kaufman, *Theorizing Masculinities*, 135–9, discusses power relations between men within a patriarchal context. For expressions of insecurity see "The Downsizing of America," *New York Times* Special Report, 77–110.
33. For an example see Elizabeth Krause, " 'The Bead of Raw Sweat in a Field of Dainty Perspirers': Nationalism, Whiteness, and the Olympic-Class Ordeal of Tonya Harding," *Transforming Anthropology*, vol. 7, no. 1 (1998), 33–52.
34. My thanks to North County union officials for insights into these Wal-Mart ads.
35. See Jürgen Habermas, *Legitimation Crisis* (Boston: Beacon Press, 1975
36. For right-wing funding of this campaign see Jean Stefancic and Richard Delgado, *No Mercy: How Conservative Think Tanks and Foundations Changed America's Social Agenda. (Philadelphia: Temple University Press)*; Chip Berlet, ed., *Eyes Right: Challenging the Right Wing Backlash* (Boston: South End Press, 1995).
37. See, for instance, Newt Gingrich, *To Renew America* (New York: HarperCollins, 1995); *Rush Limbaugh's America*, produced by Steve Talbot, 60 min., *Frontline*, Corporation for Public Broadcasting, aired February 28, 1995.
38. For details of an example of this strategy see Chip Berlet, "Clinton, Conspiracism, and the Continuing Culture War," *The Public Eye* (newsletter of Political Research Associates, 120 Beacon Street, Suite 202, Somerville, MA), vol. 13, no. 1 (Spring 1999), 1–23.
39. Quote is from Loretta Ross, "White Supremacy in the 1990s," in Berlet, *Eyes Right*, 174.
40. Anne Okongwu, personal communication.
41. For such strategies see John Nichols, "Apathy, Inc.," *The Progressive*, vol. 62, no. 10 (October 1998), 30–2.
42. John Gaventa, *Power and Powerlessness: Quiescence and Rebellion in an Appalachian Valley* (Urbana: University of Illinois Press, 1980).
43. Robert Botsch, *We Shall Not Overcome: Populism and Southern Blue-collar Workers* (Chapel Hill: University of North Carolina Press, 1980), 195–7, discussing the 1970s, describes the "incomplete" class analysis that can develop as a result of worsening conditions for working people.
44. Lori Montgomery, "Study Shows One in Seven Black Men of Voting Age Has Lost the Right to Vote Because of Criminal Convictions," *Knight-Ridder/Tribune News Service*, January 29, 1997, NewsBank Record No 008430D1D1C8D3B7C09EA.

17 Whiteness: The Continuing Evolution of a Smokescreen

1. For broad-ranging conceptualized analysis and review of the literature see Faye V. Harrison, "Introduction: Expanding the Discourse on 'Race,' " *American Anthropologist*, vol. 100, no. 3 (1998), 609–31; see also the articles collected in Faye V. Harrison, ed., "Contemporary Issues Forum: Race and Racism," *American Anthropologist*, vol. 100, no. 3 (1998).

2. Helán Enoch Page, "The 'Black' Public Sphere in White Public Space: Racialized Information and Hi-Tech Cultural Production in the Global African Diaspora" (paper presented at the New York Academy of Sciences workshop "Post-Boasian Studies of Whiteness and Blackness: Towards an Anthropological Conception of Racial Practices," March 1997); Helán Enoch Page, definition of racism provided to the American Anthropological Association, revised 1998. See also Karen Brodkin, "Race, Class, and Gender: The Metaorganization of American Capitalism," *Transforming Anthropology*, vol. 7, no. 2 (1998), 46–57.

3. Lori Montgomery, "1 in 3 Black Men in their 20s Are Under Criminal Justice Supervision, Study Says," *Knight-Ridder Washington Bureau*, October 4, 1995, NewsBank Record No 00843*19951004*07598.

4. Beverly Bartlett, "War in the Gulf," (Louisville, KY) *Courier-Journal*, January 25, 1991, 4 A, record number LVL280697, describes a North County Gulf War event featuring this song, which has also been sung at recent Workers' Memorial Day observances in North County. For presidential backing and evidence of anthem-like character see Des Ruisseaux, "God Bless Spitsbergen, Too," (Louisville, KY) *Courier-Journal*, April 21, 1989, 2A, record number LVL76040; Connie Cass, "Patriotic Airs; War Brings New Lineup to Radio Stations," (Louisville, KY) *Courier-Journal*, February 12, 1991, 1B, record number LVL284242; "School Spirit Sucks," *The New Republic*, October 1, 1984, 6, InfoTrac article A3452925.

Index

CPSIA information can be obtained at www.ICGtesting.com
Printed in the USA
BVOW08s1242150916

462235BV00001B/1/P

9 781583 670477